RCA

Also by Robert Sobel:

The Origins of Interventionism
The Big Board: A History of the New York Stock Market
The Great Bull Market: Wall Street in the 1920s
Panic on Wall Street: A History of America's Great Financial Disasters
The Curbstone Brokers: The Origins of the American Stock Exchange
Conquest and Conscience: The United States in the 1840s
The Age of Giant Corporations
Amex: A History of the American Stock Exchange
Machines and Morality: The United States in the 1850s
Money Manias: Eras of Great Speculation in American History
For Want of a Nail . . .: If Burgoyne Had Won at Saratoga
The Entrepreneurs: Explorations Within the American Business Tradition
Herbert Hoover at the Onset of the Great Depression
N.Y.S.E.: A History of the New York Stock Exchange
The Manipulators: America in Media Age
Inside Wall Street
The Fallen Colossus: The Crash of the Penn Central
They Satisfy: The Cigarette in American Life
The Last Bull Market: Wall Street in the 1960s
The Worldly Economists
IBM: Colossus in Transition
ITT: The Management of Opportunity
The Rise and Fall of the Conglomerate Kings
Car Wars: The Untold Story of the Great Automakers and the Giant Battle for Global Supremacy
IBM vs. Japan

RCA

Robert Sobel

STEIN AND DAY/*Publishers*/New York

First published in 1986

Designed by Terese Bulinkis Platten
Printed in the United States of America
STEIN AND DAY/*Publishers*
Scarborough House
Briarcliff Manor, N.Y. 10510

Library of Congress Cataloging-in-Publication Data

Sobel, Robert, 1931 Feb. 19-
RCA.

Bibliography: p.
Includes index.
1. Radio Corporation of America—History.
2. Electronic industries—United States—History.
3. Broadcasting—United States—History. 4. Sarnoff,
David, 1891-1971. I. Title.
HD9696.A3U613 1986 338.7'62138'0973 85-43395
ISBN 0-8128-3084-9

for
Linda Sobel

Contents

Introduction

> RCA is a great technical company, it's a great innovator, but it stumbles.
>
> —CEO Edgar Griffiths, 1980

In mid-December of 1985, as I began writing the final chapter of *RCA,* it appeared the strong recovery engineered by Chairman Thornton Bradshaw and President Robert Frederick was leading to a major acquisition, the betting being they would purchase MCA, that major entertainment conglomerate, paying for it in part with funds derived from the sale of CIT Financial and Hertz. It seemed quite proper and logical: MCA would make a nice fit with National Broadcasting Corporation, then in a strong recovery under the leadership of Grant Tinker. It would be a neat way to end the book, on a note of strength and sanity after a generation of bungling, blunders, and missteps that almost laid low one of America's great corporations.

I should have known better. The history of RCA has been one of high drama and, in recent years, unexpected developments. There was to be no MCA merger, but rather a reunion with a parent from whom RCA had declared its independence more than half a century ago: General Electric.

I can't think of another instance like this in American business history.

So I was left with a realization that the chapter I was writing had to be penultimate rather than concluding. A new period at RCA is beginning, and not only for the corporation and the individuals involved but for the nature of the industry. For this is not just another big takeover in a record year for such activities—more than $125 billion worth of American corporations were acquired or merged in 1985—but at $6.3 billion it was the largest non-petroleum deal to date. Moreover there was no chance of RCA disappearing into the GE maw, large though it may be. At the time of this writing it appears GE's 1985 revenues will come in at over $28 billion, while RCA's will be in excess of $9 billion. So large a company simply doesn't vanish into another.

Certainly GE is a most visible company, but only 20 percent of its business is in consumer appliances and other consumer products, while entertainment and related enterprises account for more than half of RCA's revenues. Therefore GE would hardly attempt to replace the RCA logo on TV sets, videocassette players, phonograph records, and the like. Moreover RCA will remain at Radio City, which will not be renamed GE Plaza. And Robert Frederick, who left GE for RCA realizing he hadn't much of a chance to succeed John Welch as chairman, will now find himself working for Welch again, in what will be an interesting relationship. But everything about RCA is of interest, sometimes positively, often not.

As is so often the case, the origins of this book derived from work on another project. While conducting research for a history of International Telephone & Telegraph Corporation in 1981, I was struck by the similarities between the early histories of the two companies. Each had its true beginnings in the aftermath of World War I, when Washington and Wall Street collaborated to create international telecommunications entities designed to be America's chosen instruments in this industry in every part of the globe.

They were two of the nation's most glamorous companies during the 1920s. In addition, ITT's Sosthenes Behn and RCA's David Sarnoff were two of the most celebrated businessmen of the decade, even though they had very little else in common.

David Sarnoff departed the scene at a time when RCA's reputation was at its zenith. The company that had led the way in radio and broadcasting, played a role in the development of talking pictures, and triumphed in monochrome and color television was then engaged in a struggle to gain second place in data processing and seemed to have a good chance of success. RCA was a premier research firm, well-entrenched in half a dozen major technologies, and apparently destined to continue on under the leadership of David's son, Bob.

In reality the company was already suffering from dry rot, a good deal of it caused by David Sarnoff's style and approach to business. He had neglected to develop managerial talents needed in a company that in 1969 had revenues of $3.2 billion and profits of only $151 million. The mistake of going head-to-head with IBM was becoming evident within the industry and Wall Street if not elsewhere, while at RCA the shambles in the electronic data processing sector were obvious.

Later, when the corporation declined, some would claim the problems derived from the absence of a David Sarnoff, but in fact he had been largely responsible for the debacles of that period. Long before Ronald Reagan was tagged with the label "The Teflon President," David Sarnoff became the

Teflon businessman, and his reputation remains intact to this day. That Sarnoff was a brilliant and creative individual cannot be denied. But that he and RCA's public relations staff embroidered upon this, and found willing listeners and writers to follow their leads, was also the case. Popular writers too often concentrated upon his dazzling style, vivid rhetoric, successes enjoyed during the interwar period, and the saga of television. When not ignoring the wheeling and dealing, the technological failures compensated for by political maneuverings, and the outright blunders of the 1960s, they tended to misinterpret them.

One of the great gaps in business literature is that of a decent Sarnoff biography. As will be seen, much of what we now have is hagiography.

I realized little of this at the time, however. When first becoming interested in writing a history of RCA I did know of the debacle in data processing, the mixed success of a conglomeratization program initiated by David and carried through by Bob, the revolving doors in the executive suites at 30 Rockefeller Plaza, the erosion at NBC, and the demoralization within the ranks. In 1981 RCA had just welcomed Bradshaw as its new CEO, amid talk that the company might be taken over by some raider who would carve it up and dispose of the pieces.

At that inopportune moment I approached Executive Vice President Kenneth Bilby to ask if the company might at some time be interested in cooperating in an unauthorized, unsubsidized history of RCA. It was apparent that nothing could be done unless and until things settled down, but I wanted to initiate the process then, expecting to follow up later on.

As expected, Mr. Bilby was not prepared to make any commitment, but he suggested I keep in touch with the company, since it might be willing to cooperate "in a few years."

The company did recover, and two years later I signed a contract with Stein and Day to undertake the history. Soon after, I wrote to Chairman Bradshaw and President Frederick, indicating that I intended to begin research and asking for assistance and cooperation. These letters and others were not answered, but I started out in the hope that perhaps a chance would appear for me to get through to management.

Initially most of my research was in government documents, periodicals, and a few interviews I managed to obtain from individuals who had either retired from RCA or had left there for other employment.

As I progressed in my work RCA's unwillingness to meet with me became more understandable. Most companies will cooperate with scholars if they know there is little from which to hide or for which to be embarrassed. In some instances large and powerful firms have opened their archives to independent scholars knowing there were dark periods in their pasts, in the hope of obtaining insights into their operations that would be helpful in understanding the present and planning for the future. A confident and secure management can afford to see a few skeletons pop out of the tomb, either for the first time or for a new generation of readers. The company was still a troubled one in 1983—and in 1984, when I again wrote asking for cooperation.

Nonetheless the research progressed, with additional RCA employees accepting invitations to talk about their experiences, and others who knew the company from contacts also submitting to interviews. It soon became clear that reporters for several of the nation's more important business magazines—*Fortune* and *Business Week* in particular—had well-developed sources within the company during the 1930s and after, and at first it appeared I would have to rely upon the business press for more information than was desirable; but by the time I completed the research, it had become clear that RCA's misfortune in being such a leaky operation was my good fortune.

When the manuscript was almost completed I offered to dispatch it to RCA headquarters for comments, but once again my letters were ignored. Such was the situation in the winter of 1985-1986, when work was completed and the manuscript sent to my publisher.

By then RCA had recovered nicely. Bradshaw and Frederick had disposed of many of Bob Sarnoff's acquisitions and clearly signaled their intention to return the corporation to its original businesses of consumer and commercial electronics and broadcasting. As things calmed down at Rockefeller Plaza and in the field and the corporation's financial viability was no longer in question, a mood of confidence somewhat similar to that of the David Sarnoff era appeared. But it was different this time.

With all of its problems in the period from the early 1920s through the late 1960s, RCA appeared to be at the cutting edge of change, a pioneering concern to which the nation looked for indications of what was to be, from wireless to radio, through talking motion pictures, monochrome and color television, computers, electronics, and so on. This is no longer the case, although in 1984 RCA was third in the number of American patents awarded, behind General Electric and IBM, but ahead of Bell Telephone Laboratories. The company that began when Woodrow Wilson, Franklin D. Roosevelt, and Owen Young planned for an American telecommunications giant to dominate the world now imports much of its consumer electronics products from Taiwan and sells Japanese-made television receivers with the RCA logo affixed. Today's RCA is a much strengthened entity in mature industries, with no novel technology or product in the wings. The merger with GE may change matters but hardly before the end of the decade.

David Sarnoff offered vision and promise of a bright future; Robert Frederick produced stronger balance sheets, better management and growth, but little in the way of novelty or originality. Frederick was not a dream merchant, but he never claimed to be one. And considering RCA's record in the decade and a half prior to Bradshaw's arrival in 1981, perhaps what he had to offer was the best medicine for this often troubled corporation.

It remains to be said that RCA is as complex and convoluted as almost any great American enterprise.

Ordinarily I would take space to thank those who cooperated in this venture, but this was not a conventional task of research and writing. Most of the RCA people with whom I spoke asked for anonymity, with one of the first explaining that this was "an old RCA custom." I didn't know what he meant at the time; I do today. Rumor, cliques, and careerism exist in all organizations, but from what I have discovered, they were and possibly still are a way of life at RCA. Ending or at least mitigating this condition is one of the more important tasks of management, as Thornton Bradshaw virtually conceded.

Several RCAers spoke for attribution and are so noted in the text. I thank all for their help, and I trust that from the following pages they will recognize the corporation for which they worked and are pleased by the book they helped create.

Robert Sobel
Hofstra University
May 1, 1986

RCA

1

Provenance

THAT THE TECHNOLOGY was known originally as "wireless," "wireless telephony," and "radio telephony" provides a clue as to just what was believed to be its function and future. "Wireless" implies that there were alternate forms, which were "wired," and this of course refers to the telegraph and telephone. Thus, the newer technology would perform the same functions as the old, except that it would do so without the trouble, inconvenience, and expense of a copper conduit for the electrified messages. "Radio telephony" differed from radio telegraphy in that the message would be transmitted by the human voice and not by an operator clicking away at a key.

Such was the vision of radio in the early years of the twentieth century. Readers of Sunday supplements and dime novels pondered forecasts of a time when those jumbles of telephone wires would be scrapped and offices and homes would be equipped with telephones that transmitted messages invisibly, through the air, with no worries regarding downed transmission wires.

Naval officers fantasized about being able to send orders to ships at sea, directing their movements in ways that would alter the nature of warfare.

In 1897 Guglielmo Marconi, already hailed as the premier inventor in this new technology and the head of Marconi Wireless Telegraph, a British concern, demonstrated wireless to Italian naval officers, and two years later he supervised a demonstration for Americans, when two battleships exchanged messages over thirty-six miles of Atlantic water.

Soon after, the Navy attempted to purchase the systems. The price was reasonable enough—$10,000 plus a royalty of $10,000 a year for twenty units—but British Marconi insisted the equipment not be used to communicate with non-Marconi stations. The Navy rejected this out of hand, claiming it would limit the usefulness, and so the sale did not take place. But the

American officers continued to study the technology and plan for the time when it would be theirs without encumbrances placed by foreigners.

Other navies of the world lined up to purchase Marconi equipment, but British Marconi still required the same conditions proposed to the Americans. The Germans retaliated by utilizing a rival technology devised by Adolph Slaby and Graf George von Arco and manufactured by Telefunken. The Slaby-Arco system was inferior to Marconi's, but since the Germans were prepared to sell without conditions the system was purchased by many, including the American Navy, which in 1903 had the first units installed on warships.

Even then there were troubles. Marconi Wireless controlled most of the land stations and, true to its earlier position, was unwilling to cooperate with those ships utilizing the German system.

As early as 1905 the United States Navy Department had urged passage of legislation that give it a dominant role in the development of wireless, and five years later Congress passed and President William Howard Taft signed the Wireless Ship Act, which required "apparatus and operators for radio communication on every passenger vessel carrying 50 or more persons . . . capable of transmitting or receiving a message over a distance of at least 50 miles." Army counterparts at the War Department thought the same might be done on land.

In 1912, after the sinking of the *Titanic* dramatized the use of wireless, a radio licensing law, aimed at regulating wireless communications, was enacted. Since wireless of the period was almost exclusively utilized by marine interests, the measure required that all desiring transmission stations apply for licenses to the Secretary of Commerce and Labor, who also would assign wavelengths. The frequency of 360 meters was assigned to "amateurs." The act gave the President the right to operate or close wireless stations "in time of war or public peril or disaster." There is no indication that the then-Secretary Charles Nagel (who had been born in 1849, five years after the first demonstration of the Morse telegraph, and died in 1940, when television was being demonstrated at the New York World's Fair) paid much attention to the matter.

Wireless experiments were afoot throughout much of the Western world in this period, and the names of the pioneers were known to one another. Some were giants—America's Alexander Graham Bell and Thomas Edison, Italy's Marconi, Germany's Heinrich Hertz, and Elihu Thomson of the United Kingdom, for example. But most of the younger men, the second generation of the telecommunications age, had reputations limited to their fellows. These included John Fleming of the United Kingdom, the German Adolph Slaby, Alexander Popov of Russia, Ernst Alexanderson of Sweden, the Canadian Reginald Fessenden, and Lee De Forest of the United States.

The world was in a fever pitch regarding wireless, and scarcely a nation lacked engineers and scientists who made contributions. Lacking were far-sighted businessmen who understood the ramifications of the new technology. They would come in time, and by a most circuitous path. Meanwhile the pioneers stumbled about as best they could.

De Forest was one of the group who possessed what might today be considered the proper academic credentials. Born in Iowa in 1873, he attended Yale, where he became something of a celebrity, known for his brilliance, arrogance, and dedication. In 1899 De Forest wrote a doctoral dissertation on Hertzian waves, in the process of which he became fascinated with wireless. Upon receiving his degree he took a variety of jobs, including one at AT&T's Western Electric subsidiary in Chicago, where he experimented on perfecting devices produced by Marconi and became convinced he could do better. Relocating to New York in 1902, De Forest joined with Abraham White, a small-time Wall Street promoter, and together they organized De Forest Wireless Telegraph, which for a while was a profitable and growing concern. De Forest was now a paper millionaire, with all the time he wanted for research.

In 1905 De Forest developed the audion tube, a device that, as the name indicated, enabled wireless sets to transmit words as well as telegraph signals. "Unwittingly, then, had I discovered an Invisible Empire of the Air," the inventor wrote in his diary, and two years later he organized another company, De Forest Radio Telephone, on that occasion predicting that in time each home would have a wireless telephone to replace the wired ones.

In 1911 De Forest and several of his officers were convicted of fraud in the sale of stock, and while he continued to work in the field, his company failed, and his future commercial ventures amounted to little.

In the early years of this century Reginald Fessenden's contributions were even more important. A fellow radio pioneer, Elihu Thomson, called Fessenden "the greatest wireless inventor of the age—greater than Marconi."

Born in Quebec in 1866, Fessenden attended local schools, worked as a teacher in Bermuda, took posts later on at Edison Machine Works, where he worked directly under the Great Man, at Westinghouse, and went on to teach at several universities, all the while working on wireless devices. In 1900, at the age of thirty-four, Fessenden was hired by the U.S. Department of Agriculture to develop a means of transmitting weather information by wireless, preferably by voice rather than by Morse code.

In 1902, together with several of his colleagues and with the support of General Electric, Fessenden organized the National Electric Signaling Company. Soon Fessenden developed several promising devices, including one of the more powerful alternators of its time, an apparatus capable of throwing radio waves great distances. Four years later National Electric Signaling applied for permits from the United States and the United Kingdom to establish wireless stations, this in preparation for an attempt at transoceanic operations. On Christmas Eve, 1906, Fessenden sent a message over the air, not knowing who—if anyone—would receive it, and on New Year's Eve another message was picked up by United Fruit Company ships in the West Indies, this deemed a remarkable feat.

Given a few breaks—better management and finances among others—National Electric might have become the industry leader, for it owned valuable patents and in Fessenden possessed one of the authentic geniuses of the early period, a man who might properly claim to have invented broadcasting. Fessenden was erratic, however, and like De Forest insisted upon managing his company, an area in which he was deficient. As Roy Weigant, one of his assistants, recalled, "if he had confined himself to being a discoverer and a creator and had let the commercial designing end of the business alone, his company would have dominated the world." The company all but ceased functioning in 1912, and after prolonged litigation the company fell into receivership in 1916. But Fessenden's work encouraged others to experiment and set off a wave of wireless broadcasting activity.

The most promising American firm was General Electric, which had been organized in 1892 through a merger of Edison Electric Illuminating and Thomson-Houston, and which manufactured a wide variety of products from light bulbs to marine generators to communications equipment. Ernst Alexanderson was its leading scientist in the last-named field.

Alexanderson was born in Uppsala, Sweden, in 1878 and was educated at The Royal Institute of Technology in Stockholm and the Konigliche Technische Hochschule in Berlin, where he worked with Adolph Slaby on wireless transmitters, a product and technology to which he was to devote his professional life. Arriving in the United States in 1900, he was soon employed by GE. He was there when Fessenden asked the company's help in creating a 100,000-cycle alternator, a device capable of throwing signals across thousands of miles, which was delivered in 1906. Alexanderson continued working on alternators of his own with the help of another GE scientist, Irving Langmuir, and three years later obtained a patent for the most powerful alternator yet known, capable of transmitting signals across the Atlantic.

The ideas of these men, translated into equipment, made World War I the first in which the wireless was utilized to any significant degree. Along with the machine gun, poison gas, the tank, and airplanes, wireless seemed too important a weapon to be left to the generals and admirals. Or, for that matter, to the development and control by foreigners against whom one might fight the next war.

Guglielmo Marconi had visited the GE installation in Schenectady in 1915 to see the Alexanderson alternator in action. He left convinced it would be an essential element in transoceanic communications and placed a large order for it in return for what amounted to a virtual monopoly on its use. GE refused to grant monopoly status but did sell a unit destined for a Marconi station in

New Brunswick, New Jersey, which was seen as the beginning of recouping an investment of over $1,500,000. But political events changed the situation drastically.

The United States declared war on Germany on April 6, 1917, and two days later President Woodrow Wilson ordered the Navy to take over all wireless operations in the United States. This was a touchy situation, since it involved the "temporary" acquisition of British Marconi's partially owned American subsidiary. The diplomatic maneuverings were delicate, but the British did not protest, believing as they did that things would be set right after the war, at which time British Marconi would dominate the wireless scene in Europe and "American Marconi" would do as much in the United States.

American Marconi Wireless Telegraph Company, which had been organized in 1899, was indeed in command of much of the American market. Incorporated in New Jersey with an authorized stock of $10 million par value, its purpose was to utilize the patents and expertise of the parent firm in the United States and link that country and Europe by wireless. By 1910 American Marconi was designing its own equipment, but almost all of the manufacturing was done in the United Kingdom. When its leading competitor, United Wireless, failed in 1912, shortly before the collapse of Fessenden's National Electric Signaling, American Marconi purchased its assets, and with this the company obtained an effective monopoly of the supply of wireless services in the United States. In addition the firm owned facilities in New York, Massachusetts, and Illinois, a small publishing operation in New York, and was the major shareholder in the Pan-American Wireless Telegraph & Telegraph Company, which as the name indicates planned to extend services to Latin America.

In many ways it was an American concern, British Marconi owning only around 15 percent of the shares, and most of its directors and executives were American. In the public mind and in Washington, however, it was always deemed a subsidiary of British Marconi, and thus a foreign entity. The United States Navy in particular was bothered by this and by the cavalier way it had been treated when it attempted to purchase Marconi equipment. In an attempt to find an alternate supply and in the interests of efficiency, a Navy staff officer, Captain Sanford Hooper, devised a plan whereby leading companies and independent inventors would pool their patents in a cross-licensing arrangement, which as will be seen continued after the war under a different kind of system.

American Marconi grew substantially during the war, in the process becoming a manufacturing as well as service company. A small research operation at Aldane, New Jersey, was enlarged and transformed into a factory out of which came a stream of communications gear. Its wireless operations were taken over by the Navy and upgraded. The Alexanderson alternator had not yet been delivered when the United States entered the war, so the Navy intervened in 1918 to obtain prompt delivery and in other ways supervised the relations between American suppliers and the Marconi interests.

There were others in the field, General Electric, Westinghouse, and American Telephone & Telegraph's Western Electric subsidiary among others. Then there was Federal Telegraph, Wireless Specialty Apparatus (owned by United Fruit), and a handful of minuscule plants. But American Marconi was by far the leading supplier of wireless apparatus in this period.

OPERATING STATISTICS FOR AMERICAN MARCONI, 1914–1918

figures in millions of dollars

	1914	1915	1916	1917	1918
Gross Revenues	0.76	0.75	0.86	1.20	1.90
Net Revenues	0.12	0.10	0.28	0.68	0.90
Total Net Income	0.27	0.18	0.37	0.78	1.00

Source: *Moody's Utilities,* 1919, p. 66.

The war came to an end on November 11, 1918, and a month later, while President Wilson prepared to attend the peace negotiations scheduled to open in Versailles in January 1919, several of his Cabinet members and military advisors urged him to make permanent the temporary takeover of American Marconi. At their request Representative Joshua Alexander of Missouri, a 67-year-old veteran who was about to be tapped for the post of Secretary of Commerce, was named to sponsor legislation toward this end.

Alexander was deemed one of Congress's leading experts in this area. By luck of the draw this obscure congressman from a landlocked state had been named chairman of the International Conference on the Safety of Life at Sea in 1913 and in 1918 was the senior Democrat on the House Committee on Merchant Marine and Fisheries, which seemed the logical place for hearings on such a measure to originate, as they did on November 11.

The initial witnesses appeared in mid-December. While the subject matter was controversial—among other things the Navy was advocating the expropriation of assets owned by an ally and the creation of a federal monopoly in wireless telecommunications—the hearings were calm and received little attention from the press. American Marconi's septuagenarian president, John Griggs, a former New Jersey governor and Attorney General in the McKinley administration, defended the firm's patriotism and status. American Marconi was now posting record profits, after years of struggle and deficits, and had paid a dividend in 1918 for the first time since the war began. "Just when the farmer has planted his seed, plowed his field, and harrowed it, and cultivated his crop, and the corn is ready to husk, the government comes in and says, 'We want that crop,'" Griggs complained.

Seventy-eight-year-old Congressman William Greene of Massachusetts protested that passage of the measure would lead to a government monopoly that would prevent development and expansion of radio beyond the narrow military and naval usages envisaged by the government. "I am of the opinion that it is too much to ask the people of America to punish the people of America by restraining all their abilities and opportunities and all their hopes and expectations," he said, adding that if the Alexander bill were passed any young man interested in wireless as a career would have to join the Navy. Secretary of the Navy Josephus Daniels, a leading advocate of nationalization, conceded this: ". . . passage of this bill will secure for all time to the Navy Department the control of radio in the United States, and will enable the Navy to continue the splendid work it has carried on during the war."

Nothing came of the hearings, but a beginning toward an American wireless company was made on November 30, 1918, when American Marconi sold to the Navy Department all of its forty-five low-power transmission stations and apparatus on 330 ships for $789,500. This left American Marconi with three high-power stations and equipment on 170 ships, as well as the Aldane manufacturing facility. The sale was made under duress; the Navy was already operating the stations.

Christmas was approaching. Wilson was on his way to Europe and the country's and world's attention was focused on the forthcoming negotiations at Versailles. The radio hearings ended on December 19, and on January 16, when the peace talks were in their first week, the Alexander bill was tabled; nothing more was heard of it. But the initial salvo in the battle over radio's future had been fired.

Wilson was aware of this. While traveling to Europe on the SS *George Washington* in late December 1918 he was given a demonstration of ship-to-shore and ship-to-ship communications, which he found "interesting." While in Paris he read a report from Walter Rogers, his communications expert, detailing the possibilities of global wireless and the problems entailed by what amounted to a British monopoly in the field. Wilson knew that the United States received almost all of its military reports via the British-owned but American-controlled facilities, and he must have been aware that the British monitored reports emanating from the American embassy in London.

The outlook for any future American role in radio manufacture or service was unclear. Rogers warned that "when communications facilities are controlled by one nation which gives its commerce and its press preferential service or rates, misunderstandings are sure to arise." Postmaster General Albert Burleson agreed, cabling Wilson that "our ships and merchant marine now have to depend upon the courtesy of foreign-controlled means of communication to get home connections." Secretary Daniels wondered what it would mean to the United States if it ever found itself at odds with the United Kingdom, at a time when Marconi controlled wireless telegraphy and telephony.

Such also was the view of Franklin Delano Roosevelt, the aggressive and, insofar as wireless was concerned, farsighted Assistant Secretary of the Navy. Only 31 years old when asked to accept the post, he was eager to make a name for himself, already weighing the possibilities of becoming the second Roosevelt to serve in the White House. He and Daniels weren't on the best of terms. The Secretary was a shrewd politician who ran his department in an offhanded albeit capable enough fashion, which irritated Roosevelt, who did all he could to assume authority and exercise it, just as cousin Theodore had when he had been Assistant Secretary sixteen years earlier under the inept John Long in the McKinley Administration.

Roosevelt had hoped to obtain a naval commission as a means of obtaining a war record, no small thing for one who was raised in a period when that was deemed requisite for a political career. But Wilson needed him in Washington, and so he reluctantly remained there during the war. This placed Roosevelt in an ideal position to play a role in the forthcoming telecommunications negotiations, which he welcomed. Many of the problems regarding the Navy's control of American Marconi installations and the matter of the contract with GE required legal knowledge, and Roosevelt had been an attorney while Daniels spent most of his adult life as a newspaperman, so it was only natural that the Assistant Secretary would assume responsibility for the Navy's role in radio. It wouldn't be going too far to say that more than anyone else in the President's official family, Roosevelt had become an expert in the field.

In December 1918 Roosevelt traveled with the President's party to Europe and the Peace Conference. While others went on to Versailles to negotiate the big issues, which included the League of Nations, Roosevelt remained in Paris, dealing with claims lodged against the Navy and the disposal of surplus properties, including an American installation at Bordeaux, the largest and most complex in the world. In this and other matters he maintained regular contact with the Director of Naval Communications, who bore the imposing name of Rear Admiral William Hannum Grubb Bullard. Roosevelt also spoke often with now-Commander Sanford Hooper, and others in the service who shared his ideas.

It is reasonable to assume that Roosevelt attended a conference on telecommunications convened in Paris that winter. There he would have rubbed shoulders with naval and military men eager to expand wireless telephony and telegraphy, ministers interested in developing national telephone and wireless systems, and more important, perhaps, businessmen and bankers there to discuss financing and operating such systems. At the center of it all was Admiral Bullard who, going far beyond his official interests, participated in discussions regarding transatlantic telephone cables and wireless stations capable of throwing signals from stations in Newfoundland to Ireland and from there to the rest of Europe. Bullard came away from the conference more determined than ever "that if possible this new form of international communication should remain in the hands of the Americans."

Franklin Roosevelt shared that conviction. So did Wilson, who was developing a plan to resolve the matter. One morning, prior to departing for Versailles, Wilson turned to his naval aide and physician, Admiral Cary Grayson, and remarked, "I wish you would remind me today to get in touch and communicate with the Navy Department officially or with Admiral Bullard. I have an important message that I want to send to Mr. Owen D. Young relative to the protection of American rights and possibilities in radio communications."

That the President would turn to Young in this matter was not surprising. Young was one of that generation of businessmen perhaps best typified by Herbert Hoover and Bernard Baruch, which made a great impact on the scene during the war by assisting in the mobilization effort and turning out products for the armed forces and would continue to command the public's fascination and respect during the 1920s. Young was 41 years old in 1915, at which time as GE's chief counsel he had negotiated with Marconi for the sale of Alexanderson alternators, and four years later Young was vice president in charge of policy. He generally received much of the credit for the firm's outstanding performance during the war. Young had captured Wilson's attention; later on the President would name him to chair the Second Industrial Conference charged with developing plans to avoid labor strife. In December 1918 the focus of attention was on the Alexanderson alternators, as British Marconi, expecting American Marconi's installations soon to be released from Navy control, hoped to renew the negotiations begun before the war.

Young wrote to Roosevelt in late March 1919, telling him of ongoing discussions with British Marconi regarding the sale of alternators. A few days later Marconi proposed a deal far more attractive than its prewar offer: it would purchase 25 of the devices at $125,000 each plus $1 million in lieu of royalties for an exclusive contract (this last clause was hardly necessary, since such an order would occupy GE for several years). Some $3 million was involved, a sizable sum for the time.

This too was reported to Roosevelt, who transmitted the information to Hooper, who later wrote that he considered it the turning point for an American role in wireless. Bullard had just arrived in Washington to assume the post of Director of Naval Communications and quickly suggested that he go to Schenectady to discuss the matter with Young. Roosevelt readily assented, writing to Young, "Due to the various ramifications of the subject, it is requested that before reaching any final agreement with the Marconi Companies, you confer with representative of the department."

It is significant to note that Roosevelt wrote of "the Marconi Companies," indicating that he considered them wedded, and that American Marconi was, in effect, a subsidiary of the British firm. In fact, at the time only two of the thirteen directors were resident in London and of the others ten were Americans and one a Canadian. As noted the firm's president, John Griggs, was an American, while Marconi was a very silent vice president.

Second Vice President Edward Nally, a 60-year-old veteran who had started out as a cash boy at Western Union at the age of eight, had been at Marconi since 1913 and was deemed its shrewdest observer of the political scene. He was the key figure at the firm, its most experienced field manager, a man respected throughout the industry, and the person who had the best chance of convincing Congress that American Marconi should remain under control of the prewar management.

Although the Navy wasn't aware of it at the time, Young had come around to its view regarding the necessity of an American wireless company to take the field against British Marconi, not only in the United States, but elsewhere in the world. A muscular, confident, and expansionist American capitalism had emerged during the war, eager not only to defeat the Germans but to seize opportunities presented by the weakening of the British Empire. Wireless would be only one of several vehicles in the new struggle.

The new world order would be erected upon a national triad. First of all, there were the Wall Street banks, led by J. P. Morgan & Co., National City, Chase National, and other familiar names. Eager to expand into such British economic preserves as Latin America and cognizant of America's new role as the world's leading creditor country, the banks saw no reason why they should not mount a challenge to Lombard Street.

In order to do this, they would need cooperation from a friendly and compliant President and Congress, and both were in place. By 1915 Wilson had replaced his New Freedom crusades against big business with an awareness of the need for cooperation with industrialists in the forthcoming war effort. From 1917 to 1919 the United States was organized into a giant industrial machine, directed by what for the want of a better term might be called "the new Wilsonians," men like Baruch, Young, Howard Coffin of Hudson Motors, Walter Gifford of AT&T, Julius Rosenwald of Sears, Roebuck, Frank Scott of Warner & Swasey, and scores of others. "War is no longer Samson with his shield and spear and sword," said Secretary of War Newton Baker. "It is the conflict of the smokestacks now, the combat of the driving wheel and the engine."

Wilson was as pro-big business during the war as his successors, Warren Harding, Calvin Coolidge, and Herbert Hoover, would be in the decade that followed. Congressman Greene's antique vision of antitrust was out of place in this new environment. In its place would come a positive desire on the part of Washington to aid business through tariffs, tax benefits, and encouragement against foreigners. What was involved in 1919 was nothing less than the creation of what President Dwight Eisenhower would later call "the military-industrial complex," the first element of which was to be a national wireless corporation.

The third leg of the triad was comprised of the corporations financed and supported by Wall Street and encouraged by Washington. These included such established firms as General Electric, General Motors, Westinghouse, DuPont, and U.S. Steel—all of which were known as Morgan companies and had representatives of that bank on their boards—but also some newcomers. One of the most important of these was to be fashioned out of the corpus of American Marconi.

Bullard and Hooper went to New York to confer with Young on April 7, the same day Young received the urgent letter from Roosevelt asking him to delay the sale. Young recollected the conversation in congressional testimony two years later, in a way that indicated the triad was already in place:

> He [Bullard] said that the President had reached the conclusion, as a result of his experience in Paris, that there were three dominating factors in international relations—international transport, international communication, and petroleum—and that the influence which a country exercised in international affairs would be largely dependent upon their position of dominance in these three activities; that Britain obviously had the lead and the experience in international transportation—it would be difficult if not impossible to equal her position in that field; in international communications she had acquired the practical domination of the cable system of the world; but there was an apparent opportunity for the United States to challenge her in international communications through the use of radio. . . .

Chairman Charles Coffin of GE went along with this. "We will not put this machine in the hands of foreigners without some regulation and control," he said and then asked, "But what shall we do? We have no other customers for it." To which, according to Young, Bullard responded:

> Admiral Bullard said the President requested me to undertake the job of mobilizing the resources of the nation in radio. It was obvious that we had to mobilize everything we had, otherwise any of our international neighbors could weaken us tremendously by picking out one little thing. The whole picture puzzle had to be put together as a whole in order to get an effective national instrument. . . .

What mattered at this juncture was that through Bullard, Wilson was proposing an American version of the Marconi companies and suggesting that it would be a monopoly, sanctioned by government, perhaps along the lines of AT&T. While speaking forcefully at the peace sessions of the need to subordinate the old nationalistic drives and replace them with the vision of an international League of Nations, Wilson was fashioning a highly nationalistic American program in the international wireless field.

Young met with Edward Nally the following week to inform him that the alternator sale would not be made and was told that the Navy was inconsistent, since it already had approved the sale of other important technologies, including the Paulsen Arc system, to American Marconi. A master of the possible who from the first realized that concessions would have to be made if Marconi were to survive, Nally was prepared to strike a deal. The key to it all, he thought, was to convince everyone involved, especially the Navy, that his company was truly an American concern.

What would Washington think of an American syndicate formed to purchase the British interest in American Marconi, one including and perhaps headed by GE? Under such circumstances the company would remain intact, but its shares would be wholly-owned by Americans. "I cannot say," Young replied, but he did concede that the British ownership portion was troublesome. However, he raised the specter of another issue, that of GE entering the wireless business, though perhaps for Nally's benefit he dismissed the thought. "I recognize the right of the Government to stop us from negotiating with you, but I am almost inclined not to recognize their right to force us into competition with you."

Each man was playing a cagey game. It continued for another month, during which Young traveled to Washington to confer with Daniels, Roosevelt, the powerful GOP Senator Henry Cabot Lodge of Massachusetts, and others. Compromises were made all around. Daniels would have preferred a government monopoly not unlike the postal service but accepted the idea of a private firm. Lodge, who then was in the midst of organizing opposition to the Versailles Treaty, agreed to cooperate.

Meetings followed between GE executives and their American Marconi counterparts in New York and London, with GE edging toward an American purchase of the firm and the English negotiating for some way by which to maintain it intact. Young permitted himself to be drawn to the idea of a syndicate. After a June 20 meeting he wrote that American Marconi was definitely interested in pursuing the matter, which "would probably mean the necessity of [GE's] taking over the interest of the British Marconi Company [in American Marconi]."

By now Nally had come to realize that given adamant opposition by the Navy, survival as an independent probably was impossible. All that remained was to convince the British Marconi interests that this was so and obtain the best price and settlement for the American Marconi employees. With this in mind and accompanied by a GE representative, Nally sailed for Europe in June.

In early July Congress passed a resolution ordering the return to their original owners by March 1, 1920, of all telephone, telegraph, and cable systems seized by the government during the war. Now the movement toward an agreement accelerated. By then Nally was talking about a consortium to control American wireless that would be led by a refurbished American Marconi and GE, while Young attempted to convince him of the need for an all-American firm excluding the American Marconi interests.

Many others would have to join, if only by virtue of their patent positions. "It was utterly impossible for anybody to do anything in radio, any one person or group of companies at that time," Young later wrote. "The Westinghouse Company, the American Tel. & Tel. Company, the United Fruit Company, and the General Electric Company all had patents but nobody had patents enough to make a system. And so there was a complete stalemate."

Nonetheless Young intended for GE to have the dominant role in whatever new entity appeared. The wireless business clearly would be highly profitable, and the notion was that the restructured company would become a major customer for all sorts of electrical products. If it was controlled by GE alone, critics might charge violations of antitrust laws; such was already happening. Indeed, this was to be one of the more important political considerations involved in the creation of an American wireless entity.

From the first those with sharp memories of the recent antitrust crusade charged Young and others with attempting to fashion a radio trust not unlike earlier ones in sugar, tobacco, linseed oil, steel, and other commodities. Some believed it would be patterned after AT&T, the quasi-monopoly that had been the target of antitrusters for more than two decades. In Europe and elsewhere telephone companies were owned by governments, usually operated by the post offices, and electricity too was provided by governments. Why should it be any different in the United States? Daniels continued as a strong proponent of this view, while Franklin Roosevelt inclined toward a private corporation owned by the major electric companies.

Young took the monopoly charges seriously and so from the first made it clear that the new firm would be jointly owned by other large American concerns, with substantial contributions from Washington. For the moment, however, he proposed that GE purchase the British shares in American Marconi, invest an additional $3 million for preferred stock, and most important, turn over to the new firm its wireless patents and others for an additional amount of the common stock, after which other partners would be brought in.

Meanwhile Nally was having a difficult time of it in London, but after a month and a half of negotiations and discussions the British came around to the fact that they would have to sell their shares. In the end British Marconi agreed to accept approximately $1.5 million for its holding, the only condition being that the sale would become effective upon the formation of a new entity, this to safeguard against GE's entry into wireless communications on its own, a development that troubled it. Also, British Marconi hoped to lay the groundwork for future cooperation with the new firm to be fashioned out of American Marconi, which would be similar to the prewar arrangements between parent and offspring. The sale was consummated in September, upon which Nally returned home.

The news was released on September 2, 1919. As *The New York Times* put it, GE "will become a stockholder in the company when the deal is arranged, but it is asserted positively that the wireless company will in no sense be a subsidiary of General Electric."

Although the press didn't know it at the time, Young had already decided to become the firm's chairman, while remaining on at GE. Nally would be there as president to run things. Other Marconi executives who remained included Griggs, chief counsel James Sheffield, and Edward Harden. The GE contingent would include E. W. Rice, Gordon Abbott, and Albert Davis, who was GE's counsel and the person who had negotiated the transfer of ownership. From the first, too, J. P. Morgan & Co. had a say in who would serve on the board.

Roy Weigant and Elmer Bucher, two of Marconi's most important engineers, stayed on, as did Edwin Howard Armstrong, whose work on radio tubes was almost as important to the development of wireless as Alexanderson's in alternators. New York-born and educated in electrical engineering at Columbia, Armstrong had been introduced to wireless by Michael Pupin, one of the legendary figures in the history of electricity, and at the time was considered one of the most promising researchers in the field. Alexanderson was designated chief engineer, but like Young and Davis, he devoted most of his time to GE; so in the early years, Armstrong emerged as the dominant scientist at the revamped firm.

Under terms of the charter foreigners were forbidden to own more than 20 percent of the common shares, and the government had the right to designate a nonvoting observer to sit on the board, which to no one's surprise turned out to be Admiral Bullard.

A name had been decided upon as well; the firm was to be known as Radio Corporation of America.

What was then commonly known as "the radio corporation" was chartered in Delaware on October 17, 1919, with GE advancing $287,000 in cash and providing a line of credit of $3 million. Five days later GE and American Marconi entered into an agreement under the terms of which GE's Marconi shares would be exchanged for those in RCA, and American Marconi agreed to urge other shareholders to approve of the new dispensation. This was done rapidly given the pace of business life in that period.

On November 20, American Marconi was folded into RCA and ceased to exist, although it would pay a liquidating dividend of 25 cents per share on January 2, 1920.

The transfer was relatively uneventful. For those working at American Marconi the change was almost imperceptible; it was as though the firm had received a new name, nothing else. RCA inherited Marconi's old offices in the Woolworth Building near City Hall in lower Manhattan, where it would remain for a decade and a half, expanding every year as the company grew.

According to plans, the Navy returned the last of the seized American Marconi facilities to the Radio Corporation on February 29, and at that time the firm swung into action, sending wireless messages from the United States to Great Britain. But there was a change. The old rate of 25 cents per word was reduced to 17 cents, indicating a desire to compete more forcefully with the cable companies, which were charging 25 cents. In addition Young and Nally were negotiating with other American companies regarding their role in the enterprise.

At that time and for the next year "RCA" was deemed the repository of America's hopes in wireless and in fact was categorized by Moody's Investment Service as a utility, not an industrial company. It was not allowed to manufacture electrical gear, but instead had to purchase all it needed. The company's original purpose was to engage in wireless telephony and telegraphy, with much of the business ship-to-shore and transcontinental. No one on the board appears to have given any serious thought to other possibilities.

Much of Young's time in the next year was devoted to the second industrial conference, and in 1921 he became a key figure in President Warren Harding's Conference on Unemployment. But he also moved to make RCA a force on the world telecommunications scene. He participated in an international conference in Paris attended by representatives of RCA, British Marconi, France's Compagnie de Télégraphie sans Fil, and the German Gesellschafte fur Drahtlose Telegraphie m.b.H., the purpose being to carve up South America's wireless business. Under Young's leadership the so-called A.E.F.G. consortium was organized, with each national company having a quarter share. This done, Young moved to do the same for Asia. By then RCA had established wireless contact between the United States and Japan, with Washington's assistance obtained a contract from the new Polish government to erect a wireless station in Warsaw, and was aggressively seeking business elsewhere. Young's ambition to see RCA become the dominant international force in wireless was on its way to being realized.

Now that Young was recognized as one of the nation's most prominent businessmen, demands on him intensified. At the same time GE was expanding into new areas too, and he had to devote more time to its affairs, especially since on Coffin's retirement in 1922 he moved into the chairmanship. Thus, Young had to delegate much of his authority at RCA to others, Nally in particular.

Albert Davis too was one of the key figures in 1919–1920, for with Young's and Nally's guidance he negotiated arrangements to bring the other American wireless interests into the RCA fold. His role served to reenforce the general belief that RCA was an appendage of GE. While there was some truth in this, there were other important players in the RCA game.

As noted, from the first Young intended to bring into RCA Westinghouse, American Telephone & Telegraph, United Fruit, and others holding important wireless patents and capable of making financial contributions. There was even talk of a Western Union interest, which would unite all forms of electrical communication in one entity.

All of this was being considered against the backdrop of a strong governmental concern. In January 1920, the Navy Department observed that it had "consistently held to the point of view that all interests would best be served through some agreement between the several holders of pertinent patents whereby the market can be freely supplied with tubes."

Negotiations with Western Union came to nothing, but RCA had better fortune with AT&T. That company's interest in wireless was natural enough, for before the war it was thought that wireless might prove a superior method of telephony. In 1912 AT&T had acquired some of De Forest's audion tube patents, and H. P. Arnold, a scientist at its Western Electric subsidiary, developed an improved audion tube that was the state of the art in its time. Three years later AT&T was sending wireless telephone messages from a Navy station at Arlington, Virginia, to such distant points as Paris and Hawaii. Eventually AT&T paid De Forest $400,000 for his patent rights.

Already a competitor of GE and Westinghouse in equipment through its International Western Electric subsidiary, AT&T manufactured and sold telephony products in Europe as well and had ambitions to become a worldwide operation in addition to maintaining its dominant domestic position. Might this be possible without sponsorship by the government? Hardly so, since Washington had already signaled its intention to back RCA for this role. Moreover, the Navy was pressing AT&T to come to terms with the new company, and so it did.

On July 1, 1920, RCA and AT&T signed a cross-licensing agreement that extended to GE as well, which included all radio telephone equipment for "public service uses," the term referring to wireless telephony and telegraphy. Soon after, AT&T purchased an equity position in RCA, taking 500,000 shares of preferred and 500,000 of common for $2.5 million. This was a significant move. The RCA leadership had acquired patents that earlier had been contested by AT&T, so protracted and costly litigation was now avoided. Finally, under the arrangement RCA could utilize telephone lines when necessary, and this was deemed important in the early 1920s. Still, the AT&T people mistrusted the RCA-GE combine, which at the time seemed destined to attempt an entry into some form of wireless telephony, thus initiating a telecommunications battle.

In the contract there was some mention of the possibility of transmitting "news, music, and entertainment" over the air, but it would appear neither party considered it of great moment. Moreover, given the outlook of the period, AT&T had no interest in anything dealing with radio except the manufacture and sale of specialized gear. Broadly speaking, AT&T was to have a dominant role in the manufacture and sale of transmission equipment while RCA-GE was to have a similar position in receivers. This arrangement, which might have worked well in wireless, was destined to break down once it became clear just where the technology would lead, and both AT&T and RCA-GE interpreted the contract in its own interests. Moreover, neither group devoted much attention to the possibilities of broadcasting. Later on, when it had become obvious this would be a major industry, AT&T claimed that it was meant to have a dominant role in radio telephone, and so the others were excluded, while RCA-GE held that AT&T's rights were restricted to the manufacture of equipment, and so it had to remain out of broadcasting. Interpretation of a contract designed for wireless at a time when broadcasting was growing became a bone of contention between the parties for a decade.

Another arrangement was worked out with United Fruit, whose Tropical Radio Telegraph would mesh well with RCA's Pan-American Wireless while the Wireless Specialty subsidiary owned important patents. United Fruit purchased 200,000 each of common and preferred for $1 million. Thus was born a GE-AT&T-RCA-United Fruit alliance.

Attention now turned to Westinghouse Electric and Manufacturing, GE's chief rival in the electrical equipment business. Unwilling to play a subsidiary role to GE at RCA, Westinghouse set out to create its own wireless operation. Westinghouse's assets were impressive: a good patent position (it controlled those of Fessenden, among others, including as will be seen some important ones obtained from Armstrong), adequate financing, and experienced leadership although the RCA team was stronger in all of these areas. However, Westinghouse could count on the support of antitrusters in Congress, who smiled upon competition, although with the advent of a conservative Republican administration few thought that any significant action would be taken in Westinghouse's behalf.

Westinghouse's bid for a position in wireless came through a near-forgotten vehicle, the International Radio Telegraph Company, a successor to National Electric Signaling, which it will be recalled had been put together by Reginald Fessenden as a rival to American Marconi. The company was close to failure after the World War, awaiting the return of its handful of ship-to-shore stations, when Westinghouse approached it with an offer to purchase several of its patents. Samuel Kintner, Radio Telegraph's CEO, rejected the idea, but discussions continued and in the end Westinghouse offered him a cross-licensing deal, out of which came an arrangement not unlike that which GE had with RCA. The old owners received $1.25 million for stock worth a fraction of that amount, and Westinghouse purchased additional new shares in a reorganized International Radio Telegraph for $2.5 million, of which $300,000 was paid in the next few months. All of the arrangements were completed on May 22, 1920.

Young monitored these developments. On August 25, he told a meeting of RCA's Technical Committee that "the one obstacle which might be found in the United States was the International [Radio] Company, which had now received the backing of the Westinghouse Company." But according to the minutes, Young added that "Westinghouse . . . could hardly afford to begin a patent war on the General Electric Company, and therefore this question left him without apprehension."

This was not an idle boast. Kintner had gone to Europe that summer seeking orders and found that RCA and British Marconi, working in concert, had sewn up most markets. Westinghouse's leaders, headed by Chairman Guy Tripp, vice presidents Harry Davis and Charles Terry, and especially Frank Conrad, the firm's technician most concerned with radio, were dismayed, but resolved to continue.

Conrad was particularly intrigued by the use of wireless by amateurs, and it was largely because of him that Westinghouse became one of the leaders in the area. A shy, diffident man, who was one of Westinghouse's most prized engineers, Conrad had dropped out of school after the seventh grade to take a job as a bench hand at Westinghouse in 1890, at which time he was 16 years old. Largely self-educated, Conrad was embarrassed by his lack of education. Later on, after he received an honorary degree, he was usually referred to as "Doctor Conrad" by the company and his associates. He was one of that band of engineers who at the turn of the century were creating scores of wireless devices.

Young knew about Westinghouse's interest in the amateur market, but amateur sales seemed trifling at the time. In addition he continued to believe that RCA was sufficiently strong to meet any challenge. Yet any contest between it and International Radio was bound to spark monopoly charges from the latter, especially if Kintner raised the issue of the RCA–British Marconi cooperation. Furthermore, the business spirit of the postwar period fostered cooperation rather than competition.

With all of this in mind, Young offered Westinghouse 700,000 shares each of RCA common and preferred in exchange for International Radio, plus the remaining $2.2 million yet to be paid for the firm. This would place a value of $3.5 million on International Radio and those valuable patents that were an integral part of the deal. Since Westinghouse had already put $1.55 million into that firm, and still had to pay the additional $2.2 million, the offer hardly seemed generous. Admittedly, RCA's stock was yet to be sold to the public but most seemed to think that if and when it was the price would rise to a substantial premium. More to the point, if Westinghouse accepted it would become the second most important factor at RCA, behind GE but ahead of AT&T and United Fruit.

Tripp was interested but thought that Westinghouse should be given a larger share. As though to bolster his case, he purchased options on patents owned by Armstrong and Michael Pupin while Frank Conrad was developing ideas for an experimental radio station, which intrigued several of the young men at RCA as well. For these reasons, and also because he was eager to complete the monopoly, Young raised the offer to one million shares each of RCA common and preferred, which would have given Westinghouse a larger amount of preferred than GE but less of common.

More negotiations followed, with an agreement ratified on March 25, 1921, under the terms of which Westinghouse received the shares offered in exchange for International Radio Telegraph and for placing its patents in the pool. Under terms of the understanding RCA was to sell equipment manufactured by its principal owners, with GE to have 60 percent of the market, Westinghouse 40 percent, for which RCA would pay cost plus 20 percent. The Western Electric subsidiary of AT&T would have what amounted to a monopoly in transmitters. The RCA board was restructured and was now made up of four members each from the old American Marconi and GE, three from Westinghouse-International Radio, two from AT&T, and one from United Fruit.

SHARE OWNERSHIP OF RCA, MARCH 25, 1921

COMPANY	COMMON	PREFERRED	TOTAL	PERCENT
General Electric	2,364,826	620,800	2,985,626	30.1
Westinghouse	1,000,000	1,000,000	2,000,000	20.6
AT&T	500,000	500,000	1,000,000	10.3
United Fruit	200,000	200,000	400,000	4.1
Others	1,667,174	1,635,174	3,302,348	34.9

Source: Gleason Archer, *Big Business and Radio* (New York: The American Historical Company, 1939), p. 8.

It is crucial to keep in mind that Young and the others were fashioning a *wireless* company. Up to that time almost everyone in the industry, especially Young, had concentrated on wireless telephony, and the contracts and arrangements were written with these in mind. Broadcasting, both in the transmission and in the receiving ends, was not covered by the basic accords and so could and would prove a wide-open field, and one in which bitter contention developed. More than most, early radio was a battlefield for lawyers and lobbyists as well as inventors, technicians, and businessmen.

2

From Narrowcast to Broadcast

THE EARLY YEARS of almost any new industry are marked by efforts to discover the most effective and useful means of employing technologies, creating and marketing products, and simply learning how to adjust to circumstances. Perceptions and the search for perspective are essential, as are the visions and insights of talented entrepreneurs and managers.

Such has been the case with steam power, railroads, automobiles, aviation, telephones, motion pictures, and most recently, computers. In the case of all of these one finds that the older, entrenched industries and businessmen first rejected the newcomers, then attempted to come to terms with them, and finally bowed to the new dispensation.

Governments often played important roles in the development of emerging enterprises; certainly this was so in transportation and communication industries. In few cases prior to radio, however, did government have the real and perceived power to take command, to shape the very nature of the enterprise. Then, too, in no other industry did giant older companies play so great a role at the outset, to the point of being able to control the major player, in this case RCA.

In its first half-decade RCA was faced with the quadruple challenge of establishing itself as "The Radio Trust," maintaining proper relations with its parents while asserting independence, and working out some form of compromise with AT&T, its most important potential rival. Finally, RCA had to walk the line between government regulation and control and free enterprise.

All of this had to be accomplished against the backdrop of a national mania for radio and pressure for its expansion. No other new product in the nation's history—not railroads, automobiles, motion pictures, or personal computers—has ever experienced the kind of demand there was for radio receivers and broadcasting in 1922–1923, a phenomenon that established RCA as the most glamorous and fastest-growing corporation of the decade.

As has been seen, President Wilson became intrigued with wireless during the war and took a keen interest in the technology when observing it in action aboard the SS *George Washington* on the trip to Paris. He had stressed its use for commercial and military communications, but there was more to it than that. When later that year Young met with Bullard, he asked the admiral just what it was that drew Wilson to radio.

> He said the President had been deeply impressed by the ability to receive all over Europe messages sent from this side [i.e., by radio telegraphy] across all international boundaries from this country by the Alexanderson Alternator of his "Fourteen Points." Bullard said he had been into some of the Balkan states and there found school children learning the Fourteen Points as they would learn their catechism—made possible by the Alexanderson Alternator in New Brunswick, New Jersey, which, defying all censorship, was stimulating in everybody everywhere a deep anxiety that the war should end.

In this was the first glimmering of both the creation of an American radio company and of the direction it might take: broadcasting. But none of the principal actors of the time—not Wilson, not Roosevelt, and certainly not Young, whose mind was on other things—appreciated this potential. As his daughter and biographer recalled six decades later, "Young [did not] display, either before or after the war, any noteworthy grasp of radio's commercial or cultural potentialities. Like most of his generation, he had felt the magic of this fantastic new device which needed no wires to transmit its electrical impulses overseas; its larger message was simply not for him." Edison was of a like mind, and he belittled the radio boom of 1922. "It will die out in time so far as music is concerned," he told an associate. "But it may continue for business purposes."

As noted, Frank Conrad at Westinghouse was one of the first to recognize that wireless might have uses other than telephony and telegraphy. As early as 1912 Conrad was thinking about "broadcasting," the sending of messages to anyone who might be interested in listening, as opposed to "narrowcasting," the transmission of messages from one individual to another such as with telegraphs and telephones. Legend has it that Conrad stumbled upon broadcasting that year when he constructed a radio receiver that enabled him to receive time signals sent out regularly by the Arlington Observatory. During the war he devoted much of his time to wireless, inventing the only viable airplane radio, but he also worked on the broadcasting concept.

It was hardly a novel idea. Others, including Alexander Graham Bell, had considered such possibilities. In 1877 Bell spoke of an entire nation tied together in speech through the use of telephones. The lyrics of a popular song of that year, "The Wondrous Telephone," ran:

You stay at home and listen
To the lecture in the hall,
Or hear the strains of music
From a fashionable ball.

In 1878 Edward Bellamy, in his *Looking Backward, 2000–1887* wrote of a utopian society.

> If we could have devised an arrangement for providing everybody with music in their homes, perfect in quality, unlimited in quantity, suited to every mood, and beginning and ceasing at will, we should have considered the limit of human felicity already attained.

Marconi, De Forest, Fessenden, and other radio pioneers wrote of the possibilities of such radio devices. As we have seen, Fessenden broadcast to ships at sea in 1906, and in 1916 De Forest was to broadcast music and talk from a station at Highbridge, New York. Indeed, the thought seems to have occurred at one time or another to almost every wireless pioneer.

After the war Conrad established an experimental sending and receiving station in Westinghouse's Pittsburgh facilities. In April 1920 Westinghouse obtained a Department of Commerce license for it under the designation 8XK. Soon Conrad was in contact with a circle of radio enthusiasts in the area, and to please them he would send out over the airwaves music played on a phonograph, supplied by the Hamilton Music Store. It wasn't long before the store stumbled into commercial broadcasting by providing Conrad with free records in return for which he mentioned where they might be purchased.

It appears Conrad gave little thought to the commercial possibilities of his activities. Up to that time most receivers were amateur affairs consisting of a wire, known as a "cat's whisker," which was passed over a quartz crystal to capture radio impulses from the air by means of an aerial wire, which was connected to a pair of earphones. This "crystal set" could be assembled for a few dollars and was used primarily by enthusiasts who were that generation's equivalent of today's "computer hackers." Commercialization was on the way, however. In early 1920 the Joseph Horne Company in downtown Pittsburgh sold an assembled crystal set for $10, and shortly thereafter Crosley offered a model for $14.50.

Not being commercially oriented Conrad couldn't visualize what this might mean, but Westinghouse Vice President Harry Davis did. He later wrote that this development "caused the thought to come to me that the efforts that were then being made to develop radio telephony as a confidential means of communication were wrong, and that instead its field was really one of wide publicity, in fact, the only means of instantaneous collective communication ever devised. Right in our grasp, therefore, we had that service we had been thinking about and endeavoring to formulate."

Davis met with Conrad and others to discuss establishing a station. "If there is sufficient interest to justify a department store in advertising radio sets for sale on an uncertain plan of permanence, I believe there would be a sufficient interest to justify the expense of rendering a regular service—looking to the sale of sets and the advertising of the Westinghouse Company. . . ."

Thus, Davis saw broadcasting essentially as a means of selling receivers, not realizing at the time just how important and profitable the ownership and management of stations could be.

What he had in mind was an experiment. 8XK would broadcast the 1920 election returns and as its equipment sales expanded, other stations might be established in major markets to stimulate demand. It was as though automobile manufacturers constructed roads to make their products more desirable, and in our time, microcomputer manufacturers developing software to sell their machines.

There was no reason for Westinghouse not to enter this field, since at the time its nexus with equipment manufacturing hadn't been fixed in the public mind. In fact Westinghouse produced its first receivers, known as the Aeriola Jr., in June 1921. It was a small crystal set, which could bring in broadcasts from 12 to 15 miles away and sold for $25. It was soon followed by the Aeriola Sr., the first to use a vacuum tube and priced at $60, and the Aeriola Grand, with a self-contained loudspeaker and several vacuum tubes, which sold for $170.

Davis and Conrad worked to expand 8XK, which was soon renamed KDKA, and the election broadcast was a success. Now Westinghouse moved to create new stations—WBZ in Springfield, Massachusetts, WJZ in Newark, New Jersey (soon to be jointly owned with RCA), and KYW in Chicago. In each market receiver sales rose. In late 1921 it appeared that General Electric would concentrate upon transmission equipment, RCA would look after the creation of telephony communications, and Westinghouse would open new stations and sell receivers to the public.

David Sarnoff was one of those at RCA who appreciated the importance of the Conrad efforts. In 1916, while commercial manager of American Marconi, he wrote to Edward Nally what is probably the most perceptive and certainly the most publicized memorandum in the history of radio. "I have in mind a plan of development which would make radio a 'household utility' in the same sense as the piano or phonograph. The idea is to bring music into the house by wireless." Sarnoff went on to describe the device, a "box which can be placed on a table in the parlor or living room, the switch set accordingly, and the transmitted music received." The offerings need not be limited to music, however. Lectures could be aired, thus creating what could amount to a wireless schoolroom. "Events of national importance can be simultaneously announced and received. Baseball scores can be transmitted in the air. . . . Farmers and others living a distance from urban areas could be greatly benefited. By the purchase of a 'Radio Music Box' they could enjoy concerts, lectures, music, recitals, etc. which might be going on in the nearest city within their radius."

What he was describing, of course, was the Aeriolas that would appear a few years later. Sarnoff's contribution was not in his originality, but rather the combination of vision with a sense of commercial possibilities, for he was among the first to recognize the potentials of broadcasting and harness them to the engine of a major business operation.

Sarnoff thought the profits could be enormous. He believed that the music boxes could be sold for $75 each and that if only one million families (there were about 15 million at the time) purchased one, the revenues would come to $75 million. "Aside from the profit to be derived from this proposition, the possibilities for advertising for the company are tremendous, for its name would ultimately be brought into the household, and wireless would receive national and international attention."

In 1916 then, Sarnoff was at one with Conrad, considering that broadcasting could be utilized as a vehicle to sell receivers, and not as a separate profit center on its own.

Nally scoffed at the idea. Nor did Young think it had merit, even though he later agreed to back the radio music box experiment—to the extent of $2,000. He conceded that "this interest was increased *later* when I learned from *engineers* [emphasis added] of its possibilities for entertainment."

Thus Young indicated that initially at least he was convinced by Conrad's work, and perhaps not by Sarnoff, of radio's potential. Whatever their relative roles, Conrad and Sarnoff may be considered the real fathers of broadcasting in the United States, and in the beginning at least, Conrad was the more important. More than anything else, Conrad's work turned RCA from telecommunications to radio broadcasting. Yet it isn't unusual for Conrad's role to be slighted in most popular recitals of the origins of radio or for Sarnoff's to be enlarged. This in no way denigrates Sarnoff's contributions; it is difficult to imagine radio developing the way it did were it not for his presence. More than almost any other giant American corporation, RCA was fashioned and informed by his vision and force of will, its strengths his strengths, its flaws his flaws.

Sarnoff's rise to power, fame, and celebrity has been told many times over by hagiographers, journalists, and others for the better part of a half century. There is an adoring biography, written by a Eugene Lyons, his journalist-cousin, who on the very first page states that ". . . he [Sarnoff] has probably affected the patterns of the daily lives of more Americans than anyone since

Thomas Edison," an assumption that gives the flavor of this work. Carl Dreher, a Sarnoff associate of many years, wrote a more critical study but still one that like Lyons's book places the man on a pedestal. The title gives it away: *Sarnoff: An American Success.* We also have a collection of his selected sayings and writings, entitled *Looking Ahead,* which was released in 1968, and scores of magazine articles that tend to repeat one another, but little more in print. There is, however, a remarkable source in typescript, whose contents and even size indicate much of the nature of the man and his company.

This is the 56-volume monument by Elmer Bucher, comprising 388 chapters and more than 13,000 pages. The volumes are entitled variously "Radio and David Sarnoff," "Television and David Sarnoff," "Shortwave Radio and David Sarnoff," "Voice of America and David Sarnoff," "Subscription Television and David Sarnoff," "David Sarnoff's Golden Anniversary Dinner," "Broadcasting and David Sarnoff," and "History of Radio and Television Development in the United States of America." This is supplemented by a five-volume, 1,187-page "Color Television and David Sarnoff," and a single volume, 392-page "A Tribute to David Sarnoff."

Bucher, who knew Sarnoff since the American Marconi days, appears to have started work in 1941 and ended in 1962. Some discussion of the Bucher typescript belongs here, because of its importance and the fact that Sarnoff supported the work for so long. Judging from penciled notes and corrections in what looks like his handwriting, he might even have read it carefully.

The collection is fairly well-organized for the first few volumes but then becomes repetitive and rambling. Bucher not only has collected all the myths, probably heard from Sarnoff himself, but seems to have been the source used by many other writers on the subject.

Bucher is wholly admiring, even adoring. Perhaps some of the flavor may be captured by this paragraph, which comes early in the work, on page 1,188:

> In the line of American basic industries the public is apt to identify pioneering leadership in the development of oil with the Rockefellers; of railroads with H. E. Huntington, E. H. Harriman and James J. Hill; of the electric telegraph with Jay Gould and the Vanderbilts; of the telephone with Theodore Vail; of steel with Andrew Carnegie, H. C. Frick, and E. H. Gary, and of motors with Henry Ford, Alfred E. Sloan and William K. Knudsen. Each of these pioneers picked up the fragments of a group of unrelated or isolated attempts to develop an industry, tempered them with their own enthusiasm and judgement, made coalitions of energy companies and developed thriving enterprises therefrom. Historians of the future will properly add David Sarnoff's name to the roster of America's industrial pioneers, acknowledging his far-seeing leadership in radio, television and other developments born out of radio invention.

Bucher devoted a goodly part of his life to these volumes, which he dedicated, in December 1942, "To My Friend, David Sarnoff. Please accept this story as an expression of love and affection for you, and also of a deep regard for your contributions to the cause of radio. You may use this material in any way you see fit."

Almost everything we know of David Sarnoff derives from these friendly writers and admirers, and not much of that can be verified by independent historians and biographers. We do know that some important parts of the tale are exaggerations or fabrications. For example, according to Dreher that 1916 memorandum on radio receiver potential was backdated to September 30, 1915, when reproduced in *Looking Ahead.* The reason might have been to make it appear that Sarnoff had developed the idea before De Forest introduced the audion tube.

The story of Sarnoff's early years, as related by the company, the biographers, Bucher, and the press, is a variation upon the theme of the Great American Dream. Lyons does not exaggerate in writing that "few of the scores who have written about David Sarnoff, or eulogized him on set occasions, have resisted the temptation of fitting him into the American folklore summed up by Horatio Alger." Lyons thinks that even this comparison is inadequate. "For Sarnoff's is the kind of career Horatio Alger would have hesitated to dream up—it would have seemed too much even for *his* readers. Nor could he have conceived a hero so complex in character and motivation."

The theme would be repeated scores of times in his lifetime. In 1930 he told an interviewer, "Now forget that sob stuff in my life. Remember the Alger stories are out of date." Of course they continued. Typical was an altogether admiring *Time* magazine cover story in 1951: "Horatio Alger himself could hardly have done it in one book. He would have needed *Adrift in New York, Nelson the Newsboy, The Telegraph Boy,* and *Joe's Luck: Or Always Wide Awake.*"

His biographers did not delve into the other side of the man, for Sarnoff could be brutal, stubborn, and even vicious when the occasion required. But he shares these attributes with most of other major figures of American business history.

Among Sarnoff's flaws was an arrogance born out of a knowledge that he was superior to the individuals against whom he competed and even with whom he cooperated. The story is told of how, leg in a cast, Sarnoff hobbled into an elevator in which former President Harry Truman was riding. Noting this, Truman cracked, "Well, General, I guess now for a while you'll have to kick people in the ass with the other leg, won't you?"

Much of this might have had to do with his immigrant Jewish origins. Not a particularly religious individual, Sarnoff nonetheless was aggressively proud of his heritage and aware and contemptuous of the prejudice that worked against him. He once told Dreher that "I have to be twice as good to go half as far as 'them,'" and there was no doubt to whom he was referring.

Later on, when he had become a respected and prominent businessman, Sarnoff would ride horseback in Central Park with General James Harbord, then RCA's CEO, the two meeting at a specified location after Harbord mounted his horse at a club then in the park. A transparently decent individual, Harbord once asked Sarnoff why he didn't join the club, so they could come and go together. "General, my horse might be accepted there, but they never would take me," he was supposed to have said.

Sarnoff served in the Army in World War II and for the rest of his life delighted in being referred to as "General." This was understandable. Not only was Sarnoff a patriot, but as Harry Golden, that peripatetic chronicler of Jewish life in America, observed, no Jew in czarist Russia could hold an officer's rank, and so it meant all the more to him.

Just as one cannot understand Andrew Carnegie without reference to his Scots Presbyterian background, so to attempt to understand Sarnoff without taking account of his Jewishness would be reckless.

Wedded to this trait was an inability to forgive those whose talents were less than perfect and a surprising provincialism—Sarnoff hated to travel much beyond Manhattan except when conducting business. He often demonstrated the fierce patriotism frequently seen in first generation Americans, and toward the end of his life engaged in the kind of Red-baiting that brought into question his dedication to First Amendment guarantees.

Sarnoff was an imaginative romantic who delighted in writing articles and being interviewed on such subjects as where radio would be a generation from now, the promise of television, the possibilities of electronic journalism, and even the potential of atomic power. He was fascinated by technology and given his facility with language would have made a superb scientific essayist. Joseph McConnell, who worked with Sarnoff and eventually became head of the National Broadcasting Corp., thought he was a "visionary," who "ought to be in public office or head a university." David Lilienthal, who for a while in the early 1950s considered but rejected a major post at RCA, believed him "a restless, unsatisfied man. He has received honors and recognitions till the cows come home, and yet he doesn't quite let this satisfy him. There seems no slaking the thirst for recognition, praise, honors, kudos. . . ." An associate told Lilienthal that Sarnoff was only interested in work and wouldn't tolerate disagreement, but Lilienthal recorded conversations on a wide variety of subjects, from music to military ordnance, the Talmud to electronics, and was amazed at Sarnoff's ability to leap from one subject to another. Out of this, he wrote, came "a fascinating picture of a strong but very human man, a fighter, a pioneer, and not an easy man to understand—too complex."

Sarnoff's biographers speak and write of his vision; in 1960 a writer for *Business Week* talked of him as "always being on the frontier." And so he was. But a most intriguing and little explored side of his life was his apparent lack of interest in management. Management seemed to bore him. In *Looking Ahead* are to be found Sarnoff's thoughts over a half century on a wide variety of subjects, grouped under such headings as "Wireless Communication," "Radio Broadcasting," "Black-and-White Television," "Color Television," "The Communications Revolution," and "Science, Technology, and Human Affairs." Only one of the essays contains the word "management," and that doesn't deal with corporate affairs, but rather "The Management of Environmental Forces."

From the early 1920s until his death in 1971, Sarnoff dominated Radio Corporation of America. Even after he stepped down as chairman in 1969 his son and successor felt the General was looking on and, most of the time, with the disapproval that was part of his style.

Sarnoff's flaws might have been seen during his career, if only business writers had paid closer attention to RCA's often lackluster performance. Sarnoff may have been one of the first to recognize the potential of broadcasting and radio music boxes, but even with a powerful patent position RCA rarely had more than a quarter of the receiver market. He helped fashion a major radio network, but Sarnoff's National Broadcasting Company seldom was as innovative as William Paley's Columbia Broadcasting System. A foray into motion pictures ended dismally, when the combination of NBC's talents with RKO's studios might have made it a major force in the industry. Sarnoff maneuvered magnificently to obtain for RCA a leading position in television, but other firms, including Zenith, Magnavox, and Motorola, and eventually the Japanese, took the receiver market from RCA. He lobbied effectively for RCA's color TV technology, but by so doing saddled the United States with a second-rate system.

There were other failures, such as the decision to develop and then market the 45 rpm phonograph records, another instance where CBS bested RCA. And of course there was the fiasco of RCA's foray into computers, where Sarnoff and his son came head-to-head against another father-and-son combination, Thomas Watson, Sr., and Thomas Watson, Jr., who not only could match the Sarnoffs in vision but knew how to manage opportunity, to correlate their dreams with creation of a viable business operation.

The fact that RCA reeled from one disaster to another in the years following his departure should have come as no surprise to those who knew the company's history under the Sarnoff aegis. Sarnoff's old friends and associates often talk of how things fell apart once the master was no longer there. The fact of the matter is that a good deal of the credit for the successes should have gone to others, especially Frank Folsom, who took over as chief operating officer after World War II. Bob Sarnoff's failures and those of the others who came after were in the RCA tradition. The difference between David Sarnoff and some of his successors is that they inherited his company, but lacked his vision, shrewdness, and abilities at self-advertisement. Also, RCA was David Sarnoff's company, which is to suggest that he made himself larger than the enterprise, and so stamped his personality upon it that no one else could manage effectively.

The only source we have for Sarnoff's early life is the man himself, who related it to Bucher; all the other players of that period have died and none ever attempted to alter the story in any significant fashion. Thus, it is what Sarnoff wanted the world to believe. This is not to suggest it is a fabrication; indeed, from what is known of the lives of immigrants at the turn of the century it rings true. Still, elements of melodrama are found throughout.

David Sarnoff, the eldest child of Abraham and Lena, was born on February 27, 1891, in Uzlian, a small town on the outskirts of Minsk in what is now the northeastern part of the Soviet Union. Four years later Abraham, who was a house painter, left for the United States, upon which David was sent to live with his mother's uncle, a rabbi, to study the Talmud. He later told a reporter that he spent days debating such questions as: "If you saw an article lying in the street, what rights would you have to it?" The world of Sarnoff's childhood not only was radically different from what it would be later on but was also one in which money and power counted for far less than what he termed "the possession of knowledge."

The family was reunited in 1900. Sarnoff recalled traveling by foot and cart from Uzlian to Libau, a minor port in Latvia, where they embarked for the journey. "I had never even seen a picture of a ship," he recalled. On another occasion he spoke of how his mother prepared a huge hamper of kosher food for the trip and how he saw it being lowered into the hold. Fearing all might be lost, Sarnoff dove after it, falling (as he said) some 50 feet, but regaining the hamper. Watching all of this was a sailor, who pulled him up and said, "You'll do all right in America."

"My mother, two brothers, and I had arrived in the New World via steerage to Montreal and rail to Albany and from there to New York. Two days later I was peddling papers in the streets . . . to help support my family." Sarnoff attended elementary school, sold newspapers afterward, ran errands, and even earned some money by singing in the synagogue.

It was the stuff of which the immigrant epic was created. Owen Young, who knew him better than most, said that Sarnoff had lived "the most amazing romance of its kind on record."

Abraham Sarnoff died in 1906, and this meant that David had to leave school to support the family. His first full-time job was as a messenger boy for the Commercial Cable Company. Ambitious and even then sensing the potential in this field, he saved his money, purchased a telegraph instrument, and applied for a post as operator at American Marconi. He was hired instead as an office boy, but Sarnoff persisted and in 1908 was elevated to become a junior operator at the Marconi station on Nantucket Island. A year later he was transferred to Sea Gate on Coney Island and for a while worked aboard ship. In 1912 Sarnoff became the operator at the wireless station atop the Wanamaker Department Store in New York.

Radio telegraphy was an exciting young industry, and operators cut a romantic figure. Some had become media heroes by relaying news of marine disasters and thus saving lives. For example, as early as 1899 the East Godwin Lightship was struck by a steamer, the accident was reported by wireless, and help arrived in time to save all aboard. Two years later the SS *Princesse Clementine* was grounded, and the wireless once again saved lives. Then, on January 23, 1909, the White Star steamer *Republic* was rammed by the Italian steamer *Florida* off Nantucket. The *Republic*'s radio operator, John Binns, radioed the news and, according to one publication, "demonstrated to the whole world the value of radio in such a case by bravely standing by his instruments in the dark on a sinking ship and summoning aid, which arrived in time to save all hands."

It was the dream of every operator, either on shore or aboard ship—to save lives as Binns had and achieve recognition.

This happened to Sarnoff on April 14–16, 1912, when the SS *Titanic* was struck by an iceberg. As he told it, and Lyons repeats, the ship's wireless operator, Jack Phillips, sent out the SOS, remained at his key until the power failed in the accepted heroic mold, and then clung to a lifeboat until, overcome by exposure and cold, he died. Sarnoff stayed at his post for three days nonstop, relaying messages and directing rescue operations to the scene. All other wireless operations ceased, to clear the air for him, and during this period Sarnoff was the center of national attention. Now 21 years old, he was a celebrity when it was all over.

This is not quite the way Carl Dreher recalled the episode. Dreher observed that Sarnoff received little press attention at the time. One reason might have been that the Wanamaker station not only was closed at night but also lacked the power to communicate with distant ships, having been designed to reach only as far as Wanamaker's other facility in Philadelphia. In all probability Phillips's messages were picked up by the Marconi station on Nantucket Island, and it was from there Sarnoff obtained the information he relayed to the press. But the tale, as recited in Lyons's biography, helped burnish the image.

The name of the Nantucket operator is unknown. Jack Phillips is forgotten.

The experience marked Sarnoff as a comer at American Marconi, and he rose rapidly thereafter.

In 1913, when he became assistant chief engineer, Sarnoff decided on a career change. Until then he had attempted to absorb technology from books and occasional lectures, but he had learned enough to realize the limitations of such an approach. Moreover, Sarnoff had an interest in becoming an executive, which clearly would be a more remunerative position than technician.

Dreher relates how Sarnoff spoke of this to a mutual friend. "An engineer or scientific experimenter is at the place where the money is going out. The place to make money is where the money is coming in," Sarnoff reasoned. "I am going to quit trying to be an engineer, therefore, and am going to solicit the sale of contracts and service that will bring money into the company."

There was more to it than that. Sarnoff noticed that executives and salesmen had offices next to those of the chairman and general manager, while the technicians were further down the hall.

All went well. In 1914 Sarnoff was named contract manager and the following year, assistant traffic manager. On the eve of the United States' entry into World War I in 1917 Sarnoff was elevated to the post of commercial manager, which gave him authority in the purchase of equipment and operations. In effect he was second in command to Nally.

Sarnoff attempted to volunteer for naval duty, despite having recently been married. He recognized the importance of wireless to the Navy and might have suspected that uniformed personnel would be at the center of the industry so long as the war was on. But he was rejected, nominally because of his role in American Marconi's war effort, but also perhaps because of the prevalent anti-Semitism in the armed forces, the Navy in particular, during this period. In any case, Sarnoff spent the war working on wireless in New York, and after the Armistice he went into RCA along with other Marconi leaders.

By then Sarnoff had become the *de facto* chief operating officer while Nally assumed duties customarily performed by chief executive officers. With a board comprised of officials who owed their prime loyalty to their parent firms and Nally acting as liaison between RCA and the owners, Sarnoff was in a position to recommend and push for policy as well as implement it.

Sarnoff had become convinced that as promising as were RCA's prospects in wireless telephony it had a brighter future in commercial radio. While Young and the rest of GE management planned for the sale of electrical equipment, Sarnoff bent his efforts toward the creation and marketing of radio music boxes, which he hoped in time would be produced by RCA in its own factories. In addition he pondered the future of broadcasting, trying to figure out a means whereby RCA could enter the field and perhaps even in time dominate it. One might say that he was actively conspiring against the interests of RCA's two most important shareholders. Of course he had to move carefully since Young was still the most powerful force at the firm.

In March 1920 Sarnoff wrote to GE's President E. W. Rice, Jr., about the music boxes, arguing that a $75 set could be marketed with ease. In the first year, Sarnoff wrote, one might expect sales of 100,000, bringing in revenues of $7.5 million, in the second year sales and revenues would rise to 300,000 and $22.5 million respectively, and in the third, 600,000 and $45 million, for a total of 1 million sets and $75 million.

These estimates appeared farfetched. What Sarnoff had in mind were relatively small and not particularly powerful battery-operated models like the Aeriola Jr. then being planned at Westinghouse, and not the more grandiose but equally weak $200 sets some Westinghouse and GE engineers were talking about. The major electrical firms' top managements were not interested in such devices at the time, and Sarnoff bided his time. Patience was rewarded; in May 1921 he became RCA's general manager, in a stronger position to put forth his views.

The growth of stations and sales of receiving equipment provided the best evidence of radio's vitality and soon caused a change of mind in the executive suites. In September 1921 the Department of Commerce began issuing broadcasting licenses. In the first three months only five licenses were issued, but the floodgates opened in December, when 23 new stations appeared, after which there was a decline to 8 in January, by which time there were 36 stations nationwide. There was a veritable explosion of applications in February, which gathered steam during the rest of the year, so that by the close of 1922 the United States had 576 stations and it was transparently evident that broadcasting would become a powerful industry. Now the 360-meter band assigned to amateurs under terms of the 1912 Radio Licensing Act became jammed, prompting the Commerce Department to open the 400 meter frequency to low-level, local broadcasters.

Many of the stations were owned and operated by receiver manufacturers, but many others also entered the field. Newspapers and magazines accounted for 70 stations and educational institutions another 65. Thirty stations were established by department stores, both as advertisements and as a curiosity that would draw customers. There was even one station owned by a laundry, and four were owned by stockyards. It was a yeasty field at the end of 1922, with no one certain where it would go.

As broadcasting grew, so did the demand for receivers, catching everyone unprepared, RCA included. During the first eleven months of 1921 GE and Westinghouse between them had produced for RCA approximately 5,000 vacuum tubes apiece, and this not only met the demand but created a surplus. The surplus vanished late in the year, as demand far outstripped supply. Sarnoff acknowledged this in a national advertising campaign, headlined: "Meeting the Demand that Grew Overnight," and promising a greater supply of tubes. Production reached 40,000 a month in December, and in January, 60,000, but even this wasn't enough. Only in June, when 200,000 units were shipped, did the backlog of orders start to shrink.

Until then Owen Young's attention had been focused upon transatlantic communications, for he still believed this to be RCA's major area for growth. That opportunities existed there was obvious. Revenues from this area rose from $2.1 million in 1921 to $2.9 million in 1922, and in the same period marine services (ship-to-shore) went from $553,000 to $630,000. But this paled alongside the expansion in radio, which rose from $1.5 million to $11.3

million. "Radiolas" and related equipment provided most of the firm's growth. That radio was the fastest expanding industry in the United States in the early 1920s can be illustrated by comparing total receiver revenues with those for another industry, automobiles.

VALUE OF OUTPUT FOR RADIOS AND AUTOMOBILES, 1921–1926

figures in millions of dollars

Year	Radio Sales	Increase Over Previous Year	Auto Sales	Increase Over Previous Year
1921	12.2	—	1115.5	—
1922	26.9	113%	1546.1	38%
1923	50.3	87	2188.8	41
1924	139.3	177	1922.5	(14)
1925	168.2	21	2340.2	22
1926	206.7	23	2504.3	7

Source: *Historical Statistics of the United States,* p. 700.

Of course these figures are for radio receivers alone; during the period many individuals cobbled together sets from components. In 1922, when $26.9 million worth of receivers were sold, the Federal Trade Commission estimated that $60 million was spent on all receivers and that $11 million of RCA's revenues of $14.8 million derived from Radiolas. Thus, while RCA was the leader in the field, it had only an 18 percent market share. The rest was accounted for by a wide variety of smaller companies, including Atwater Kent, Grebe, Crosley, Grigsby-Grunow, Fada, Philco, Zenith, and scores of others, almost all of whom were soon to be charged with having violated GE and Westinghouse patents assigned to RCA.

Had wireless become RCA's dominant business it is probable that the firm's development would have been smooth and untroubled as it evolved into a public utility along the lines of AT&T. In such a case the original agreements between the major corporate stockholders might have been extended for decades while harmony ruled. The rapid and unanticipated growth of radio altered the situation.

Secretary of Commerce Herbert Hoover perceived this. An engineer and businessman himself, Hoover had a good reputation within the business community prior to the war, and during the fighting he became a world celebrity as a result of his efforts at Belgian relief and then as United States Food Administrator. He attended the peace negotiations and, according to John Maynard Keynes, was "one of the few who left Versailles with added luster."

In 1920 Young—and Franklin Roosevelt—urged him to seek the Democratic presidential nomination. Hoover declared himself a "progressive Republican," but he and Young remained on the best of terms. The following year Hoover entered the Harding Cabinet as Secretary of Commerce, where he was generally deemed representative of the new breed of American businessmen who had emerged after the Progressive era and who were more concerned with cooperation than competition, convinced that big business required not only harmony between capital and labor but a friendly input by government as well. Hoover and Young cooperated on Harding's Conference on Unemployment in 1921, during which Hoover was seen as the kind of person "enlightened businessmen" might easily support for the presidency. The following year he published *American Individualism,* a paean to the old verities but at the same time a call for cooperative efforts.

Why did Hoover represent the government's interest in wireless and radio? The simple answer would be the mandate of the 1912 Radio Licencing Act, but that was not the only reason. The man who was known as "Secretary of Commerce and undersecretary of everything else" believed government had to take a role, perhaps a major one, in an instrumentality that clearly would become important in the future. Hoover was known to oppose commercial broadcasting, saying it was "inconceivable that we should allow so great a possibility for service to be drowned in advertising chatter." Throughout his tenure at the Commerce Department he would advocate private ownership with government regulation, continually altering his position to take into account technological changes and alterations in the rapidly expanding and evolving industry. Within his mind there was a struggle between a belief in free enterprise and a conviction that government had to play a role to protect the public. Unlike those businessmen who spoke glowingly of laissez-faire, Hoover considered the doctrine out of place in the post-World War I period. In addition he saw chaos developing in the new industry, as stations elbowed each other aside in a struggle for the airwaves in which the public interest seemed hardly to be served. The patent situation complicated matters, with pirating becoming the rule, and above all were the developing tensions between AT&T and GE-Westinghouse-RCA.

In the hope that the federal government might harmonize differences and create order, Hoover called a Radio Conference, which met in Washington in February 1922. Representatives of all the important companies were in attendance, in addition to hundreds of "amateurs," convinced the big players meant to crowd them out of the industry and in some way limit the free growth of independent broadcasting.

In his introductory comments Hoover spoke of "the astonishing development of the wireless telephone" and later referred to Radiolas as "receiving stations," indicating that even then the term "radio" hadn't come into common currency. Hoover went on to suggest that the participants consider the role his department might play, expecting that he might be asked to decide upon the allocation of stations and related matters. All of this would have pleased Young and his group, since they saw little to be gained by permitting the amateurs a larger role.

Young trusted Hoover, but more important, he knew that the Navy was still interested in playing a role in the industry, and he much preferred regulation by a friendly Commerce Department. On most matters Young's ideas and those of the Secretary jibed.

Young welcomed Hoover's intervention; any regulation would pertain to broadcasting, not manufacturing, and so might precipitate a clash between the Administration and AT&T, but the Radio Group would not be affected. So Young supported Hoover's call for another conference and in the meanwhile restructured RCA to meet the new challenges.

It now seemed inappropriate for the firm to be headed by Nally, whose entire career and major concern had been with wireless. In addition he had no real experience in sales and was deemed an ineffectual lobbyist. While still vigorous and wanting to continue on, Nally was made to understand the RCA board expected his resignation. To those within the Radio Group this signaled not only a Sarnoff victory over the CEO but more important perhaps, the acceptance of the notion that RCA's future was tied to Radiolas and broadcasting far more than to wireless operations.

In September 1922 Sarnoff was given the title of vice president and what amounted to complete control of the radio end of the business, while Nally was reduced to tending to wireless and acting as go-between for Sarnoff with the GE and Westinghouse interests, his chief duties in this regard being to attempt a speedup of receiver manufactures.

Apparently Sarnoff was not considered for the succession at this time. He was still quite young and inexperienced in boardroom politics, and while knowing as much about radio as anyone in the country he was deemed unprepared for the delicate battles to be waged in Washington and with AT&T over the next few years. In addition, this was a period in which Jews did not move easily in industrial circles. Sarnoff understood and gave every indication of approving of Young's selection of General James Harbord as President.

While hardly as knowledgeable as Sarnoff insofar as business matters was concerned, Harbord was a highly respected individual who if not among the leading ranks of war heroes was at least a familiar name to the public. Like Sarnoff, he had had one of those Horatio Alger lives. Born on a farm in 1866, a year after the end of the Civil War, Harbord aimed for a military career but failed to enter West Point even though he tied for first place on a competitive exam. After waiting for an opening and failing to obtain one Harbord enlisted in the Army as a private hoping to rise through the ranks. This he did and after the Spanish-American War served in a variety of posts. Harbord gained a reputation as a natural diplomat, a quiet and scholarly individual who excelled in dealing with congressmen and senators and knew his way around the War Department.

A major at the outbreak of World War I, Harbord went to France as an administrative officer, asked for duty at the front, and led a Marine unit at the Battle of Belleau Wood. By now a major general, Harbord was a leading figure in the second Battle of the Marne, this resulting in a promotion to become General John Pershing's chief of supply and, soon after, his chief of staff. The assignment suited him; Harbord worked well with his British and French counterparts, many of whom had been irritated by the fiery Pershing. Over the years Harbord had honed these diplomatic skills, and so seemed a natural for a top post in the civilian world. That several corporations considered Harbord for a major position was fairly well known.

After the war Harbord headed a division and in 1921 became deputy chief of staff of the Army under Pershing. Only 55 years old at the time, he might have hoped for even more were it not for the fact that he had not graduated from West Point, and this effectively barred him from further advancement.

Since Young had important connections within the Wilson Administration, he was familiar with Harbord's record and reputation. He knew, for example, that one of the conditions Pershing had placed upon his appointment as chief of staff was that Harbord serve as his deputy.

Secretary of the Army Newton Baker strongly supported Harbord for the RCA presidency, as did such businessmen as Charles Dawes, who had served with him during the war, and Gerard Swope, Young's colleague at GE and RCA. Earlier, Young had indicated in a letter to Nally that the person he wanted would have to be nonpartisan, know his way around Washington, and not be identified with Wall Street. "It is particularly important in this connection that no one should be able to question his Americanism, such as they have done in several instances in the case of our international bankers."

Young arranged a meeting, and the two hit it off. When Young offered him the CEO position at RCA, Harbord accepted even though he not only knew nothing of radio but didn't even own a receiver.

He joined RCA as president effective January 1, 1923. At the time the corporation was negotiating with Secretary of Commerce Hoover about its future and that of broadcasting and was about to be investigated by the Federal Trade Commission on charges it had violated the antitrust acts. Harbord devoted most of his time to these matters, and like Nally before him permitted Sarnoff much leeway in running the company.

We have seen that the agreements between GE, Westinghouse, and RCA on the one side and AT&T on the other covered wireless transmission and inferentially permitted AT&T to do what it wished in the manufacture of radio receivers and broadcasting. Chairman Harry Thayer of AT&T pointedly observed that while the 1920–1921 agreements specifically granted GE rights to manufacture AT&T equipment for use by amateurs, the army of Radiola purchasers did not quality under the meaning of the term. Moreover, AT&T insisted it alone had the right to establish commercial radio stations—radio telephony—and in fact was erecting two transmission towers in New York toward that end. The gap in the 1920s agreements between RCA-GE and AT&T, namely the failure to realize the potential of broadcasting, was about to cause warfare between the two groups.

Other broadcasters were put on notice: bow before AT&T or expect litigation. In fact, all of the independents fell into line, for within a year some forty stations were paying franchise fees to AT&T ranging from $300 to $3,000 a year for the use of its patents. The money itself was a minor consideration. What really mattered was the principle. In essence AT&T meant to create and preserve a monopoly in radio telephony by whatever means were necessary.

With all of this, Thayer lacked a strong commitment to broadcasting. Sixty-four years old at the time and a year from retirement, Thayer had been born before the Civil War, had known Alexander Graham Bell, and had started working at Western Electric as an office boy in 1881. From the start he was a telephone man who had little interest in anything else. However, Thayer was intrigued by wireless. He delivered the first transatlantic speech in 1923 and before that had installed ship-to-shore equipment in his home. Thayer did not doubt that there was a place for wireless in AT&T's future, but broadcasting was another matter. He would support pilot programs so long as they did not divert attention, manpower, and financial resources from the main business, but he would go no further than that, especially if it involved a competitive struggle with others. But Thayer would soon depart the scene. Others at AT&T, more interested in the new technology, felt differently.

The GE leadership protested AT&T's initial foray into broadcasting, for it violated the 1920–1921 accords, and Harbord consulted with Sarnoff as to the best way of dealing with the situation. By all means negotiate, Sarnoff said, but if that fails accept arbitration since "I believe that despite the present ambiguities of the contract, our position is sufficiently clear and meritorious to justify resting our case on the decision of competent and impartial arbitrators." Should arbitration be declined, Sarnoff recommended the filing of a suit against AT&T for violation of contract.

Harbord accepted this advice, and after an impasse was reached in negotiations the companies agreed to conciliation efforts on the part of an outsider, Charles Neave of the law firm of Fish, Richardson & Neave, which had wide experience in such matters. Fish was a former president of AT&T, while Neave had been assigned patent work by GE and AT&T, and together they had drafted the original agreement whereby AT&T had taken its participation in RCA.

Neave concluded that AT&T indeed did have the right to manufacture radio receivers and operate stations, but came down on GE's side in the matter of exclusivity of licenses in broadcast receiving apparatus. Both companies rejected the decision, and it appeared that a struggle would soon begin between the Radio Group and AT&T. The conciliation effort had failed, but Thayer and Young continued correspondence on the matter in the months ahead.

To this intercompany conflict was added a contest within AT&T itself regarding the future of broadcasting. One group, made up for the most part of traditionalists, believed in what at the time was known as "public radiotelephone broadcasting," which would be the transmission of programs over telephone wires, this being deemed vastly superior in reception and reliability to wireless telephony. In fact several stations could be tied together by wires, not unlike long distance telephones, and so they dimly perceived the possibilities of a network. Another, younger and more technologically-oriented, cadre talked of wireless broadcasting.

The former group planned for "toll broadcasting," by which AT&T would provide studios and other facilities but not programming. "Anyone who had a message for the world or wished to entertain was to come in and pay their money as they would upon coming into a telephone booth," said one of this group. Such a person would "address the world and then go out," to be followed by the next "subscriber."

The AT&T executive vice president, Walter Gifford, sympathized with the traditionalists. What he had in mind for radio was a variety of public telephone, which he referred to as "radio telephone broadcasting." Music was to be played between announcements, merely to indicate to listeners that the station was in operation. "For my part," Gifford said years later, "I expected that since it was a form of telephony, and since we were in the business of furnishing wires for telephony, we were sure to be involved in broadcasting somehow." But he concluded that "nobody knew . . . where radio was really headed."

Moreover, Gifford was occupied with other matters in this period. He and Western Electric President Charles DuBois were being considered for the succession to the AT&T presidency after Thayer stepped down, and neither man wanted to commit himself to any program that might prove contentious and divert AT&T assets from its main business.

A compromise of sorts between the AT&T traditionalist and the pro-telephony forces was arrived at. All stations, both those already operating and new ones coming on line, would operate on a wireless mode, but several would be joined by telephone wires. There would be no AT&T programming initially but rather toll broadcasting. Management decided to charge $50 for use of the airwaves for 15 minutes in the evening and $40 for the afternoon period.

The first station, based in New York and known as WBAY, was ready by summer 1922, while a second, WEAF, was announced soon after. As it turned out the two operations were combined under the WEAF designation and went into operation in August, in direct competition with the Westinghouse-RCA New York station WJZ on the 360-meter band.

That the two stations would battle it out had become evident even before then, as had the growing enmity between AT&T and the Radio Group. In June, Gifford and Frederick Stevenson, the other AT&T representative, resigned from the RCA board, and soon after AT&T announced it would sell all its RCA holdings. In its 1922 *Annual Report,* AT&T stated this was consistent with its policy "to hold permanently only the stocks and securities directly related to a national telephone service," and that "ownership of stock in the Radio Corporation of America has not . . . proved to be necessary for cooperation." That a fight was brewing was obvious to all.

On November 2, 1922, AT&T established the parameters of the conflict when it presented a list of five specific complaints to the Radio Group. Key among these were allegations that RCA and its allies were "using their broadcasting stations in a manner not contemplated or intended," and that RCA's vacuum tubes were being used by "outsiders in broadcasting transmitting stations, and are being used by the Magnavox people, and perhaps others, in loud speaker amplifiers."

The charge was justified; in 1922 RCA shipped 1.6 million vacuum tubes, most of which were sold through jobbers, and many of these were being used by the approximately 200 companies then in the business of manufacturing receivers.

The situation hardly was one RCA relished. In order to halt this practice the company dealt only with dealers who offered Radiolas. In this way, RCA hoped to exclude all dealers not directly connected with the firm from obtaining tubes to use in their own sets. Yet the practice continued.

In addition AT&T knew that its sales of certain kinds of transmission equipment, for which it was supposed to have a dominant position, ran far below industry placements. In February 1923 it would be learned that of the roughly 600 stations in operation only 35 had purchased transmission products from AT&T's Western Electric subsidiary, while the others in violation of the 1921 agreements utilized equipment turned out by members of the Radio Group. It wasn't surprising, then, that AT&T would indicate an intention to fight the Radio Group's efforts to expand further into broadcasting and to hold RCA to its responsibility to monitor companies manufacturing equipment under AT&T licenses.

The RCA position, as set down by Sarnoff for Harbord the following June, was that the original agreement was meant to apply solely to wireless. "Under the present contract," he wrote, "we find the Radio Corporation Group saying, in effect, to the Telephone Company, that in the field of radio telephony, for tolls, as a public service, 'we not only recognize your patents and agree not to infringe them, but we also grant you an exclusive license to use our patents in this field, from which we exclude ourselves under your patents and ours.' In the field of wireless telegraphy as a public service, we find the Telephone Company saying, in effect, the same thing to the Radio Corporation."

Sarnoff recommended meetings of representatives in order to clarify the situation and resolve ambiguities.

As for the allegation that RCA was not preventing others from using its vacuum tubes in manufacturing transmission equipment, Sarnoff observed that pirating was epidemic and that he was doing all he could to prosecute violators. Indeed, he threw the charge back to AT&T, observing that Western Electric was producing amplifiers, loudspeakers, tubes, and other accessories that were being sold to receiver manufacturers and "should cease such operations and conform to the intent and letter of the contract in this respect."

Sarnoff knew he couldn't go too far with this, since Harbord and Young feared AT&T's power. Albert Davis, GE's chief counsel, warned Harbord that AT&T had a strong case and that if the matter went to arbitration AT&T might obtain many advantages. Moreover, if the arbitrator decided AT&T could enter the radio receiver business it "would possibly put us out of business."

The matter was complicated by a new device invented by Edwin Armstrong, who had become one of Sarnoff's warmest allies. They had met in 1913, when Armstrong was a student attempting to interest the American Marconi executive in a powerful radio circuit he had invented. Sarnoff didn't make the purchase, but they drew closer to one another. Later it would be said that while Sarnoff had many acquaintances, Armstrong was one of his few friends.

During the war the Germans utilized shortwave transmission for trench communications, and Armstrong, now a Signal Corps major, was asked to design a version of it for the Allies, which he did. Out of this and related experiments came the superheterodyne. ("Heterodyne" meaning it mixed signals within the vacuum tube in such a way as to improve reception greatly.) This involved him in the first of several litigations with De Forest, who claimed to have developed the technique earlier, and won him support from Westinghouse, which purchased his patents for $335,000, making Armstrong both wealthy and independent.

Soon thereafter Armstrong started work on an improved Radiola utilizing superheterodyne features, the first capable of receiving programs without an antenna, and it did away with much of the static that was the bugaboo of radio. He demonstrated this receiver to Sarnoff late in 1922. Recognizing in it a product that not only would make obsolete every other radio on the market but would also provide a gold mine in licensing fees, Sarnoff purchased the patents for $200,000 and 60,000 RCA shares, making Armstrong the largest noncorporate shareholder in the company.

By then Armstrong had achieved recognition as one of the more important inventors in the industry and was embarked upon a spectacular career—a quarter of a century later *Fortune* would call him "the greatest American inventor since Edison and the most important of all radio inventors, including Marconi." The superheterodyne, which established his reputation, gave RCA a strong technological edge over its competitors. Sarnoff adopted the Armstrong machine as the basic RCA offering and helped revamp the Westinghouse and GE radio facilities for its production.

Other manufacturers soon learned of the new radio, and as they had done with earlier sets, prepared to pirate the receiver and produce similar models. Licensing did begin, however, and by 1923 it provided RCA with yet another revenue stream.

Rumors soon made the rounds that AT&T was readying an advanced version of the superheterodyne and, in fact, had assembled several of them, which were distributed to officials for testing. It was believed that Western Electric would soon market such receivers under its own nameplate, the goal being to dominate that product area.

RCA knew of this and proceeded along a double path.

Harbord proposed mediation, while requesting AT&T to supply transmission equipment for its new facilities in New York. He also asked AT&T to provide long distance telephone lines for networking, in this oblique fashion informing the company that he intended to disregard repeated demands that RCA quit commercial broadcasting. After being rebuffed, Harbord notified Young that in his view "the Telephone Company is each day getting more aggressive and is consolidating its position in violation of our rights as I see them to such an extent that every day of delay will make it more difficult for them to accept any compromise which we suggest."

At the same time Sarnoff struck out on another front. He authorized the initiation of legal action against A. H. Grebe Co., charging the firm with patent infringement. This move had been planned since the previous August, when Sarnoff recommended such action as a shot across the bow of those who were violating the patents. "Great pains should be taken not to have a multiplicity of suits," he wrote. "Pains should, however, be taken to bring enough [of them]."

Grebe probably was singled out for two reasons. It was a prominent manufacturer whose models often were blatant imitations of the Radiolas. In addition the firm's founder, Alfred Grebe, was generally thought of as an AT&T ally. Some 90 percent of the parts used in his receivers came from Western Electric, and Grebe advertised on WEAF. The suit was to be taken as a warning that pirating of the superheterodyne would not be tolerated. There was a message in this for AT&T as well; the Grebe litigation might easily be expanded to include AT&T itself as a codefendant.

But there were no further suits, perhaps because Sarnoff came to realize that multiple actions might encourage new charges that RCA was seeking a monopoly position. Instead, the company took pains to maintain as low a profile as possible, working for accommodation rather than entering easily into litigation.

Sarnoff also knew of a more effective way of combating AT&T. He hoped to capitalize upon RCA's influence in Washington and Hoover's well-known dislike of toll broadcasting, which was central to AT&T's plans. But this meant that the Radio Group would have to be united on an alternative acceptable to Hoover, and this would be difficult, given the growing attractiveness of toll broadcasting. Sarnoff knew that any important show of interest in toll broadcasting on their part might alienate powerful allies in the Commerce Department.

By then the lines between the Radio Group and AT&T were well drawn. The Telephone Company meant to erect around WEAF a toll network, while the Radio Group continued on with public service broadcasting. WEAF was profitable, while Westinghouse and GE had started questioning the worth of their stations.

Plans for networking were being formulated, however. Sarnoff urged GE's honorary chairman E. W. Rice, to consider such a possibility. "Let us organize a separate and distinct company," he began, "to be known as the Public Service Broadcasting Company or National Broadcasting Company or American Broadcasting Company, or some similar name." Control of the network would be in the hands of RCA, with representatives of GE and Westinghouse on its board. Into the new company would go all the stations owned by the three parents. For the moment, however, nothing came of this.

Harbord continued to seek a compromise with AT&T. Perhaps the 1920–1921 agreements might be amended so that Western Electric could be permitted to manufacture radio receivers for sale under the RCA nameplate, in the manner of the GEs and Westinghouses. He thought a fair division would be 20 percent, with GE retaining 48 percent and Westinghouse 32 percent. In return for this concession AT&T would be expected to drop its accusations that the Radio Group was acting improperly in the broadcasting area.

Young went along with this, but Westinghouse Chairman Tripp, irate at what he considered AT&T's high-handed manner and still interested in setting up a network of his own, decided to attack. On May 13 he fired off a letter to AT&T Chairman Thayer, asserting his view that AT&T had no right "to establish or maintain any so-called 'broadcasting stations' nor to make, use, sell or lease any receiving apparatus for 'broadcasting stations.'" Tripp went on to inform Thayer that any use of Radio Group inventions in this regard "must be infringement of our patent rights." He concluded by asking for a conference to determine the rights of each party.

Thayer accepted the invitation. In a response directed not only to Tripp but to Harbord and Young as well, he wrote that "our views are directly opposed" and concluded that there indeed were "differences which for a long time I have felt should be cleared up." And with this, negotiations reopened, but this time without an arbitrator.

None of this had any relationship to the developing struggle over broadcasting. The AT&T vice president, A. H. Griswold, who was placed in charge of radio broadcasting, was quite clear on this point when addressing the matter in 1923. "We have been very careful, up to the present time, not to state to the public in any way . . . the idea that the Bell System desires to monopolize broadcasting; but the fact remains that it's a telephone job, that we are telephone people, and that we can do it better than anybody else. . . . In one form or another, we have got to do the job." Others might broadcast only if they paid AT&T's franchise fee.

Within days of WEAF's opening it clashed with WJZ, which by then had been transferred *in toto* to RCA, over airwave allocation. Station WEAF had many advantages over its rival. In the first place it had the AT&T wires while WJZ's signals went out on wireless, and the wires provided far better reception. It attracted advertisers; the Queensborough Corporation, a real estate operation, paid $50 for a ten-minute pitch, which fetched several thousands of dollars of business, and others followed. Finally, WEAF had intelligent leadership in the person of George McClelland, a dynamic executive who arrived from the Association of National Advertisers to lead the sales campaign, and who turned out to be one of the most imaginative and innovative broadcasting figures of the decade.

Within a year McClelland was broadcasting manager, and under his leadership WEAF became the nation's best known and run station. Station WJZ, which was run by men who talked of performing "public service" and selling Radiolas, couldn't match McClelland when it came to technology, programming, and later on, networking. It was a feeble affair, with a small 500-watt transmitter whose signal couldn't be discerned outside of a twenty-mile radius, and then only when atmospheric conditions were right. Moreover, WJZ had inferior programming, and often the station was unable to deliver on programming commitments. Meanwhile WEAF's signals went over the wires and were stronger, more dependable, and clearer. Given the state of the technology at the time, WEAF was in a far stronger position to conduct network operations than was WJZ. The key element was the telephone wires; so long as wireless remained an inferior technology, AT&T would have a decided edge in the field.

Since both stations were using the same wavelength—the government had yet to make allocations—it became necessary for them to share it, and in another compromise, WJZ operated from 7:00 P.M. to 9:00 P.M., with WEAF taking much of the rest of the time.

Nor was this the only struggle. In January 1923, AT&T linked WEAF with its Boston station, WNAC, the first instance of networking or, as it was more commonly known at the time, chain broadcasting.

Five months later AT&T tied together WEAF, WGY in Schenectady, and KYW in Chicago via telephone lines, in the first important demonstration that networking was possible. During the next two years the AT&T network (which had no official name) expanded; by 1924 it had an experimental coast-to-coast operation consisting of twenty-three stations, which was inaugurated with a speech by President Calvin Coolidge. Advertisers were charged by the minute; an hour was billed at $2,600, and the young network had gross revenues of around $750,000. The following year the twenty-six-station network broadcast Coolidge's Inauguration, heard by an estimated 18 million people.

At the same time RCA was also working along this line. The company had connected WJZ and WJY in Hoboken through an agreement with Western Union. The experiment succeeded, but it was hardly as dramatic as the AT&T entry. By 1925 the RCA network had only four stations, all of them in the Northeast. Others were even less successful. Westinghouse strove to develop an alternate method of networking by means of wireless, since AT&T denied its lines to the Radio Group.

All the while AT&T continued to insist that it alone had the right to broadcast commercially. Attempts to do so by WJZ or KDKA would constitute a violation of contract by RCA and Westinghouse. The showdown between the parties drew closer.

The Radio Group was unclear as to just who would pay for broadcasting. It was unwilling to advocate toll broadcasting, public service offerings by set manufacturers, or government subsidies. Sarnoff once suggested that wealthy individuals might endow stations as they did university chairs or libraries, but nothing came of this. It was becoming more apparent daily that broadcasting could evolve into a highly profitable enterprise, perhaps even more so than the sale of receivers.

In the meantime each side charged the other with patent violations and reneging on agreements while advocating their particular form of broadcasting, with neither side quite certain regarding long-term objectives.

Another force was about to enter the arena. The federal government frowned on the idea of toll broadcasting, and Hoover was monitoring the British Broadcasting Corporation, then embarking upon a system of charging licensing fees to set-owners and banning commercials from the airwaves. In this period technological breakthroughs and political decisions could sharply alter the history of the industry.

There were three major players in the broadcasting field: the Radio Group, AT&T, and the Commerce Department. The first two would struggle toward some kind of arrangement regarding how to carve up the broadcasting and equipment industries, while Hoover, true to his belief in working arrangements between government and industry, sought the proper relationship with both. And all the while smaller players—broadcasters and manufacturers of transmission and especially receiving equipment—attempted to elbow their way into both industries. These two struggles, and those of the secondary companies, would dominate RCA's attention for the next five years, even while the American people continued their infatuation with the new medium.

And what of wireless, which after all had been the reason for RCA's existence? The company continued these operations and even expanded somewhat. Rumors had it that there would soon be a takeover of Western Union's cables by RCA, with GE and Westinghouse providing the financing, but nothing of the sort happened. By 1922, RCA had become far more concerned with broadcasting and receiver sales than telecommunications and was no longer willing to expend its entire resources on becoming the American flag carrier in the international wireless field.

3

RCA Transformed

SELECTED RADIO STATISTICS, 1921–1924

YEAR	Radio Receivers Produced	Value of Production	Households With Radios
1921	—	$1,469,920	—
1922	100,000	11,286,489	60,000
1923	500,000	22,465,091	400,000
1924	1,500,000	50,747,202	1,250,000

Source: Archer, *Big Business and Radio,* p. 200; *Historical Statistics,* p. 796.

THESE STATISTICS INDICATE how fast radio grew during the industry's early years, when most involved were still struggling to understand its capabilities and limitations and devise the business structures into which the new medium might be channeled.

The numbers are all the more impressive when one considers that the average price of a receiver in 1924 was around $80, a sizable amount for the time. Families would put off the purchase of almost anything besides food, clothing, and shelter in order to buy a radio.

Moreover, the figures are not for the industry as a whole, but only radio sets. Not included are broadcasting revenues, for example, though these were quite minor; AT&T, the only real force in the field, had gross revenues of less than $750,000 from toll broadcasting. Toward mid-decade, however, it began to be recognized that these could be potentially far greater than revenues obtained through receiver sales. In 1925, which was the breakthrough year at WEAF, the station turned in a profit of $150,000.

That radio was a powerful new medium was evident to leaders of government, the Radio Group, and AT&T, but most of all to Sarnoff and others at RCA, who perceived that their company had an opportunity to become one of the largest and most influential in the world. The technology was there and being improved steadily. Money was a relatively minor problem, since GE and Westinghouse were relatively liberal in making allocations. But AT&T was a growing force in broadcasting and a potential rival in manufacture; working out a way of living together would occupy executives of both companies. There also could be problems from Washington. While Commerce Secretary Hoover was generally considered friendly toward RCA, his attitude regarding broadcasting could pose problems. And there were stirrings on Capitol Hill as well.

It was evident that the chaos on the airways that had developed in 1922 was if anything becoming worse, and Congress intended to act. Some twenty measures to regulate radio were introduced from 1921 to 1923, ranging from outright nationalization of the airwaves to greater regulation of AT&T to the breakup of what was perceived as a GE-Westinghouse-RCA monopoly in patents.

The most important of these was one offered in 1922 by Maine Congressman Wallace White. A forty-five-year-old Republican whose interest in wireless had led Hoover to invite him to attend the first Radio Conference, White had decided to concentrate upon the medium, and from his entry into the House of Representatives in 1917 to his retirement from the Senate thirty-two years later he was considered a leading congressional expert in the area.

The White draft proposed giving the Secretary of Commerce sweeping powers over broadcasting, including the granting of licenses and assignment of frequencies as well as the power to withdraw them should he decide the licensee was acting against the public interest. Given Hoover's outlook, this would have served the interests of the Radio Group. In any case the White Bill failed to pass the House, which was one of the reasons for the calling of another radio conference.

Hoover convened the second Washington Radio Conference in March 1923, at a time when AT&T and the Radio Group were preparing to renew negotiations regarding their respective roles in manufacture and broadcasting, Sarnoff was pressing the suit against Grebe, and discussions were taking place at the FTC regarding antitrust activities. Networking was expanding, and receiver sales were soaring as the nation was in the midst of a radio mania.

While there was some discussion of the White draft, a more pressing issue, that of allocation of the airwaves, took up most of the sessions. There had been 60 stations at the time of the first conference; by early 1923 the number had grown to 581. In the same period the number of receivers had grown from 600,000 to approximately 2 million. The first conference had dealt with generalities; the second struggled with the real problems that had developed as a result of the 1922 boom in stations and receivers.

The sessions were confused; as had been the case at the first conference, few truly appreciated the potential of the medium, the rapidity of change, or even the problems involved. Credo Harris, a novelist who had been inveigled by a newspaper-owning friend into managing his new plaything, WHAS in Louisville, Kentucky, thought Hoover, too, was groping for a rationale.

> Both he and they foundered in possibilities, nodded sagely over probabilities, and spent hours discussing supposedly known principles which a year later were discarded in as many minutes. . . . While we slept, unexpected theorems sprouted, bloomed and had dropped their seeds by the time we came down to breakfast. . . . Before luncheon new and untried mechanical appliances had, from all sides, sprung upon the Art with a confusion of madness, and by evening a visitor could instantly recognize the station manager by the wild, roving look in his eye.

With all of this the beginning of order was being created. The stations were divided into three groups according to their transmission power, with most of the local stations in the second and third category, leaving the majors—RCA, GE, Westinghouse, and AT&T—the first and most important sector. Concluding the proliferation of stations might be uneconomical, the Conference recommended future licenses be limited, a policy that would make those already granted more valuable. This decision was widely regarded as a signal that Washington expected the big companies to dominate broadcasting.

At least as important as what was decided, however, were the areas Hoover did not touch upon. He had no intention of entering the thicket of cross-licensing and technology, and despite earlier protestations from small manufacturers, there were no significant decisions made by Hoover regarding commercial broadcasting. Since AT&T continued franchising new stations, all operating on the toll principle, with no protest from the Commerce Department, it had won this contest by default. The Radio Group now realized that it too might utilize commercials on its stations, and this perception in time would result in a new profit stream for RCA. Sarnoff decided to press ahead more vigorously with toll broadcasting.

A number of measures embodying the Hoover approach were introduced in Congress in spring 1923, but the waters were muddied by the decision of the United States Court of Appeals in the District of Columbia in the case of *Hoover v. Intercity Radio* that the Secretary might assign wavelengths, but in no other way could he control radio. This all but assured the calling of yet another radio conference. Before one could convene, however, there were further developments in the conflict between the Radio Group and AT&T.

Each claimed rights the other denied existed under the original agreement.

In mid-June 1923, Sarnoff sent all involved a memorandum outlining what he hoped would become the basis for a new agreement, but which was clearly favorable to his company and interests. It called for AT&T to have exclusive rights in transmission equipment, though with a reservation: the Radio Group could manufacture transmission apparatus for its own use. In return AT&T would have the right to manufacture receivers upon payment to the Radio Group of a royalty of 50 percent of the selling price. Further, AT&T was to make its wires available to the Radio Group under "reasonable terms of payment."

This represented a realistic view of the industry as it existed. It also indicated that both parties realized what it would take to coexist in radio set manufacture and broadcasting. Had it been implemented and augmented, an industry centered upon the two giants, with a host of smaller entities in their wake, might have developed.

Thayer rejected the plan, still clinging to the hope that AT&T could control broadcasting and also win an important position in set manufacture. After some additional parrying both sides agreed once again to submit the matter to binding arbitration.

All of this was carried out in the utmost secrecy; as far as Washington was concerned, the AT&T and Radio Group interests were united against all outsiders. Thus it came as little surprise when in December 1923, the Federal Trade Commission issued a report indicating that both might have violated the antitrust acts in both receiver and transmitter manufacture and broadcasting.

There was irony in all of this. Patently, AT&T had been deemed a government-sanctioned, regulated monopoly since 1913, while RCA had been established specifically to function as a monopoly. Now the FTC was preparing to prosecute both for being what earlier governments had intended them to be!

Perhaps recognizing the need for action in the face of this threat from Washington, both parties agreed to an arbitrator, Roland Boyden. That Young accepted Boyden came as no surprise; the two men had been associated with one another in the international arena for a number of years. Thayer, Gifford, and others at AT&T must have known this, when they acceded in the selection.

In January 1924, when the FTC filed its complaint against the parties, they were preparing to meet for the arbitration, which after some postponements was initiated on May 20. The trial would not begin until October 1925, by which time the arbitration appeared to have reached a conclusion, but in reality it had bogged down and would drag on until the end of the decade.

Public knowledge of the FTC action and ignorance of the arbitration arrangements affected the politics of the situation. Congressman White reintroduced a Radio Control Bill in the House in February 1924, which would give the Secretary of Commerce sweeping powers over radio broadcasting, but while the measure was reported out of committee, like so many others it failed to pass. Meanwhile Hoover set into motion the calling of the third radio conference, which convened on October 6, 1924.

Just as the industry changes had dictated the agenda for the second conference, so they did for the third. Hoover opened the meeting by proclaiming his belief that broadcasting should be left in private hands and hoped the parties would be able to come to an agreement on their own. As before he offered his assistance in the establishment of "radio traffic rules" should it be needed. Earlier President Coolidge had said he had no desire to see government play an important role in the development of radio, and his comment, combined with Hoover's, appeared to indicate such would be the case. But it was also evident that Hoover supported regulation.

Hoover also believed the FTC might have to step in to prevent the formation of a Radio Trust. He warned of intervention "if its [radio's] control should come into the hands of any single corporation, individual, or combination." By now recognizing the similarities between radio and the press, the Secretary went on to suggest that "it would be in principle the same as though the entire press of the country were so controlled."

Then as before and after, Hoover deplored the growing commercialization of radio, indicating some sympathy for the Radio Group's past stance. "If a speech by the President is to be used as the meat in a sandwich of two patent medicines, there will be no radio left." He had a clear-cut approach to radio, based upon the belief that a trust existed, which would involve the government in broadcasting to no little degree and would mean it would have a say in programming and commercialization.

The following day Sarnoff announced that RCA planned to develop a "superpower broadcast station" to serve the New York region, with a far wider range than any previously known. If the experiment worked others would follow, the goal being a networking through shortwaves to cover the nation.

Negotiations with AT&T proceeded all the while, and indications were that important breakthroughs were being made. Specifically, Sarnoff was recommending that the Radio Group purchase AT&T broadcasting interests, with AT&T to receive benefits from providing it with services. "Put all stations of all parties into a broadcasting company which can be self-supporting and probably revenue-producing," he wrote, and "the telephone company [would] furnish wires as needed." Sarnoff was not only suggesting unification of interests but acceptance of the toll broadcasting principle. Given the mixed signals out of Washington, this was bound to create discussion and perhaps an antitrust blast, but it would bring an end to the acrimonious struggles between the Radio Group and AT&T.

During the next year and a half parallel developments in Washington and New York determined the nature and future of broadcasting for the next half century. The Radio Group and AT&T moved slowly toward an agreement whereby their interests would be merged to create a major chain, while Hoover and Congress struggled to develop legislation to regulate the new industry.

Hoover called the fourth radio conference into session on November 9, 1925, hoping that out of it would come an operational plan that would guide the industry for several years at the very least, along with a structure whereby government might play an appropriate role. Hoover told some 400 delegates that they should consider the matter of limiting stations to prevent congestion of the airwaves. He also wanted to determine guidelines for public service broadcasting, since he was determined this should be a factor in awarding licenses, and provide a means whereby the general citizenry could make its views known both to the Commerce Department and to the stations. What he had in mind was the creation of a body somewhat similar in structure and purpose to the Interstate Commerce Commission, which regulated the railroads. In addition, the stations would have to solicit opinions from a broad spectrum of the listening audience and respond to them, though how this might be done was left vague.

On other matters, Hoover now spoke favorably of superpower stations and networks in general, telling the delegates that all indications were that they would not interfere with regular broadcasting, and he looked forward to the time when intercontinental broadcasting via short waves might be possible. On the other hand, he remained adamant regarding advertising. "I wish our engineers and inventors would invent another knob on our receiving sets by which we could express our feelings to the fellow who is broadcasting," he commented. "Tuning out in disgust is an uncompleted mental reaction."

Agreeing with the Secretary, the conferees called upon Congress to create a regulatory body. However, they rejected the notion that in some ways broadcasting was a public utility like the electric company. Thus they opposed direct government control, while affirming the principle of freedom of speech. Finally, they agreed to oppose any attempt to monopolize the airwaves.

All of these recommendations suited Sarnoff since they pointed the way toward his national network based upon toll broadcasting. In all, the fourth conference was a triumph for his vision of the future. Order was to be created, government's role was to be limited, and at no time was there indicated a strong opposition to networks by either the Secretary or a sizable number of attendees. Congressman White, who attended most of the sessions, indicated he would prepare legislation embodying these recommendations, and Hoover offered his support.

In 1925 Sarnoff decided to take a step to demonstrate that RCA did not intend to be a monopoly: in the future the company would license its technology more freely to others.

This wasn't as political a move as it might appear, but rather a simple coming to terms with reality. It was close to impossible to attempt to monitor for patent violations an entire industry that by then was made up of thousands of small to medium-sized companies. So licenses would be granted liberally, and the first of these went to All America Radio Corp. in March of the following year. This policy had the additional value of meeting objections detailed in the FTC complaint.

The terms were stiff. Sarnoff demanded 7½ percent of the wholesale value of the set, not just the components under its patent. So if a radio had a $50-cabinet not covered by patents, RCA expected a royalty on that as well as the equipment it housed. Most paid, and in the first year RCA awarded twenty licenses for which it received $3 million. Simultaneously Sarnoff moved to further placate and woo AT&T. He gave in on the matter of AT&T's manufacturing receivers and vacuum tubes, an area from which that company had been barred under terms of the 1920-1921 agreements, in return for a generous royalty of 50 percent on all sales above $3 million per year on receivers and $2 million on tubes.

All of this satisfied the FTC, which in 1928 dropped the antitrust suit.

With this out of the way, RCA and AT&T turned to the more important matter of creating a national network out of their respective holdings. One problem involved the price to be paid for WEAF. AT&T wanted $2.5 million for a property with assets of $200,000. Clearly AT&T considered its goodwill, listenership, and the right to use airwaves granted by the federal government to be worth $2.3 million. After some discussion Sarnoff got the figure down to $1 million. This was low considering that, as indicated, WEAF's revenues for 1925 came to $750,000 and had the potential of twice that amount at current rates, which were certain to be raised once networking was expanded.

Sarnoff might also have reflected that since between them RCA, GE, and Westinghouse had expended $1.4 million on broadcasting that year (with RCA's total coming to $370,000), and that with WEAF in, with the switch to toll broadcasting put into effect, that figure could be reduced, according to one estimate to $410,000 the first year, $350,000 the second, and $250,000 the third.

At the same time AT&T, too, benefited from the arrangement, since it had the sole right to supply the new chain with land-lines. Even if RCA failed in its attempt to create a monopoly in networking, it would become AT&T's largest single customer. In the first year of the agreement AT&T received $800,000 in rental fees and more than $1 million in 1926. Network payouts to AT&T in 1930 came to $4.4 million and in 1935, $4.5 million.

STATION OPERATION BY THE RADIO GROUP, 1925

CALL LETTERS	LOCATION	OWNER
KGO	Oakland, Cal.	GE
KOA	Denver, Col.	GE
WGY	Schenectady, N.Y.	GE
WRC	Washington, D.C.	RCA
WJZ	New York	RCA
WJY	New York	RCA
WEBL	[Portable]	RCA
WEBM	[Portable]	RCA
KYW	Chicago, Ill.	Westinghouse
WBZA	Boston, Mass.	Westinghouse
WBZ	Springfield, Mass.	Westinghouse
KFKX	Hastings, Neb.	Westinghouse
KDPM	Cleveland, Ohio	Westinghouse
KDKA	Pittsburgh, Pa.	Westinghouse

Source: Archer, *Big Business and Radio,* p. 244.

CITIES SERVED BY AT&T NETWORK, 1925

New York	St. Paul-Minneapolis
Philadelphia	St. Louis
Washington	Akron
Providence	Pittsburgh
Worcester	Chicago
Boston	Cincinnati
Buffalo	Davenport
Detroit	Cleveland

Source: Archer, *Big Business and Radio,* p. 246.

On December 30 a subcommittee established by RCA and AT&T to iron out details advised that the "American Broadcasting Company" centered around WEAF could be established almost immediately. There were a few minor problems remaining, which were dealt with in January 1926. It was decided, for example, that the entity would be 50-percent owned by RCA, and 30-percent by GE, with Westinghouse having a 20-percent interest. This out of the way, matters proceeded smoothly and rapidly.

Four months later, in preparation for the transfer to the new network,

AT&T reorganized all of its broadcasting operations into Broadcasting Corporation of America. All that remained was to arrange for the use of AT&T wires, which was done in July. The formal announcement of what had happened was made on July 31. In the interim the name of the network was changed from American to National Broadcasting Company, which was incorporated in Delaware on September 9, 1926, and soon afterward the public learned of it through advertisements placed in major newspapers.

Announcing the

NATIONAL BROADCASTING COMPANY, INC.

National radio broadcasting with better programs
permanently assured by this important action of the Radio
Corporation of America in the interest of the listening public

There were to be two networks, one erected around the former AT&T holdings with WEAF as the flagship station, the other with WJZ at the core to include the Radio Group's holdings. These were known as the "Red" and "Blue" respectively, after the colors of the crayon lines used by RCA's executives and engineers in setting them down on a map. Along with WEAF in the Red network went WSB (Atlanta), WHAS (Louisville), WMC (Memphis), and WSM (Nashville); by the end of the year there were 25 stations in all, stretching in a band from New York to Kansas City. Station WJZ served as the Blue anchor for WBZ (Springfield, Mass.), Pittsburgh's venerable KDKA, KYW (Chicago), and twelve other stations. There were also NBC Gold, Green, and Orange networks on the West Coast and three other minor entities, but these were relatively insignificant and worked independently.

Under the plan, the networks were made up of two categories of stations, those that were wholly-owned and others that were affiliated, the latter being independents that "signed on," taking network-originated programs for which they paid a fee. Later on there would be a third group, which might be considered "quasi-affiliates," that were more numerous than the others combined, consisting of stations that purchased individual programs.

Actual relations between networks and affiliates would later become a source of problems for both sides and require governmental regulation. At the time, however, all were delighted with the arrangement as might be seen by the rapid growth during the next few years.

As before, and in accord with their differing traditions and missions, the Red Network tended to concentrate upon commercial broadcasting, while the Blue prided itself on public service although it also sought advertising. From the start the plan was for the Red stations to seek programs supported by sponsors, while the Blue often permitted a program to build up an audience

NBC STATIONS, 1926–1936

YEAR	NUMBER OF STATIONS
1926	19
1927	48
1928	56
1929	69
1930	72
1931	83
1932	85
1933	85
1934	86
1935	87
1936	103

Source: United States, Federal Communications Commission, "Report on Chain Broadcasting" (USGPO: Washington, 1941), p. 15

in the hope of eventually attracting a sponsor. These were known as "sustaining" programs. In practice, however, the tendency was to have sponsored programs in the prime early evening hours, with the unsponsored "sustaining" ones on the air during mornings, afternoons, and late evenings. That the two networks had different missions was underlined by the fact that seven cities beside New York housed both a Blue and a Red station. The Red attracted more affiliates and charged higher fees.

While the Red and Blue were supposedly independent of one another, in fact they worked in tandem. They utilized the same studios and equipment, even announcers, musicians, and engineers, all of whom were under contract to NBC and not an individual network.

Affiliates signed on directly with NBC too; these contracts did not specify which network the affiliate was to join, and on occasion NBC would shift an affiliate from one to another. A move from Blue to Red was viewed as a promotion, while one in the other direction was deemed far less desirable. Thus, the two networks hardly competed with one another, in the process realizing important economies of scale.

In 1926, when the future seemed bright for all aspects of radio, it was said that RCA held the Blue in high esteem, as the creator of the radio art, while the Red was looked upon as a secondary, money-grubbing organization, alien to the Radio Group because of its origins with AT&T. This attitude could be seen in the September announcement in which RCA reasserted its belief that broadcasting's major commercial function would be to stimulate receiver sales. "The market for receiving sets in the future," it stated, "will be determined largely by the quantity and quality of the programs broadcast," adding, "We say quality because each program must be the best of its kind. If that ideal were to be reached, no home in the United States could afford to be without a radio receiving set." While 5 million homes had radios, "21 million remain to be supplied."

Whether or not the company really believed this (and all evidence is that Sarnoff did), it made good reading for Hoover who as always was wary of commercial broadcasting.

The Red Network went into operation without any significant publicity, understandable perhaps since it had been networking for years. The Blue made its debut on November 15, 1926, with a coast-to-coast program emanating from the Waldorf-Astoria and feeds from stations across the nation, an event that made the front pages in many cities. The offering was a huge technological and artistic success.

Although NBC was the most powerful network, it was not the only one. In early 1927 Arthur Judson, a violinist turned talent agent, and George Coats, a salesman in sound equipment, organized United Independent Broadcasters, which for a while attracted the attention of Adolph Zukor of Paramount and radio receiver manufacturer Atwater Kent. There were discussions with Victor Talking Machine Company as well, but nothing came of them.

Judson and Coats had more success with Columbia Phonograph Co., and when it later became evident that RCA would unite with Victor Talking Machine, Columbia came to terms with UIB. From this came Columbia Phonograph Broadcasting Company, which after several additional changes fell under the control of William Paley and was renamed Columbia Broadcasting System. A small factor in 1928, CBS was destined to become NBC's main rival, the force that insured there would be no monopoly of the airwaves.

Regulation was a continuing problem. In April 1926, the Supreme Court considered the case of *United States v. Zenith.* At issue was whether the Commerce Department had the right to regulate the airwaves. Eugene McDonald, the feisty founder and president of Zenith Radio, also owned a station in Chicago, whose wavelength was shared with GE's Denver affiliate. Chafing at regulations, he sought a test case by moving to another frequency and challenging Hoover to bring a legal action against him. This the Secretary did, and the Supreme Court decided for Zenith, observing that nothing in previous radio acts gave Hoover the authority to allocate air space. The Secretary was chastised for "the display and action of purely personal and arbitrary power." After some talk of yet another case Hoover conceded defeat, but even before then passage of some kind of act appeared probable.

The reason was obvious to all in the industry as well as to owners of receivers. Immediately after the decision scores of stations attempted to elbow into new and more attractive frequencies, and hundreds of new, unlicensed stations appeared throughout the country. The situation was chaotic and bad for business. Listeners unable to obtain clear reception abandoned radio. During the rest of 1926 receiver sales dropped more than 12 percent while purchases of phonographs and records soared. Along with other radio leaders, Young, Harbord, and Sarnoff called for legislation to regulate the industry.

This is where matters stood on December 8, when an amended version of the White Bill, initially known as H.R. 5589, was introduced into the House. In its final form, the draft reflected some of the antimonopoly attitudes of Hoover and White, though it wasn't quite what they had had in mind during the fourth radio conference. The legislation embodied three basic concepts. First of all, the airwaves belonged to the public, with the government its trustee. Next, the stations were to be privately owned and operated. Finally, free speech was to be safeguarded, though at the time no one was quite certain what this meant, and certainly the framers had no idea of considering radio on a par with newspapers in this regard.

The measure was now sent to the Senate, which while accepting the gist of the House measure made a significant addition. As Hoover had wished, an independent regulatory agency was created to enforce the Radio Act.

Senatorial Democrats went along with him on this, perhaps because they viewed Hoover as a likely presidential nominee in 1928 and had no desire to permit him additional powers—and exposure—before then, especially control over so powerful a means of disseminating news and opinion as radio. Democratic Senator Clarence Dill of Washington, who had emerged as one of RCA's strongest critics in Congress, introduced the measure designed to establish such an agency, to be known as the Federal Radio Commission, and after some negotiation with White the two drafts were merged into the Dill-White Bill.

The power formerly wielded by the Commerce Department was vested in the FRC's five commissioners. Among these were the right "to refuse a license to any applicant found guilty by a federal court of unlawfully monopolizing or attempting unlawfully to monopolize radio communications." The Act affirmed the principle of private ownership of the airwaves; in the public interest licenses would be continued for periods of good behavior. Advertising was mentioned only briefly, for even then it was uncertain that commercial radio would be universal. Implicit in the Act was the notion that stations would not be as independent as newspapers. "Chain broadcasting" was hardly touched upon, indicating that the framers hadn't a clear idea of how to deal with the likes of the emerging new broadcast form.

The measure emerged from conference in January as the Radio Act of 1927. President Coolidge signed it into law on February 3. After more than six years of debate, radio finally had clear legislation to guide it.

Taken as a whole, the legislation pleased the Radio Group. There was nothing in it to hinder networking and toll broadcasting, or anything else

Young, Harbord, and Sarnoff had in mind to increase their power or influence. They were pleased by the creation of the FRC, which was bound to give them more leeway than Hoover. The Radio Group's satisfaction increased on learning who would man the Board.

Heading the Commission was Admiral Bullard, whose sympathies for the Radio Group and special kinship with Owen Young were well known. The other four commissioners—Orestes Caldwell, Eugene Sykes, Henry Bellows, and John Dillon—were nonentities who could be easily swayed. Bullard died shortly after accepting the post, and Sykes, an elderly former Mississippi judge who was a political appointee and knew almost nothing about the technology or industry, served as temporary chairman. Caldwell edited various industry publications, all dependent upon advertising placed by the industry. One of these, *Radio Retailing,* had been a leader in supporting virtually every demand made by the Radio Group. During his first year on the Commission, Caldwell continued to receive a salary from that magazine. Bellow's confirmation was held up because several senators objected to his pro-industry sentiments. Recognizing that he would have a tough time of it and lacking a salary while awaiting confirmation, he stepped down in October 1927, to accept a position as a Columbia Broadcasting System vice president. Dillon, who had been a colonel during the Great War, had little to say. Neither did the men who replaced Bullard and Bellows: Harold Lafount, a radio manufacturer on good terms with RCA; and Sam Pickard, who directed radio matters for the Agriculture Department.

All were favorable to the concept of commercial broadcasting, and in fact virtually every other concept that assisted the Radio Group and other large interests. In common with most regulatory bodies, the FRC became a captive of the industry it was supposed to guide but did so faster than most.

RCA had been born in 1919 through a marriage of convenience between private corporations and the government, to function as the American entry in the wireless competition and to serve the Navy in any future conflict. Seven years later it had been transformed into the major force in broadcasting and the marketing of consumer receivers, and government's role had been diminished. In 1925 RCA's gross revenues from wireless came to $4 million, while the sale of Radiolas and related equipment was $46 million. And the gap was growing; three years later wireless would fetch the firm $6 million and radio equipment, $86 million. Would the government that sanctioned the wireless monopoly stand still as RCA gained dominance in radio? This was the industry's most important unanswered question.

4

Annus Mirabilis

HAD SARNOFF DESIRED the top management post at NBC it doubtless would have been his. By 1926 he had emerged as RCA's most important and innovative executive, with Young and Harbord content to let him run the day-to-day operations and take charge of what today would be called research and development while they concentrated upon political problems. But the same principle that had caused Sarnoff to switch from engineering to management dictated that he remain at RCA, which is to say that while NBC was bound to become an important but specialized part of RCA, the locus of real power would be at the parent firm.

It fell to Owen Young to locate the proper chief executive for NBC. Young knew he needed a person capable of dealing with the Federal Radio Commission, possessed of a finely honed political instinct, a pleasing style, and preferably some knowledge of radio, though this last wasn't of primary importance since Sarnoff would be there to provide guidance. What was required, then, was another person like Harbord, selected for his reputation, intelligence, and personality.

Young selected Merlin Aylesworth, the managing director of the National Electric Light Association, a lobbying organization that represented the utilities industry. At the time Aylesworth knew little about broadcasting, but he possessed all the requisite characteristics and talents for the post.

A tall, well-built, and handsome man with erect military bearing and sharp features, Aylesworth was 40 years old in 1926 and well known in industrial circles, though not to the general public or the radio industry. Young had observed him at close range. As the leading supplier of equipment to the electric utilities, GE had a strong interest in maintaining cordial relations with them and often did so through Aylesworth. It was not unusual for Young and Aylesworth to testify in tandem before congressional committees, bump into one another at industry and political functions, and appear on the same platforms.

Both men strongly opposed public power, Aylesworth portraying advocates of government power generation and distribution as crypto-Bolsheviks, quite a popular stance in the mid-1920s, and one that put him in favor with Republican congressmen and the Administration.

Aylesworth's background was in the best American business tradition of the time. Born in Cedar Rapids, Iowa, in 1886, he grew up in Colorado, graduated from the state university there and went on to law school. After practicing for a while in Fort Collins, he became head of the Colorado Public Utilities Commission in 1914. Four years later he was picked to head Utah Power & Light, the state's leading electric company, and the following year took his post at the NELA. Aylesworth's entire career after the brief stint in private practice was in areas in which government cooperation with the private sector was of paramount importance.

Aylesworth had a realistic notion of his own talents. He did understand public relations; it was he who organized that first coast-to-coast NBC broadcast. Aylesworth also strove to provide the network with an aura of public service by creating an advisory council that included such distinguished individuals as John W. Davis, Charles Evans Hughes, Dwight Morrow, Elihu Root, and Julius Rosenwald, none of whom as far as can be known was ever called upon to offer opinions.

In April 1930 Aylesworth told Sarnoff that he was interested in having an important say in RCA's public relations. Sarnoff deciphered the message: Aylesworth intended to serve as a PR man for the entire organization, meaning he would defer to others in matters of substance. Sarnoff quickly agreed to this relationship, which merely reiterated what was already known, that he was the *de facto* CEO at NBC. For day-to-day guidance he would have McClelland, who was named vice president and general manager. Popenoe, WJZ's station manager, became treasurer and secretary while Harry Davis, the Westinghouse radio veteran, filled the largely ceremonial post of chairman of the board. Above them all, of course, was Sarnoff, who made all the important decisions.

The company's progress in revenues and earnings in the late 1920s were truly phenomenal, and its stock was the outstanding feature in the Great Bull Market of the 1920s. That radio had a glorious future seemed beyond doubt, and that RCA was destined to become the preeminent company in the field was also evident. Little wonder, then, that investors rushed to buy and speculators made it their plaything. Mike Meehan, one of Wall Street's most colorful characters, a former theater ticket broker-turned speculator, became a celebrity through organization of pools to manipulate RCA's price and in the process made the stock the market's bellwether issue.

SELECTED STATISTICS FOR RCA, 1921–1929

figures in millions of dollars

YEAR	REVENUES	EARNINGS	EARNINGS PER SHARE	STOCK PRICE
1921	4.2	0.4	—	2½–1½
1922	14.8	3.0	0.28	6¼–2⅛
1923	26.4	3.0	0.28	4¾–2¾
1924	54.8	3.3	2.91	66⅞–19*
1925	46.3	4.3	3.72	77⅞–39¼
1926	56.1	3.3	2.85	61⅝–32
1927	61.6	7.1	6.15	101 –41⅛
1928	101.4	18.5	15.98	420 –85¼
1929	182.1	10.3	7.90**	572⅞–130**

* reverse split: 1 new share for 5 old ones. ** before 5–1 split.
Source: Moody's *Utilities,* 1925, Moody's *Industrials,* 1928, 1932.

The network was one of the main reasons for this performance. The rapid development of NBC and its superior radio fare prompted an acceleration of receiver sales. In 1926 1.75 million receivers were produced, down 250,000 from the previous year. The figure jumped to 2.35 million in 1927 and 3.25 million the following year. In 1929 the industry turned out 4.42 million sets, and the number of households with radios passed the 10 million mark. In 1928–1929 Americans purchased 7.5 million radios and invested $1.5 billion in receivers and parts. During these years RCA's revenues came to $283.5 million and profits to 34.4 million, more than the combined totals for the previous nine years.

By the time of the 1929 stock market crash the network had been in operation for two years and had developed more rapidly than anyone had dreamed possible. But while broadcasting still seemed a highly profitable enterprise, other enterprises had surfaced that offered almost as much appeal. The company was on the way to becoming what amounted to an entertainment conglomerate through a venture into motion pictures, and it was now big enough to consider breaking away from its corporate parents and going it alone. Finally, in a bold, controversial move RCA attempted to divest itself of the original wireless business. All of this occurred within a period of one year.

The foray into motion pictures was both logical and contentious, just as had been RCA's entry into broadcasting, and like that business, it involved Sarnoff in a conflict with AT&T.

In 1925 AT&T had entered into an exclusive agreement with Warner Brothers, under which that small studio would produce a talking picture using Western Electric apparatus. The system was to be known as Vitaphone and controlled by a new Western Electric subsidiary, Electrical Research Products, Inc. (ERPI). Several demonstrations of the new system were held the following year, and some films utilizing Vitaphone musical sound tracks were produced. In October 1927 Warner released the first full-length talking picture, *The Jazz Singer,* which created a sensation and marked the beginning of the end for the silent movie.

Others moved in to challenge ERPI, with Phonofilm, the most important of these, sold by Case Fox Films. Phonofilm, in which the sound waves were actually recorded on the film was developed by the ubiquitous Lee De Forest and William Case. Fox organized Fox-Case Movietone in 1927 and entered into an alliance with ERPI, increasing AT&T's grip on the new technology. Barely a year after it had relinquished its interest in broadcasting to RCA, AT&T appeared destined to control talking films.

But Sarnoff also hoped to take a leading position in talkies. He had an indirect interest in a version of the phonograph, the Visual Photographic Recorder, that GE scientist Charles Hoxie had invented in 1917 to record high speed telegraph messages on light-sensitive film. Utilizing the Hoxie principle, GE developed what it called the Pallophotophone, which later was known as the Photophone, the name of the GE subsidiary organized to exploit it. During the late 1920s the company's research in this area was led by Elmer Engstrom, an owlish young engineer who had joined the company in 1923 and was already carving a reputation in the field. Westinghouse had also created a system of its own. So Sarnoff was elbowing his way into talkies, in tandem with GE and Westinghouse.

Sarnoff also attempted to enter the field on his own. In the autumn of 1927 the RCA board approved his recommendation to purchase 14,000 shares in a studio, Film Booking Office (FBO), for $400,000. This made RCA a partner of Joseph Kennedy, who controlled the company.

Kennedy purchased a controlling interest in FBO in February 1926. He had ambitions for the studio but like most small producers needed financial backing if he was to make talkies, which was where RCA came in.

In order to do anything at FBO Sarnoff needed a strong technology, which was lacking. So he devised a clever strategy that would enable him to obtain it and at the same time gain some independence from GE and Westinghouse.

By this time a number of GE scientists had concluded that Photophone's system was inferior to ERPI's and apprised Young of their opinion. Possibly because of this Young had initiated preliminary discussions with Fox regarding the purchase of the Phonofilm system, which of course were dropped when Fox came to terms with ERPI. Young considered talkies a serious matter, for he had concluded that it would be a growth industry, ideal for GE and RCA, and wanted both to have a strong position in it. It was then that Sarnoff stepped in, arguing that GE's system was every bit as advanced as Phonofilm, a rather unusual stance considering that it not only went against the opinion of the vast majority of technicians but was patently untrue.

So as to underline and give credence to his view, Sarnoff suggested that RCA purchase a 60-percent interest in Photophone from GE and take over direction of its operations. Young agreed and, in order to sooth ruffled feelings at Westinghouse, arranged for it to have a share as well. Amended articles of incorporation were agreed upon in early April 1928, with RCA having its 60-percent interest, GE 24 percent, and Westinghouse, 16 percent.

As had been the case with broadcasting, RCA was a late entry into the field. It found a solidly entrenched ERPI, which had signed up "the Big Five" (Metro-Goldwyn-Mayer, Paramount, United Artists, First National Pictures, and Universal) in addition to retaining its original position at Warner Brothers, and had already started to wire theaters. But AT&T didn't benefit as much as it anticipated; the decision to sign an exclusive contract with Warner Brothers proved a mistake, since that company now reaped royalties from the ERPI patents and equipment. Still, ERPI possessed a near-monopoly position in what everyone agreed was a rapidly growing industry that rivaled broadcasting in promise.

Sarnoff assumed the presidency of the new RCA Photophone, with Elmer Bucher named vice president in charge of sales and one of his most prized scientists, Alfred Goldsmith, as vice president for development. Provided with a mandate to crack the ERPI facade, Bucher approached the Big Five as well as several others but was unable to sway any of them from ERPI. Discouraged, he decided to enter film production on his own, organizing Gramercy Studios and actually turning out a series of shorts before abandoning the effort.

Sarnoff considered this a futile gesture, knowing that far more would be required if Photophone were ever to succeed. Independent production wasn't the answer. What the firm needed was an alliance with an established operation. What NBC was to RCA, a studio could become for RCA Photophone. FBO, which would be the key to all of this, had already moved into the RCA orbit.

While Sarnoff planned for a union between radio and motion pictures, Kennedy was attempting to create a large, vertically integrated company that would control production, distribution, and exhibition, in this way realizing significant economies. Needing additional theaters in which to exhibit his movies, he had borrowed $4.2 million from the Rockefeller-dominated Chase National Bank and Lehman Brothers and purchased a majority interest in Keith-Albee-Orpheum Theaters, which in turn controlled newsreel producer Pathé Pictures. At the time KAO was a 200-unit chain of mostly second-rate houses, none of which was wired for sound, an operation that would require far more capital than Kennedy intended to invest or could possibly borrow on the collateral he had to offer.

Seeking an alliance as well as the best financial deal possible, he agreed to have several KAO theaters wired by RCA Photophone. Bucher was delighted; this was his first major victory over ERPI.

Some 4,000 theaters either had been wired or were in the process of making the change by early 1929, and $37 million had been expended on equipment and services. The leader by far was ERPI, with more than 90 percent of the installations, so Photophone's prospects were bleak.

Sarnoff realized that RCA Photophone had virtually no chance of winning business away from ERPI. Bucher had signed up only a handful of minor studios—such forgotten names as Tec-Art, Standard Cinema, Van Buren, and Tiffany—along with Mack Sennett and the Kennedy interests. Photophone licensees had produced 20 talking films in 1928, and that year the company installed its first theater equipment. But far more than that was required if Photophone was to become a credible entity. Unable to crack ERPI's market, Sarnoff set out to create a new one for Photophone. Looking back at the experience in his 1934 Report to Stockholders, Sarnoff said:

> One of the main purposes of the investment was to provide at least one major motion picture producing and reproducing organization free to use RCA equipment in the motion picture field. RCA had developed a sound-on-film system of recording and reproducing of motion pictures, but when the apparatus was ready for the market it found that nearly all the large producers and exhibitors of motion pictures were under contracts to others, with the result that RCA found itself substantially without a market for its equipment.

The Sarnoff-Kennedy negotiations to create a major studio around FBO and KEO holdings came to fruition on October 25, 1928, with the purchase of FBO by RCA. This was arranged by Morgan and Chase. (The previous month Paramount had purchased a 49-percent interest in CBS, and so the RCA-FBO nexus wasn't the first linking of radio with motion pictures.)

In exchange for its Photophone patents and the equipment installed in approximately 200 theaters, RCA received 500,000 shares of a new Class B common stock, which gave it a 20-percent interest in the new company, known as Radio-Keith-Orpheum. Into RKO also went FBO and KAO, creating an entity with assets of $72 million and making it if not a major motion picture-theater company, at least one that was a more important force in the industry than FBO alone might ever have been.

Thus, Sarnoff obtained a major stake in a promising studio-theater complex, for which he did not have to invest any additional funds or issue more RCA shares. In terms of assets he received more than $15 million in RKO equity for installations and patents that at the time were worth only a fraction of that amount. Little wonder that within the industry it was said that Sarnoff had received "a free ride." Kennedy departed the scene, having received a $150,000 fee for arranging the deal. The RKO shares he obtained for his FBO and KAO holdings were soon sold.

Sarnoff assumed the chairmanship of RKO with Aylesworth as president. Young, GE President Herbert Bayard Swope, and other GE executives joined the board but for the most part devoted little time or thought to the enterprise.

Seeking a chief executive to replace Kennedy, Sarnoff settled on Joseph Schnitzer, who had been with FBO since 1922. Schnitzer was given a relatively free hand in production with the understanding he was to stress the connection with RCA. This was done in several ways, the most apparent being that the logo, which appeared at the beginning of all movies, was a giant radio tower atop a globe, flashing the signal, "A Radio Picture," and in the titles one would see the name of the company as "RKO Radio Pictures." The company and Photophone licensees between them produced 354 movies in 1929 and 613 in 1930.

With RCA money behind him Schnitzer signed up new talent, mostly minor actors and actresses such as Richard Dix, Sally Blane, Betty Compson, and Bebe Daniels. Sarnoff urged him to unify radio and movies whenever possible, hoping to use his radio stars in films and so enhance their popularity. Rudy Vallee was signed to a contract, and one of the early RKO movies was *Check and Double Check,* which starred Freeman Gosden and Charles Correll, the Amos 'n Andy of radio fame. Other radio-based movies followed.

Meanwhile RCA Photophone's engineers proceeded to wire the KAO (now RKO) theaters. Playing the Kennedy role, Sarnoff sought further acquisitions, especially theaters into which would go RKO sound equipment. The following April RKO purchased the Pantages's vaudeville circuit and in May New York's Proctor chain. The large Cincinnati-based Libson-Heidingfeld-Harriss operations were purchased in May 1930.

By now RKO was one of the four top exhibitors in terms of numbers of theaters. Moreover, the company was profitable; in its first full year of operation RKO took in $51.7 million in theater admissions and film rentals and sales and showed a gross profit of $3.2 million and a net of $1.7 million. (Comparable 1929 figures for RCA were $182.1 million and $10.4 million.) Motion picture equipment, theaters, and film production might not have been as important in RCA's scheme of things as radios and network operations, but in 1929–1930 the outlook for both appeared bright.

The negotiations to create RKO had been important, but Sarnoff devoted even more time to another acquisition, that of the Victor Talking Machine Company. Not only would this open to RCA yet another related industry, which meshed with radio even better than did motion pictures, but it might be considered another step toward one of his longtime goals, cutting his company loose from GE and Westinghouse.

Victor Talking Machine Company, organized in 1901, was considered a pioneer and industry leader. In Eldridge Johnson, Victor had the most original and innovative executive in the industry. Johnson would be the first to place the horn inside the machine and offer phonographs in cabinets that were aesthetically pleasing and acoustically correct. Under Johnson the word "Victrola" became more a generic term for the product than a brand, and it wasn't unusual for would-be purchasers to ask salesmen to show them a "Columbia Victrola" or a "Majestic Victrola," or even a "Victor Victrola."

Opera was an early staple, and Johnson managed to obtain exclusive contracts with leading international stars such as Enrico Caruso, Antonio Scotti, Maurice Renaud, John McCormick, and Lucrezia Bori. He even had his own recording orchestra. Victor's Red Seal label, which was licensed from its English affiliate, Gramophone & Typewriter, Ltd., was considered the class of the field. Victor's corporate symbol, the fox terrier "Nipper," head cocked, listening to a Victor record played on a Victor phonograph, with the legend, "His Master's Voice," was one of the most recognizable in the nation.

Within a year of organization Johnson claimed to have 10,000 dealers and sold $2 million worth of phonographs and records. By 1914 Victor had retained earnings of $16.8 million, and in 1919, $27.9 million. Three years later the company declared a six for one stock split and reported income of over $7 million on revenues of $47 million.

Radio changed all of this. Victor's revenues fell from $6.6 million in 1922 to $1.2 million the following year, and in 1924 the company reported a deficit of $141,000. Industry-wide phonograph sales evaporated, going from the 2.2 million in 1919 to 596,000 in 1922, and purchases of records declined almost as dramatically.

The reason was obvious: not only was radio new and exciting while the phonograph was old and familiar, but music over the air was free.

The manufacturers seemed paralyzed, unable to develop a strategy to deal with radio. In 1925 Victor slashed the prices of its single-faced Red Seal Records, the $1.50s going to $0.90 and the $1.00s to $0.65, but sales continued to fall. Victor took a $4 million inventory loss. Faced with ruin, Johnson took the obvious and necessary step: Victor entered into alliances with both AT&T and GE.

As with wireless and then radio, AT&T was concerned with all technologies dealing with sound. In 1924 two of that firm's leading scientists, J. P. Maxwell and H. C. Harrison, developed new techniques for recording music to eliminate distortions, and these were quickly adopted by Victor. But AT&T had little interest in the technology other than the ways it might be utilized in telephony and so was willing to listen to Johnson's suggestion that Victor purchase exclusive rights to the equipment.

So advanced were the AT&T patents that had this been done, Victor might have gone on to obtain a monopoly in the industry. But AT&T withdrew at the last moment and sold licenses to virtually every recording company in the United States. As a result Western Electric became the leader in this field as it already was in that of developing sound equipment for motion pictures, while Victor suffered.

Sarnoff realized that rather than being in competition with one another, radio and phonograph could be complementary. In April 1922 he wrote a memo on the subject. After noting that important economies could be realized if some of the parts, such as the horn or loudspeaker, could be used by both instruments in a single cabinet, Sarnoff went on to observe:

> Technically the Radiola and the phonograph are both trying to do the same kind of job, i.e., to reproduce, as faithfully as possible, speech or music. The phonograph employs mechanical means to accomplish this result; the Radiola, the electrical means. The former is old and has about reached the limits of its capabilities. The latter is new, has just begun, and the future holds for it untold possibilities. . . . Radio may be expected, in the course of developing its own business, to produce inventions and improvements which will not only be applicable to the phonograph industry but which may indeed technically govern or control the future of the phonograph.

As early as 1924 Sarnoff had suggested a merger to Victor's board but had been rebuffed at that time and on several subsequent occasions. As one who had spent his working life with phonographs, Victor president E. E. Shumaker couldn't come to terms with radios, even then considering them a regrettable fad he somehow hoped would fade, and certainly incapable of producing sound as clear and vivid as phonograph records produced with the new AT&T technology.

In 1925 RCA entered into negotiations with Brunswick-Balke-Collender, then a major force in phonographs and licensee of GE's Pallatrope, a new and improved method of recording sound. The companies signed a $1.5 million contract under which Brunswick would be provided with radios (presumably manufactured by GE) for a combination radio-phonograph to be sold under the Brunswick label.

At the same time Victor and GE were coming closer together, this doubtless prompted by interest in the Pallatrope. They agreed to combine superheterodyne radios with a new phonograph, which would be provided by RCA. Out of this came a five-year contract signed on May 1, 1925, under which the two companies agreed not only to cooperate in the design and manufacture of combination receiver-phonographs but also to have Victor artists appear on NBC programs. The firstfruits of this arrangement appeared later that year. These models, and an "Orthophonic Victrola" based upon AT&T technology, sold well, and it appeared Victor had been saved, the company reporting a profit of $7.7 million in 1926.

Feeling it couldn't last and perhaps weary of operating in so precarious a position, Johnson and his associates sold their two-thirds interest in the company to the Wall Street investment banking houses of Speyer & Co. and J. & W. Seligman for approximately $27 million. The brokers had no desire to run a business, but rather expected to resell the shares to the public at a profit. Orthophonic Victrola sales continued strong, and Victor earned $6.6 million in 1927, but public perception of the phonograph industry's future was such that the bankers couldn't obtain the price they had anticipated. Late in the year the block was sold for $15.8 million.

Then the Great Bull Market entered its last and most volatile phase. Victor common, which was selling in the low 50s in January, started to rise, and believing he might obtain a premium price, Victor President E. E. Shumaker was prepared to talk seriously about a merger.

Sarnoff realized that radio, movies, and the phonograph could become complementary rather than rival products. Moreover, just as Sarnoff had recognized the similarities between radio and motion pictures, so he perceived the same kind of situation with the phonograph. In radio the more programs available on the air, the more attractive receivers would be, and the more receivers there were in homes, the more listeners could be claimed for programs, which meant higher rates charged advertisers. Similarly, the sale of a phonograph implied the purchase of records, and owners of record collections would be encouraged to buy still more acoustically refined players.

From the marketing of radios RCA had entered broadcasting and then had created NBC, which soon would loom more important than manufacturing. Already the motion picture studios were coming to dominate the theaters. So it was with phonographs; by the mid-1920s it had become apparent that record production and sales had more potential than the instrument itself.

Then there was the intriguing synergistic relationship the three mediums might enjoy. Victor's contracted artists were naturals for radio and sound films; indeed, there was no reason why Victor couldn't package programs for radio and participate in the creation of movies.

That Sarnoff wanted to wed the technologies was understandable. But he was at least equally interested in Victor's manufacturing capabilities. The company owned a 2.5-million-square-foot facility in Camden, New Jersey, and branch plants overseas that could be converted to the manufacture of radios. This in hand, RCA might push for freedom from GE and Westinghouse, which still manufactured all of the receivers marketed under the RCA logo.

Although the leading force in broadcasting, RCA had only 20 percent of the radio receiver market. We have seen how other corporations pirated licenses and became aggressive marketers. Sarnoff yearned to slug it out with them in the marketplace and felt hindered from so doing because of the ponderous arrangements between RCA and GE and Westinghouse—two companies producing receivers, one marketing them, and all requiring the kind of coordination in research, design, manufacture, and sales difficult to achieve. Duplication of effort was common. This could be rectified by unification of all operations under one umbrella, which Sarnoff meant to be RCA.

Sarnoff's ambitions were hardly secret; he had discussed them with Harbord and Young, neither of whom supported the idea. In 1927, however, Young was willing to bend to a small degree. He agreed that a new entity might be established to manufacture receivers in which RCA could play a role. Known as the Radio Manufacturing Corporation (RMC), it would be made up of all of the receiver facilities then operated by GE and Westinghouse, which would receive 60 percent and 40 percent of the stock respectively, with RCA given the right to purchase up to 20 percent, the goal being a 48–32–20 percent division among the three parties. One of the shrewdest negotiators and judges of people in American business, Young hoped this would slake Sarnoff's thirst for independence—and perhaps also dissuade antitrusters in the Justice Department who he knew were fairly aching to indict "The Radio Trust." In fact RMC was never formed owing to changes in the relationship with Victor.

Although GE and Westinghouse might oppose any attempt on RCA's part to enter manufacturing on its own, they approved the merger with Victor, providing that company limited itself to phonograph and phonograph-radio combinations, of course on condition that all the radios came from their plants.

Shumaker and Sarnoff agreed that Victor's physical assets were worth $69 million, and the Radio Group would pay an additional sum to be negotiated, with payment to be made in the form of RCA stock.

Word leaked to the press in late summer of 1928, and Victor common started to rise, going to the 140 level by early autumn. In the same period RCA catapulted from 85 to 226. By the end of the year Victor was at 145 and RCA had gone to 380.

Anything seemed possible in such a heady atmosphere. Indeed, RCA common was deemed a jewel on the Street and a fine currency to effect a merger. What Sarnoff wanted to do was what many tycoons do during major bull markets, namely exchange their overvalued paper for undervalued physical assets.

Sarnoff was in a whirl at that time. The Victor discussions took place while he was negotiating to form RKO, and even before that deal was concluded Young invited him on a joint mission to Paris to help restructure the German war debt payments, in what came to be known as the Young Plan. As will be seen, Sarnoff was also holding informal discussions with International Telephone & Telegraph regarding the establishment of a new American telecommunications entity. So in a span of one month he negotiated with Kennedy,

Shumaker, ITT's Sosthenes Behn, Morgan's Thomas Lamont, and the German banker Hjalmar Schacht, and came out with pretty much what he wanted in each case.

That Sarnoff was able to keep all of these balls in the air at the same time was another indication of his abilities and capacities. Not only was 1928–1929 a watershed in RCA's history, but it was also one of Sarnoff's most impressive periods.

On January 4, 1929, it was agreed that each share of Victor would be exchanged for one share of a new RCA preferred, the total value of which came to $64 million, and one of common, worth another $70 million, in addition to $5 per share in cash, this totaling $4.1 million. Also, RCA would retire Victor's preferred stock, which added $19 million to the price. The total value of the package was around $157 million. Since RCA lacked funds for the cash payment and preferred stock buy back, it borrowed $32 million from GE and Westinghouse, the understanding being that they would have the right of approval of any disposition of Victor property.

Shumaker wanted Victor to produce receivers as well as phonographs, all to be utilized in combination sets. Sarnoff approved this condition, which was in line with his own plans. But the GE and Westinghouse representatives vetoed it, insisting upon the old arrangement under which they provided radio sets. Still, matters were proceeding smoothly enough for Sarnoff to accompany Young, Lamont, and other financiers and businessmen to Paris in early February 1929.

In their absence negotiations were continued by Harbord, Swope, and Westinghouse CEO Andrew Robertson, who appeared to believe that they could put into operation the plan for a Radio Manufacturing Corp. by using Victor instead of the existing GE and Westinghouse plants. Perhaps because he misunderstood the situation and assumed all three companies were acting in unison, Shumaker agreed that GE and Westinghouse would continue to provide Victor with receivers.

As a result, that April GE, Westinghouse, and RCA organized the Audio Vision Appliance Company (AVA), which took over the Victor properties, with GE and Westinghouse slated to own it on a 60–40 basis and RCA granted the right to purchase 20 percent of its stock from them. A second firm, to be known as Radio-Victor Corp of America, which would incorporate the Victor and RCA sales organizations, would be wholly-owned by RCA and charged with selling the combination radio-phonographs.

Sarnoff was informed of the plan upon his return and rejected it out of hand. His leverage had increased as a result of success in Paris, where he was generally acknowledged to have worked out the details of the plan for which Young received most of the credit. Young was quite willing to share credit with Sarnoff; on May 17, 1929, he sent a radiogram to Mrs. Sarnoff, saying:

"David did the job of his life last night and if we succeed here it will be due to his persistence and skill intelligently applied."

Already told he soon would be named president of RCA, well aware of his value to the corporation, and knowing he never again would be in so strong a bargaining position, Sarnoff let it be known that unless changes were made he would resign his post. Considering what happened next, it also appears that he presented Young, Swope, and the Westinghouse contingent with a demand that RCA finally be permitted to manufacture receivers on its own at the Victor plant, a program he called "unification" in that it would unify production with distribution.

According to Bucher, this decision was made in the summer of 1929, when the two discussed it during a taxi ride. Sarnoff turned to Bucher and said, "We have reached the point when I think we can have either participation or unification. Which shall it be?" and with this slammed his hat to the floor in frustration. To this Bucher replied, "Why ask me? Your mind has always been set on complete unification." Sarnoff interrupted. "Yes, yes, I know. Complete unification. But can we get it?" "Why not?" asked Bucher. Picking up his hat and clamping it on his head, Sarnoff answered, "Well, boy! Unification it is."

That October 4, in a gesture of independence from GE and Westinghouse, the RCA board voted for unification, and the report was presented to GE and Westinghouse eleven days later. Under ordinary circumstances the parent firms might have protested; they certainly had the votes to block Sarnoff. But rumors persisted of a forthcoming antitrust suit, in which the Justice Department would demand divestiture. Young knew Washington and gauged the temper of the time accurately; he would accept unification in his way, and not that of the Hoover Administration.

Bowing as gracefully as they could to the inevitable, Young and Westinghouse's Robertson went along with the plan. Sarnoff would obtain unification, and with it a greater degree of independence than ever. Essentially, RCA would own 50 percent of the New RCA Victor Co., GE would have 30 percent, and Westinghouse, 20 percent, which would be the same ratio as decided upon for NBC. Furthermore, GE and Westinghouse would retain their stock interest in RCA, but Young would resign as chairman to be succeeded by Harbord, with Sarnoff assuming the presidency and office of chief executive.

Everything had fallen into place. What had begun slightly more than a decade earlier as a wireless company had been transformed into an entertainment complex erected upon a triad of radio receiver manufacturing, networks, and motion pictures, all of which were deemed growth areas. There was the phonograph too, a technology and business that Sarnoff clearly believed might support the other three. Soon thereafter RCA purchased two large music publishers, Leo Feist, Inc. and Carl Fisher, Inc., this taken as a sign of Sarnoff's desire to expand upon these operations.

On December 26, RCA Victor was incorporated, and simultaneously Sarnoff organized RCA Radiotron, which was to engage in the manufacture and sale of tubes. A week later, on January 3, 1930, Young resigned as RCA's chairman and assumed the chairmanship of the Executive Committee. One of Sarnoff's first acts as president was to arrange for the purchase of his two partners' portion of RCA Victor stock. After three more months of negotiations it was agreed that in return for 6,580,000 new RCA shares (which almost doubled the total capitalization) distributed on the usual 60–40 basis, GE and Westinghouse would relinquish rights, licenses, royalties, factories, and even the $32 million advanced RCA earlier. Now GE owned 32.1 percent of RCA's common and Westinghouse 19.2 percent, the total coming to 51.3 percent, a majority of the shares. Thus, RCA may have become an independent producer, but it still was under the control of GE and Westinghouse.

Almost overlooked in all of this was the original wireless business, which as noted had leveled out at $6 million per year. What once had been RCA's sole reason for existence had been relegated to a sideline Sarnoff was interested in disposing of, the funds realized to be used to develop the entertainment triad.

There was a willing and eager purchaser who held to the original vision as set forth by Wilson, Roosevelt, Bullard, Lamont, and Young, namely the creation and operation of an American telecommunications entity to vie with those fashioned by the Europeans. In International Telephone & Telegraph Sosthenes Behn had created a corporation even more impressive than RCA in its growth.

At its core ITT had Behn's telephone companies in Puerto Rico and Cuba, which he and his brother had operated before the war. As a Signal Corps lieutenant colonel during the conflict, Behn envisaged what amounted to an international version of AT&T, a holding company for global telecommunications, the stress being on telephones rather than wireless. Later he would call this "The International System"; his national telephone companies would purchase equipment from ITT factories and be tied to one another by ITT cables.

Toward this end and with aid from Wall Street and Washington, Behn competed against European interests, such as Ericsson and Siemens & Halske, and won rights to own and construct telephone companies in Spain, Mexico, Chile, Uruguay, Argentina, and Brazil. He acquired AT&T's overseas manufacturing operation, International Western Electric (which he renamed International Standard Electric), which gave him plants in Europe and Latin America. In 1927 ITT purchased All America Cables, which connected the Latin American companies with one another and provided a base in New York as well. Then came a merger with the Mackay Companies, which operated Western Union's only significant rival in the United States, Postal Telegraph, and also Commercial Cable, which owned and managed seven cables between the United States and Europe, and one that connected San Francisco to Hawaii, the islands of the western Pacific, and went on to Japan.

In 1928 ITT had assets of more than $389 million, earnings of $21.2 million, and had developed into the kind of global power RCA was intended to become. That RCA had put aside its original and intended function was obvious, and there seemed no reason why this shouldn't be assumed by ITT. Yet nothing happened until 1928, when ITT's acquisition of the Mackay Companies set things into motion.

An Imperial Conference was held in London in the autumn of that year, at which time ITT's development was discussed. Correctly interpreting Behn's actions as a challenge to their interests, several British companies, most notably British Marconi and Eastern and Associated Cable, announced their intention to form a new entity, to be known as Cable & Wireless, to "work in the common interest."

This would pose a clear challenge to ITT but also to other American telecommunications companies. Western Union was also in the cable business while, albeit with diminishing enthusiasm, RCA attempted to market equipment overseas. For a while in late 1928 it seemed RCA might strike a deal with Western Union whose president, Newcomb Carlton, feared the new British combine and didn't think his ailing company could meet the challenge alone.

Thomas Lamont of Morgan & Co. knew of this and during a recess at the Paris negotiations spoke with Sarnoff about the possibility of a merger between RCA and ITT, both of which were his clients. The idea was appealing, and after a luncheon with Young, the three agreed to pursue the matter "if and when the laws of the United States permit," this necessary because under existing legislation there could be no merger between wireless and cable companies. Still, negotiations proceeded to the point where Lamont and Sarnoff agreed that Morgan would float a new bond issue for ITT, the proceeds of which would go to buy RCA's wireless business. That done, ITT would attempt to do the same with Western Union, the object being to organize a single entity capable of doing battle with the forthcoming Cable & Wireless.

This was very much on Sarnoff's mind in late December 1928, as he prepared to leave for Paris.

On January 3, 1929—the day prior to making the tender offer for Victor—RCA organized RCA Communications Inc. as a wholly owned subsidiary, into which was placed its entire wireless operation. The reason was obvious: this would make its disposition simpler.

On March 29 *The New York Times* carried a front-page story entitled: "International T.&T. Acquired R.C.A. Communications, Inc., to Add to

Great World Chain," the price to be $100 million in ITT stock. Harbord and Behn denied the deal was settled—there was that matter of the law to consider. But the next day they issued a joint announcement, stating they were "in accord as to the desirability of a consolidation of their communications interests," and that a plan of that kind indeed did exist.

No measure to alter the law was introduced in Congress that session, but hearings were scheduled before the Senate Committee on Interstate Commerce for the following October. Young, whose reputation after acceptance of the Young Plan was at its zenith, was to testify in favor of legislation that would enable RCA to sell its telecommunications business for a large amount of ITT stock.

The situation changed during that autumn and early winter. The stock market collapsed in late October, casting a pall over business. Confidence had been replaced by fear, and legislators who earlier might have been willing to accept alterations were turning dubious, unwilling to sanction changes that might further unsettle business. Moreover the prices of both RCA and ITT stocks had declined badly; in mid-August ITT was quoted at 115 and RCA at 85 (after its five for one split). Four months later the prices were 70 and 40 respectively. Still, a recovery was taking place, and when Young appeared before a senate committee in mid-December it seemed the worst of the decline was over and the bull market was about to resume.

Nonetheless, Young was on the defensive. He did the best he could under the circumstances. Young spoke of the national interest in ways that echoed his statements of 1918–1919. He suggested that fears regarding the creation of a unitary telecommunications company could be mitigated by creating a nationalized one in its place, indicating his willingness to support any plan to meet the challenge he believed had been posed by Cable & Wireless.

There was opposition to this from the business community, Western Union in particular, as well as from antimonopoly-minded senators. By early 1930 it seemed evident that no legislation would be passed, and the possibilities of a deal between RCA and ITT faded.

Even so, RCA's outlook had never been brighter. Consider the company's position at the time. The radio receiver business was booming, as were the NBC Red and Blue networks. RKO was engaged in a record number of new productions, and several of its movies, *Syncopation, Street Girl,* and *Rio Rita,* were successful, with the last-named playing at the Earl Carroll Theater in New York to standing-room audiences. Profits that year would come to a record $1.7 million. Theater wiring was proceeding rapidly, and Sarnoff earmarked $33 million for the purchase of additional houses, which within a year would bring the chain's total to 175.

The unification with Victor had been completed, and RCA was about to become a manufacturing concern, with the "Micro-Synchronic Radio," and the "Electrola," already being advertised nationally as "RCA-Victor" products. A decision had been made to concentrate upon the higher priced end of the spectrum, to make Victor the class of the field, and this seemed both sensible and achievable given the outlook in autumn of 1929. Reception of the new high-performance, high-priced products was excellent, with the company reporting $2.5 million in advance orders.

Furthermore, there was a new combination with General Motors, which in 1929 decided to enter the radio business and applied to RCA for licenses. Out of this would come a joint venture, General Motors Radio Corporation, to which GM contributed $5 million, thus creating a firm that was supposed to dominate the market for car radios. The contribution made by RCA would be its patents, for which it would receive 51 percent of the stock, while Sarnoff would become GMRC's chairman. Once again, he entered a new field at little cost.

He continued to be tantalized by the idea of NBC's radio performers appearing in RKO movies and (perhaps) recording songs published by Leo Feist or Carl Fisher for Victor Red Seal, and all of this without having to obtain approval from GE and Westinghouse. Finally, the relationship with Chase National, begun through RKO, had matured to the point where Sarnoff might have concluded that it would be a proper ally if and when he managed to divorce RCA from GE and Westinghouse.

Sarnoff and Harbord had every reason to congratulate themselves on their accomplishments and expect better things in the 1930s. But of course this was not to be. RCA's prospects and performance would soon turn downward and remain that way until the coming of World War II. The company that had symbolized growth and glamor during the 1920s would be a victim of the Depression in the 1930s. If it fell further than most, the reason might have been because it had soared so spectacularly earlier.

5

Independence and Decline

UNDENIABLY RCA ENDED its first decade with a greater degree of confidence and optimism than most older corporations its size, but the situation changed dramatically from 1929 to 1935. The company underwent severe business traumas in these years and was forced to abandon Sarnoff's master plan to unite motion pictures, the phonograph record business, and broadcasting. To compensate for this the corporation finally won its complete separation from its parents and was on its own, this accomplished—as were so many developments in RCA's early history—through the intercession of government.

Ever since passage of the Radio Act of 1927 there had been rumors of an impending antitrust action against the Radio Group. It was well known that Hoover's doubts regarding the industry structure hadn't changed since he entered the White House in 1929. Still, the Federal Trade Commission had been investigating the matter for close to three years without coming up with negative findings, and so it was generally believed the company was safe from prosecution.

The failure of the government to file an action prior to 1929 was taken as a sign that none would be forthcoming. In that year RCA notified the Justice Department of negotiations toward unification, and this drew no protest. That the Department might bar the sale of RCA's wireless operations to ITT was well known, and in early 1930 this seemed the only antitrust matter the firm needed to consider.

But in 1930 President B. J. Grigsby of Grigsby-Grunow testified before the FTC that his company had paid RCA $5.3 million in royalties during the past three years and owing to this had been hampered in competing in the field of radio receivers. "No licensee can long pay 7½ percent royalty to its competitor," he said. In addition he complained that his company was obliged to purchase RCA tubes for use in its receivers. Others charged RCA with patent violations, while independent broadcasters argued that NBC should be prosecuted under terms of the Clayton Antitrust Act for alleged monopolistic practices.

One RCA spokesman responded that the corporation had only 20 percent of the receiver market and 40 percent of that for tubes and other replacement parts, while Young observed that Grigsby-Grunow's Majestic brand radios had outsold RCA's in its price category the previous year, hardly an indication that RCA was a monopoly or prevented trade. Sarnoff denied the patent violations, while Aylesworth challenged broadcasters to produce proof of their allegations.

And of course there was that unspoken argument: RCA had been established by government action, its charter approved by the White House and the Navy Department. How could the government argue that the company was in violation of the antitrust act when it had only a fraction of the radio receiver and broadcasting business when it had not objected when RCA enjoyed a monopoly of wireless?

While GE and Westinghouse maintained their controlling interest in RCA, the ties that held the Radio Group together had been weakened by unification, and presumably this would lessen rather than increase the chances of prosecution. Finally, while it by no means was clear that the nation had entered a prolonged period of economic decline, the Wall Street crash and indications of a business slowdown appeared to have eliminated the chances for such prosecution.

But there was a political dimension to the situation that deserves mention. As noted, owing largely to his well-publicized efforts at working out the German debt payment, Owen Young was at the peak of his popularity during this period. He denied having any interest in politics but was definitely attractive to the Democrats in the aftermath of the Al Smith defeat in 1928. Young had an international reputation and was known as an "enlightened businessman" at a time when the Democratic Party appeared short of such talent. And he was visible. In January 1930 *Time* magazine named him "Man of the Year," and scarcely an issue thereafter failed to mention him. Yet to come was a three-part biography in *Fortune,* indicating that powerful publisher Henry Luce among others considered him "presidential."

Already some Democrats were contrasting Hoover's beliefs in rugged individualism with Young's pragmatic capitalism, witnessed by his willingness to accept governmental entry in the international telecommunications industry if unable to affect the RCA Communications-ITT merger. It seemed a winning basis for a 1932 campaign. Influential Republicans agreed. None of this is to suggest that in some way the White House sent down the word to "get Young." Indeed, Hoover and Young respected one another; just prior to his inauguration Hoover had written Young that he would give five years of his life to have him a Republican, and Young agreed that Harbord could have an unpaid leave of absence from RCA to work for Hoover's election. In addition, to seek to punish Young this way would be out of character for the President. But some within the administration might have seen in an antitrust action against the Radio Group a means of crippling any political ambitions Young might have entertained.

Whatever the motivation, on May 13, 1930, the Justice Department brought a suit against GE, Westinghouse, RCA, General Motors Radio, and Western Electric, charging them with violations of the Sherman Antitrust Act, specifically attacking the patent pool in equipment manufacture. The Antitrust Division claimed that ever since RCA's origin in 1919 the defendants had conspired to restrain competition, that they "have continuously refused, except on terms prescribed by them, to grant licenses under said patents and the patent rights to any individuals, firms, or corporations for the purpose of enabling the latter to engage in radio communication, radio broadcasting, or interstate commerce in radio apparatus, independently or in competition with the defendants."

Senator Clarence Dill was delighted, saying the action was "more comprehensive than anything I expected in the course of five years' fight on the issue." He went on to charge Young with attempting to create a worldwide wireless trust through RCA Communications and ITT as well as monopolizing domestic equipment manufacture and broadcasting. Grigsby cheered the filing, apparently believing it would end in lower licensing fees. Young released a statement: "The Radio Corporation of America welcomes the suit of the government of the United States to test the validity of its organization, which has now existed for more than ten years, and in every step of which the government has been advised."

The news had virtually no impact on the financial markets, and in fact the stocks of all companies involved actually rose somewhat in the next few New York Stock Exchange sessions. Parrying continued for more than a year, during which the issue was erased from the common consciousness. But in this period the government developed its plan to restructure the industry, while the Radio Group considered its response.

The Justice Department's solution was simple and straightforward: GE and Westinghouse should divest themselves of all of their RCA holdings, RCA should make available its licenses to them and others at lower rates, and AT&T and all three former parents should enter the receiver manufacturing field on their own. This was immediately rejected by GE and Westinghouse, while AT&T made no response and indeed was the least troubled of all, having disposed of its RCA stock. From the first Gifford indicated a willingness to go along with whatever the other parties could decide upon.

As for RCA, it was in a touchy position. Sarnoff considered divestiture a natural next step after unification and so was with the government on this issue. But it had to be on his terms, which meant that GE and Westinghouse would receive as little as possible in return for relinquishing their interests in the corporation. Moreover, he wanted RCA to maintain the traditional relationship with its licensees and broadcasting rivals, namely to continue ownership of patents and enjoy a dominant position in broadcasting. As Eugene Lyons put it, "his strategy was to accede to the order for separation—but without abrogating the unification agreement or dismantling the patent structure."

This he proposed to Young and Westinghouse's Andrew Robertson. Painting the picture in stark hues, he noted that if the Justice Department succeeded in dismantling the unification agreement and in other ways acted against RCA the corporation would be in dire straits, and so any governmental attempt to cripple RCA had to be opposed by all. At the same time he hoped to settle matters before the case reached the courts, this scheduled for late 1932. With their support, he rejected the government's demands, and all agreed that Young was best suited to respond to the government's initial proposal.

To bring the kind of competition called for was both unrealistic and unwise, Young observed on October 1, 1931. Not only did it fly in the face of prior agreements, but it would disrupt a sensitive and vital industry when the entire economy was in a shambles. "To attempt to make the readjustment at this time . . . when the hope of improved industrial conditions not only remains unrealized but when the country is in an unprecedented economic and industrial crisis, would be to court financial and industrial disaster."

In speeches, articles, and interviews Young indicated a generalized belief that the times called for industrial cooperation, not competition, and went so far as to suggest temporary suspension of the antitrust laws until the emergency ended. "Throughout the country large radio plants owned by competing manufacturers stand idle today because of overproduction resulting from ruinous competition." Dozens of manufacturers had been forced from the market, and others would follow. Sales of radios and receivers had become profitless in this kind of environment. "Thousands of men and women, the large majority of whom might have remained employed if stable conditions existed, are out of work today, and hundreds of thousands today find their investment depreciated, not by restraint of competition but because of competition so great as to have demoralized prices and to have made profitable operations largely impossible."

The Justice Department remained adamant, however, and matters dragged on for another year, the only progress being an agreement that AT&T should be separated from the suit. But in September 1932, with court appearances scheduled for November 15 and the economy in still worse shape, all parties became more willing to compromise. More than that, a whiff of influence-peddling appeared.

Eight years later it was revealed that in this period RCA had paid two former Republican senators, George Moses of New Hampshire and Daniel Hastings of Delaware, to assist in lobbying activities. Moses, who had served as president pro tem of the Senate, was particularly well connected, and it was alleged that he helped sway the administration to RCA's point of view. Sarnoff conceded that lobbying indeed had taken place but denied any wrongdoing. In any case the antitrusters took positions on several occasions that suited RCA's ends.

Given the Justice Department's interest in a compromise, the corporations set to work creating one. Sarnoff, Young, Robertson, and squadrons of their lawyers met daily to work out an arrangement, and this time the parties talked as adversaries in what amounted to an action for separation rather than as partners against the government.

There were four points at issue. A division of patents was of prime consideration, for this was the core of the government's case. As might have been expected, Sarnoff attempted to retain all of them at no cost. He also wanted GE and Westinghouse to agree to remain out of the manufacturing field for at least two years, to enable RCA Victor to establish itself as a profitable entity on its own. Then there was the matter of moneys owed GE and Westinghouse, which amounted to some $18 million. Initially Sarnoff hoped the debt could be canceled in some mutually agrecable fashion, but when this was rejected he sought the least painful method of repaying the loans. As for broadcasting, GE and Westinghouse would keep their stations, severing the connection with NBC, but Sarnoff wanted NBC to be granted management contracts there, which would return additional profits to RCA.

While the Justice Department was willing to concede some points, it continued to insist upon complete divestiture, acting as though it did not recognize that RCA actually wanted this to occur and that the others would go along with it. Skillfully, Sarnoff convinced the government's attorneys that the key to the entire proposed settlement was to make certain RCA would remain a viable enterprise and that too much should not be ceded to GE and Westinghouse.

Judge Warren Olny, who was scheduled to try the case, agreed with Sarnoff. On October 8, 1932, he wrote to GE's lead attorney, Charles Neave, that he believed "the only way in which the Radio Corporation may be properly protected, in case of a divorce, is to put it at the outset in such a position, financially and otherwise, that it can stand on its own feet and take care of itself in the case of competition without the existence of agreements or arrangements designed to protect it against competition."

In early November, with the court appearance only days away, Sarnoff proposed the following financial arrangement: GE, which was owed $11.5 million, would receive a building RCA owned on Lexington Avenue and 51st Street in New York (which at the time was operating at a loss) for an assigned value of $4.7 million. Another $5.9 million of the debt would be canceled, leaving $875,000, for which it would receive that amount of RCA debentures. Westinghouse was to cancel $3.9 million and obtain $2.2 million in debentures. This plan was accepted as the basis for negotiation.

That Young would agree to what by any interpretation must be considered a major victory for both RCA and Sarnoff may have resulted from his strong attachment to the firm but also to preoccupation with other matters. At the time his own financial affairs were in disarray because of the market collapse, and much later it was learned that Young had been obliged to liquidate personal holdings and borrow funds in order to remain afloat. Financial writer and publisher B. C. Forbes visited Young in this period, and wrote, "His appearance shocked me. He has aged. The lines on his face have deepened. . . . He looks tired, burdened, contemplative." It well might have been that in 1932 Young welcomed the chance to relinquish one of his many roles.

The settlement was concluded on November 13, generally on Sarnoff's proposed terms. Of the debt RCA owed GE and Westinghouse, $8.9 million was canceled, $4.7 million was accounted for by the Lexington Avenue building (which soon after became GE's headquarters), GE obtained $1.6 million in debentures, and Westinghouse's share came to $2.7 million in debentures. In what was the most startling concession, GE and Westinghouse accepted Sarnoff's suggestion that RCA was to retain all radio patents and that they wouldn't produce radios under their own nameplates for two and a half years, and then only after becoming RCA licensees. Otherwise, GE and Westinghouse agreed to distribute half their RCA shares to their own stockholders within three years, but as it turned out the entire distribution was completed by February 1933. Under terms of the divestiture agreement cross-licensing of patents would no longer be made on an exclusive basis.

By then important changes in the makeup of the boards of both RCA and NBC had been effected, indicating the end of GE, Westinghouse, and Morgan influence. Departed were Melvin Traylor, Paul Cravath, and most important, Gerard Swope, and in their places came Cornelius Bliss, Frederick Strauss, and Mark Woods. Young remained, but only as a member of the advisory council, content to follow Sarnoff's lead, and as before the two men had good rapport. This isn't to say Sarnoff finally had a free hand; banker support was crucial during the Great Depression, and banks were represented on the board too, in the form of nominees from First National City Bank and other Rockefeller-dominated institutions. But all were willing to defer to Sarnoff on operational matters.

There were changes in the field as well. For several years Sarnoff had chafed at George McClelland's inability to counter the growth of the Columbia Broadcasting System, even while conceding he had managed to lure the leading advertising agencies to NBC and maintained excellent relations with Lord & Thomas, the nation's largest radio advertiser. He replaced him now with his own man, Richard Patterson, former commissioner of correction for New York. Two years later Aylesworth would go over to RKO on a full-time basis, permitting Sarnoff to name Lenex Lohr, who had just completed organizing the Chicago World's Fair, as his replacement at NBC. Gradually and with a minimum of disruption, Sarnoff remade the personnel more in his own image.

The company entered 1933 as an independent force, with Harbord still chairman and Sarnoff president. "RCA had been praised, damned, investigated, stipulated," wrote *Variety.* "It had been multiplied, augmented, expanded, revised, reorganized, refinanced, reoriented, and reformed." The writer might have added it was now being "Sarnoffized" as well.

Soon after, referring to the antitrust suit, Sarnoff cracked, "The Department of Justice handed me a lemon and I made lemonade out of it." As Eugene Lyons wrote, "excessive modesty was not among his cardinal virtues." But it was true that RCA was independent by virtue of Sarnoff's ability to sway events his way. And as usual, he was involved in several battles simultaneously, the most important of which after divestiture being survival through the Great Depression.

The aggregate economic statistics for the first half of the 1930s reveal a nation in which the great progress of the late 1920s had been reversed. Although there was a recovery in 1933, economic performance remained far below that of the predepression period. In fact, the 1929 level wouldn't be matched until 1941, when because of the pressures of war America finally recovered.

SELECTED ECONOMIC STATISTICS, 1929–1935, 1940

figures in billions of dollars

Year	Gross National Product	Disposable Personal Income	Personal Savings	Corporate Profits
1929	103.1	83.3	4.2	10.5
1930	90.4	74.5	3.4	7.0
1931	75.8	64.0	2.6	2.0
1932	58.0	48.7	–0.6	–1.3
1933	55.6	45.5	–0.9	–1.2
1934	65.1	52.4	0.4	1.7
1935	72.2	58.8	2.1	3.4
1940	99.7	75.7	3.8	9.8

Source: *Historical Statistics,* pp. 224, 234.

In common with most other industrial companies RCA went into a sharp decline in the early 1930s, posting deficits in 1931, 1932, and 1933 before staging a modest recovery. Sarnoff slashed the work force, and those who remained took pay cuts; by the end of the decade personnel had been reduced by half.

The price of RCA common collapsed from an unadjusted $572 per share in 1929 to $55 in 1930, and then sank to $10 in 1931, as the most spectacular success story of the Bull Market was followed by the Bear Market's most dismal flop.

SELECTED RCA STATISTICS, 1929–1935

figures in millions of dollars

Year	Revenues	Net Income	Earned Surplus
1929	182.1	10.4	29.7
1930	137.0	0.3	30.0
1931	102.6	–3.5	11.3
1932	67.4	–1.5	9.9
1933	62.3	–0.6	9.3
1934	78.8	4.2	13.5
1935	89.2	5.1	12.4

Source: *Moody's Industrials,* 1933, 1936.

The company's operations in this period may be divided into six areas: broadcasting, communications, manufacturing, royalties, and through RKO, motion picture production and theaters. The results for some were dismal, for others spotty. While RCA did not break down its statistics by activity, it is possible to approximate them based upon whatever do exist plus interpretations of industry-wide figures.

As noted, RCA Communications, which was the company's original business, had leveled off in terms of revenues and income toward the end of the decade. In 1928, the last year of this period for which RCA reported income by segment, Communications posted revenues of $6.1 million and appeared to have earnings of around $1 million. Since a good deal of its business was commercial, there was a falloff in revenues in 1930, probably to below $6 million, while earnings remained level. The company disclosed its 1930 earnings—$661,000—to historian Gleason Archer, who indicated that for the first half of 1932 these came to $202,000. Communications required little in the way of new investment, however, while labor costs remained constant and relatively low. It would appear that this segment of the company's business remained profitable throughout the depression.

Manufacturing was the sole activity that was capital rather than labor intensive, requiring heavy investment in plant and equipment and inventories. A glut of radios developed early in the depression, and total sales declined from 4.4 million in 1939 to 2.4 million in 1932 before turning upward. In this period price wars and cutthroat competition became commonplace, and profit margins were slim.

Receiver prices had been coming down ever since the mid-1920s while performance improved, a familiar enough development, which was also taking place at the same time in autos and later on would be repeated in such items as ballpoint pens, digital wristwatches, and most important, computers. In 1923 a three-tube model might cost $100; a like-powered model in 1930 might sell for $20, while six-tube sets were available for as little as $50. Still, in 1929 the average price for a radio was $133, but most of the sets purchased that year were large consoles, the centerpiece of the middle-class living room.

The situation changed with the onset of the Depression, when customers sought lower-priced models. Answering the demand were several minor companies such as Fada, Emerson, DeWald, and Crosley. Emerson was the first on the scene, with what was called "the pee-wee," a tabletop set introduced in 1931. It weighed only five pounds, sold for $25, and was a huge success. Others followed, so that by early 1933 pee-wees were taking more than half the nation's unit sales, with some retailing for as little as $10. Now the majors joined in; RCA Victor's pee-wee, which cost $12.95, legitimized the small sets. By 1935 the average price was down to $55, and by 1940, $38.

Furthermore, RCA Victor suffered setbacks even in its familiar niche, as more innovative and aggressive marketers, led by Philco, elbowed it aside. In fact Philco seized sales leadership from RCA in 1931 and remained the leading company in its segment for the rest of the decade.

In 1926 RCA had announced it was the world's largest manufacturer of radio receivers, but at no time in that decade had it commanded more than 25 percent of total sales. It was plagued by overcapacity caused by ambitious expansion programs of the late 1920s. The giant Camden plant, considered one of the most modern in the industry, had been upgraded in 1928–1929, and again in 1930 at a cost of $7.5 million, to meet what was believed to be a growing market for radios and combination sets. The collapse of the radio market in 1931–1932 pushed this segment into the red, contributing the greatest share of the company's deficit.

Squeezed by the likes of Emerson on the lower end and Philco on the upper, Victor was a troubled concern through much of the decade.

Yet radio outperformed the general economy, and the 1933 recovery was impressive. A CBS survey indicated that there were more than 16 million receivers in operation, and $300 million worth of receivers were sold in 1933, the figure rising to $350 the following year. Writing in 1936, sociologists Robert and Helen Lynd observed that radio had emerged as the nation's most pervasive medium. "It is likely that this inexpensive form of leisure, like the reading of free library books, has involved a relatively larger amount of time per radio during the depression."

However, RCA more than compensated for manufacturing setbacks through the collection of royalties. In 1928 these amounted to almost $6.4 million, and they remained close to that level the following year. Total payments dropped to $5 million in 1931, after which they appeared to rise once again.

Sarnoff cut back on ancillary activities and sold assets to realize additional economies. In 1931 its 50-percent-owned European operation, Gramophone Co., which had been part of the old Victor, united with Columbia Gramophone to form Electric & Musical Industries, giving RCA a 29-percent ownership. Needing funds and in any case having little interest in the British market, four years later RCA sold its shares to investors in that country for $10.2 million, intending to plow the funds into domestic operations. In 1940, in a little-noted move, RCA sold its interest in Victor Talking Machine of Japan for $2 million in cash, payable over a five-year period.

By themselves royalties and asset sales couldn't keep RCA profitable, but without them the corporation would have been in trouble. This situation would continue even after RCA recovered from the Depression. Always a fine research operation, RCA had become accustomed to selling the fruits of its laboratories to most takers. This practice enabled domestic rivals to flourish. As will be seen in time, the corporation's penchant for licensing would become the means whereby the Japanese all but defeated the Americans, RCA included, in consumer electronics.

Broadcasting underwent important changes because of the advent of bad times. There was a steady decline in sustaining programs and an increase in sponsored ones, especially during prime-time evening hours. The Red Network had such old and new programs named after sponsors as "The Cliquot Club Eskimos," "The A & P Gypsies," "The Gold Dust Twins," and the like. Chase & Sanborn coffee, Ipana toothpaste, Lux soap, Texaco gasoline, Lucky Strike and Camel cigarettes, Coca-Cola, and dozens of other brand-name products had programs with their names affixed.

As was to have been expected, most of the programs were light, escapist dramas, variety shows, and musicals. News programs remained pretty much on a sustaining basis, a situation that wouldn't change until later in the decade. Regulations regarding the amount and tone of ads were altered. In the late 1930s sponsors weren't permitted to mention price, and some products, such as suppositories and certain pain relievers, were deemed in bad taste; this eventually went by the boards.

As a result of increased listenership and greater sponsor demand, the networks were able to raise their rates even while the cost of almost everything else declined. By 1933 a network hour on NBC Red cost $12,880, and on

Blue, $11,740 (CBS charged $16,160). This was just for time, exclusive of programming, for which the networks also took responsibility, putting together packages for potential sponsors. Increased revenues meant that the networks could offer more lavish programs, and so they did, in the hope of attracting more listeners, more sponsors, and higher fees.

In 1930 NBC became RCA's major source of profits, with revenues of $22.2 million and earnings of $1.9 million. The following year, when RCA's total revenues came to $102.6 million and posted a loss of $3.5 million, the network contributed revenues of $29.6 million and showed a profit of $2.3 million. A two-year decline followed, but there was a sharp recovery in 1934. Indeed, NBC was consistently profitable, and were it not for this contribution, RCA might have been forced to the wall.

NATIONAL BROADCASTING COMPANY, 1928–1935

figures in millions of dollars

YEAR	GROSS RECEIPTS	NET PROFITS
1928	7.2	0.4
1929	11.4	0.8
1930	15.7	2.2
1931	20.5	2.7
1932	20.9	1.2
1933	18.0	0.6
1934	23.5	2.4
1935	26.7	3.6

Source: Archer, *Report on Chain Broadcasting,* p. 17

There was a fallout at the theaters during the early years of the Depression. While admissions held up pretty well initially, they declined once the fascination with talkies faded. Then ticket prices were slashed, hurting profits. One after another of the major studios went into bankruptcy, not to recover until later in the decade.

The falloff affected and included RKO. The company seemed strong enough in early 1930, when most believed the Depression would be short-lived and the talkies craze would result in ever-increasing admissions and profits. In fact, RKO common was a feature in Wall Street's small bull market that February and March, when one brokerage predicted it would earn $10 million and soon depose Metro-Goldwyn-Mayer to become the industry's leader.

SELECTED MOTION PICTURE STATISTICS, 1929–1934

figures in millions

YEAR	MOTION PICTURE ATTENDANCE	BOX OFFICE RECEIPTS
1929	4.2	$720
1930	4.7	732
1931	3.9	719
1932	3.1	527
1933	3.1	482
1934	3.6	518
1935	4.2	556

Source: *Historical Statistics,* p. 400.

Toward the end of the year RKO purchased Pathé Exchange for $4.6 million, obtaining its Culver City studio, equipment, talent roster, and three uncompleted films. At the time it appeared a sensible enough move. Pathé was generally deemed a more prestigious operation than RKO, with such stars as Ann Harding, Helen Twelvetrees, and Constance Bennett, and it was a profitable operation.

Costs soared and attendance declined in 1931, in large part owing to an extremely hot summer that kept audiences away in those pre–air conditioner years. Production now went into the red. Attempting to place the best face on the situation in the 1931 *Annual Report,* RCA announced that 1,690 theaters had been wired for Photophone along with 413 nontheatrical installations and that twelve studies were using the technology. It was evident, however, that RKO and the entire motion picture segment was in trouble.

Management was shaken up in a move to restore confidence. But attendance again declined sharply in 1932, when virtually all the exhibitors did poorly. Set beside Warners' loss of $14 million and Paramount's $21 million, RKO's $10.7 million deficit may have appeared a relatively decent showing, but there were more troubles ahead. As a result of its commitment to Pathé Radio City and the continuing upgrading of theaters, RKO had to increase spending, at a time when its credit was poor.

This was complicated by RCA's and RKO's involvement in one of the nation's most spectacular real estate projects. In 1930 John D. Rockefeller, Jr., announced that the project later to be known as Rockefeller Center would involve RCA and include one or more RKO theaters. Sarnoff derived particular pleasure in having the project referred to as Radio City. But in a

SELECTED RKO STATISTICS, 1929–1934

figures in millions of dollars

YEAR	THEATER ADMISSIONS	FILMS RENTALS	OTHER	TOTAL	OPERATING INCOME	NET INCOME
1929	37.1	10.4	4.1	51.7	3.2	1.7
1930	50.6	16.5	4.2	71.4	5.5	3.4
1931	50.4	24.4	4.5	79.2	–1.7	- 4.6
1932	—	—	—	59.9	–6.6	–10.7
1933	23.3	18.4	2.3	44.0	–0.7	- 1.4
1934	18.3	21.3	2.1	41.7	2.2	- 0.3

Source: *Moody's Industrials,* 1935.

year when attendance actually rose industry-wide, the company's films were badly received, with RKO posting earnings of $3.4 million and revenues of $71.4 million.

The financial interest in Radio City proved a severe strain. Ground breaking took place in 1931, close to the bottom of the depression. The project was plagued by difficulties and by then had taken on the appearance of a white elephant, which would drain the resources of all involved, RKO in particular. Rumors of deep deficits and a general awareness that RKO had borrowed to the hilt, combined with stock rigging and a generally poor market, caused the price of its common to plummet from 50 to under 1 in less than three months.

In response RKO tried to restructure its debt and equity, to little avail. Cutbacks became the rule, including the cancellation of one of the two proposed theaters at Rockefeller Center, as well as sharp reductions in the amount of office space the company had contracted to lease. In order to insure occupancy, RCA had to make a $300,000 loan to RKO. To satisfy other claims, the motion picture firm had to issue 100,000 new common shares, worth $350,000, to the Rockefeller-controlled Metropolitan Square Corporation.

In this way the Rockefeller interests achieved dominance at RKO. The Rockefellers were becoming a more important force at RCA itself, as Sarnoff also canceled RCA leases and issued 100,000 shares of preferred stock, worth $2.2 million, to Metropolitan Square as a settlement. The aforementioned new directors at RCA and NBC—Strauss, Woods, and Bliss among them—were directly or indirectly associated with the Rockefeller interests. Most important, as much for its symbolism as anything else, soon Young would leave both boards, to be replaced by Newton Baker, a prominent member of the Rockefeller interests.

Did this mean RCA had rid itself of GE and Westinghouse only to come into the Rockefeller orbit? Not really, since the Rockefellers were interested in finance, not management of RCA. Sarnoff continued to have a free hand in all important matters, while the bankers were given a say in financial matters, which suited both. The latter wanted a clean balance sheet and a return on their investment and were there to see that both were accomplished.

This interest became evident in 1936, when RCA engaged Joseph Kennedy to restructure its capitalization. Kennedy called in preferred stock for redemption and through other juggling managed to reduce the preferred dividends from $5.6 million to $3.2 million. This was a prelude to the clearing up of arrears on RCA's Class B preferred stock (a large amount of which was owned by Rockefeller interests) by paying a dividend of $31.25. Then Sarnoff declared the first dividend on the common, $0.20 per share. Wall Street took note of this, considering it a sign of strength, and the prices of both issues rose.

The dividend payout also marked the beginning of a new period in the way RCA viewed the capital market. During the 1920s Sarnoff and others at the firm watched the dazzling rise of RCA common with great pleasure, knowing their own holdings were increasing in value. Yet RCA itself did not profit from the strength of its equity, since not once in the decade did the corporation even consider selling additional shares to the public. If RCA needed funds it would borrow from Morgan and his allies, doing so with GE and Westinghouse as its nominal guarantors. The change in the dividend policy signaled RCA's arrival as an independent entity even if it was wrongfully considered a Rockefeller satellite.

The new partnership might have been seen in the name of the construction project. By agreement it still would be called Radio City, and the prime theater would be named Radio City Music Hall, but Sarnoff was careful to refer to the project as a whole as Rockefeller Center. The company moved there from its old offices at 7611 Fifth Avenue in 1933, and so did NBC. From his 53rd floor office Sarnoff could look out at one of the most ambitious real estate developments in American history, completed at the bottom of the nation's worst economic crisis.

By then the motion picture business had reached its nadir, while a slump in New York real estate meant that offices in Radio City remained vacant. Reluctant to sink additional funds into RKO, and troubled about a Securities and Exchange Commission investigation of stock trading and corporate practices, all involved were willing to see RKO go into receivership, which it did in January 1933, at a time when creditors had claims against it of $35.4 million against free assets of only $5.2 million.

The company retained its equity position in RKO, but from that point onward it had only a minor say in its operation. Within a year Aylesworth had been relegated to a minor role, and in 1935 the Atlas Corporation and Lehman Brothers purchased half of the RCA holdings for $5 million while receiving an option for the rest at $6 million. Meanwhile RKO continued to founder, and while the option was extended it was not exercised, so that at the end of the decade RCA continued to own approximately 15 percent of its stock. By then Sarnoff's interest in RKO had become relatively minor, and the company passed from the RCA universe. The loss was regretted but was hardly as important as other negative developments of the period.

However, RCA's concern with sound equipment remained. Even while withdrawing from RKO, the company made a strong effort to wire independent theaters and sell equipment to minor studios. In 1937 Sarnoff threatened AT&T with an antitrust action unless ERPI ceased collecting royalties on certain devices for which it lacked clear licenses. AT&T backed down. Thereafter RCA's position in theater installations increased, to the point that by the end of the decade it was the major force in that field.

What was significant for the long run was that with the RKO collapse RCA ceased to be a highly visible player in motion pictures while remaining the central one in radio networks. This would have important implications for yet another technology in which Sarnoff was interested. Throughout the 1930s RCA experimented with television; as early as 1929 it appeared to be the entertainment medium of the future, with a potential as great or greater than either films or radio. Had RCA remained a force in motion pictures, Sarnoff might have considered it an adjunct of RKO. As it was, with only NBC his vehicle, Sarnoff came to see television as a logical outgrowth of radio.

In the 1930s television stood at a crossroads. It would be deemed either radio with pictures or movies in the home. The bankruptcy incurred by RKO helped insure it would be the former.

6

At War with the FCC

THE LAST HALF of the thirties was a time of recovery, expansion of existing businesses, development, and a cautious and measured entry into a new area. While RCA continued to evolve, its focus in these years was not so much on the creation of new products or exploitation of new markets, as on the maturing of older ones and relations with government.

The company's recovery may be traced in the corporate statistics. We have seen that after three years of deficits RCA turned profitable once again in

SELECTED RCA STATISTICS, 1935–1945

figures in millions of dollars

YEAR	REVENUES	NET INCOME	EARNED SURPLUS
1935	89.2	5.1	12.4
1936	101.2	6.1	15.3
1937	112.6	9.0	16.5
1938	100.0	7.4	20.0
1939	110.5	8.1	20.5
1940	128.5	9.1	23.6
1941	158.7	10.2	28.0
1942	197.0	9.0	33.3
1943	294.5	10.2	41.6
1944	326.4	10.3	43.6

Source: RCA, *Annual Reports,* 1935–1944; *Moody's Industrials,* 1939, 1944, 1946.

1934; never again during the David Sarnoff period would there be another loss quarter.

By now RCA had taken on the appearance of two networks with manufacturing sidelines. The company did not break down its revenues by sources in the 1930s, though business magazines and industry analysts offered what appear to have been fairly accurate assessments. All observers agreed that the networks provided the corporation with the bulk of its revenues and earnings, while production of receivers and combinations turned in relatively drab performances. While national sales of radio sets recovered, rising from 3.6 million in 1933 to 5.7 million in 1935 and then to 7.7 million in 1937, RCA never became the dominant force in the industry it had once hoped to be. It was unable to become a leader in tabletop radios and continued to lag in other product categories.

To complicate matters Philco brought a legal action against RCA in 1936, not only charging unfair licensing practices but alleging RCA had tried to steal trade secrets through espionage and other illegal actions, including the attempted seduction by RCA operatives of several of Philco's female personnel. The complaint alleged that the agents "did provide them from time to time with expensive and lavish entertainment at hotels, restaurants, and night clubs . . . did provide them with intoxicating liquors, did seek to involve them in compromising situations, and thereupon and thereby did endeavor to entice, bribe, persuade, and induce said employees to furnish them . . . confidential information, designs, and documents. . . ."

It was an embarrassing, messy, and complicated case that eventually was settled out of court and, as will be seen, was involved more with television than radio. It did more to damage RCA's already tarnished reputation and detracted attention from NBC, which rode the crest of changes in advertising budgets.

Advertising was steadily shifting from print to radio during the 1930s. In 1928 radio accounted for only $20 million of the approximately $1.1 billion spent on advertising. Newspapers then were the prime medium, accounting for $760 million, with magazines in second place with $215 million. That year outdoor billboards accounted for more than four times the amount of revenue as radio.

Along with almost everything else, advertising declined during the early years of the Great Depression, going to $665 million by 1933, of which $65 million went to radio. In 1935 radio took $130 million of the $1.7 billion expended on advertising, this working out to 7.5 percent of the total; radio advertising accounted for $215 million of the $2.1 billion, or more than 10 percent, expended in 1940.

Increased advertising and higher time charges enabled NBC to boost revenues to $38.5 million in 1937, approximately one-third of RCA's total and a quarter of the industry's business. Industry sources estimated profits at $3.7 million, also a third of the parent's figure.

By mid-decade approximately one-third of all radio programs were on a fully sponsored basis. Most of the increase went to the networks, of which NBC was the undisputed leader. Under McClelland and then Richard Patterson both NBC networks expanded their advertising, with Lord & Thomas's Albert Lasker, who was one of Sarnoff's closest friends, accounting for some half of all billings. Among Lasker's clients in the late 1930s were such heavy advertisers as American Tobacco, General Electric, Cities Service, Commonwealth Edison—and RCA and RKO. L & T-created shows for the Red Network included Eddie Cantor (Chase & Sanborn Coffee), Ed Wynn (Texaco), Rudy Vallee (Fleishman's Yeast), Jack Pearl (Lucky Strike), Charles Winniger (Maxwell House Coffee), Ken Murray (Royal desserts), and Al Jolson (Chevrolet), while the Blue had the Marx Brothers (Esso) and a handful of other top-line stars and offered a larger array of newscasters and analysts. There was little in the way of news programs on the Red Network and much more on the Blue, this in keeping with their characters. In 1937 Blue's revenues came to $11 million, while Red's were $27 million.

In those years sponsors preferred variety, comedy, and drama programs, shying away from news and public events. But this soon would change, owing to the crises in Europe and Asia and persistent prodding from a new government agency.

DISTRIBUTION OF PROGRAMMING BY TYPE, 1929–1939

YEAR	MUSIC	DRAMA	TALKS and NEWS
1932	63.0	10.8	10.1
1933	67.3	11.2	9.0
1934	67.7	12.6	8.3
1935	63.3	13.3	10.7
1936	63.0	13.6	10.9
1937	59.7	17.4	11.4
1938	58.2	17.8	13.1
1939	57.2	20.1	13.4

Source: Kenneth Bartlett, "Trends in Radio Broadcasting," *Annals of the American Academy,* Spring, 1940, pp. 16–17.

As always, regulatory matters were of prime concern for RCA, more so in the 1930s than before since so much of its profit derived from NBC. Much of Sarnoff's time in the early 1930s was devoted to observing and attempting to influence developments in Washington when reformers were laboring to strengthen the Federal Radio Commission or replace it with a stronger agency, which in the end they did by creating the Federal Communications Commission.

The origins of the FCC may be found in outcries of those who considered the Radio Act and the FRC creations of network forces that opposed the early public service mission so desired by Hoover and others. Reformers specifically rejected all suggestions that the FRC members had acted in an impartial manner in dealing with broadcasters, especially when it came to awarding franchises. The rapid development of commercial broadcasting in 1930–1932 had distressed them, and demands were made for reserving a minimum amount of prime time for nonsponsored programs.

President Hoover sympathized with these positions and in Senator Simon Fess (R, Ohio) found an individual who thought along the same lines. A former history and law professor who had served as president of Antioch College prior to entering Congress in 1913, Fess long had been an advocate of educational radio. Seeing the concept falling into disfavor, he sponsored an omnibus measure in 1932 calling for the reservation of 15 percent of station time for educational purposes (which included news and public events) and alterations in the way franchises were granted. This measure failed to be reported out of committee. Another bill that would have combined the Commission with the radio division of the Department of Commerce passed Congress only to fall before a Hoover pocket veto. This set the stage for reform under Franklin Roosevelt.

Roosevelt had said little on the subject during the 1920s, but in 1932 he had indicated a willingness to support the reform position and was not appreciably different from Hoover in this regard. However, radio hardly was high on his agenda in 1933; far more pressing were problems of economic recovery. But to consider framing a new policy, Roosevelt's Secretary of Commerce Daniel Roper did create an Interdepartmental Committee on Communications, which among others included Dill and Representative Sam Rayburn (D, Texas). Out of this came a recommendation for an enlarged, more powerful commission that would regulate not only radio but telephone and other forms of communication as well and unite the FRC with some portions of the Interstate Commerce Commission in a superagency dominating all forms of communication. The final report spoke of "the transfer of existing diversified regulation of communications to a new or single regulatory body, to which would be committed any further control of two-way communications and broadcasting." This was seen as consistent with the New Deal's tendency toward government regulation and central control.

The President called the proposed entity the Federal Communications Commission and in early 1934 said, "The new body should, in my opinion, be given full power to investigate and study the business of existing companies and make recommendations to the Congress for additional legislation at the next session."

Senator Dill introduced such a measure soon after, but as might have been expected from the author of the Radio Act of 1927, it was a mild, generalized draft. This prompted the writing of an amendment by Senators Robert Wagner (D, New York) and Henry Hatfield (D, West Virginia). Where Dill merely wanted to revamp the FRC and give it some of the ICC's powers, Wagner and Hatfield intended to start fresh, making a new distribution of stations, in effect breaking up the networks. Passage in this form not only would have revolutionized the industry but shattered NBC and severely crippled RCA.

Dill agreed that the networks represented a problem in that they so dominated the industry. "The bill specifically sets out as one of the special powers of the Commission the right to make specific regulations for governing chain broadcasting," he said. "Power must be lodged somewhere, and I myself am unwilling to assume in advance that the Commission proposed will be servile to the desires and demands of great corporations of this country." Dill assured Wagner, Hatfield, and others in their camp that under the terms of his draft the new agency would have "the power to protect against a monopoly," hinting that they might expect vigorous action against the networks.

The reformers intended to alter content as well as structure. Drawing upon the work of Senator Fess, they would oblige all stations to devote a quarter of air time to news, public affairs, agriculture, labor—in fact the whole panoply of informational programming—in what appeared to be an attempt to recreate radio somewhat in the form of Great Britain's British Broadcasting Corporation.

While sympathetic to such ideas, Dill wouldn't go so far since he believed it was too late in the game for so radical a change and in any case was troubled by First Amendment considerations. Of course the networks opposed these reforms, as did their trade association, the National Association of Broadcasters. "The NAB was in a panic checking off names of Senators and trying to pull wires and get votes," wrote *Variety*. The Association pleaded with them "not to destroy the whole structure of American broadcasting."

After a short debate—again, other matters were more pressing—the Wagner-Hatfield amendment was defeated, and the Dill bill, now called the Communications Act of 1934, sailed through the Senate.

Meanwhile a similar measure, written by Rayburn, was being debated in the House of Representatives, and the experience there was similar to that of the Senate, as reformers called for more sweeping legislation. Louis McFadden (D, Pennsylvania), a longtime network critic, was typical in his denunciation of the industry and demanded a tougher approach. "The strong hand of influence is drying up the independent broadcasting stations in the United

States and the whole thing is tending toward centralization of control in these two big companies. . . ." But the Rayburn bill passed, was harmonized with the Dill measure in committee, and was signed into law.

Hyperbole aside, there was little in the measure to trouble RCA. It was assumed the members would insist upon more public service programming, but the networks in anticipation of this already had put more news and educational programs on the air. The Commission also would have regulatory and licensing powers; unlike the Radio Act of 1927, the new legislation specifically discussed the networks, though in vague and imprecise terms. Even so, that NBC could be dealt with more effectively by the FCC than it had been by the FRC was obvious. All that was needed were tough, reform-minded commissioners.

Two members of the FRC were named to the FCC, and Roosevelt selected five new ones. None was particularly distinguished; like the FRC, the FCC appeared destined to serve as a political dumping ground. Only one member, George Henry Payne, was deemed an activist, repeatedly criticizing "the broadcasting monopolies."

A rotund, choleric, fast-talking Republican who seemed to pattern himself after Teddy Roosevelt, Payne had switched to Roosevelt in 1932, and the Commission nomination was his reward. He railed against the broadcasters on many occasions. "Gentlemen! Radio shall not be allowed to stop the growth of the American mind! There must be nobler programs instead of the jazz and trash of today!" he shouted, charging the networks with promoting questionable food and drugs in advertisements. Payne was particularly critical of "nerve-racking children's entertainments" and "indecent programs." His utterances might be construed as attempts to violate the broadcasters' First Amendment rights, but this didn't seem to be an issue at the time.

The question certainly did not bother a majority of the commissioners, such as Eugene Octave Sykes, who prior to coming to Washington had been a judge in rural Mississippi. Did the networks engage in chicanery? "One of the cleanest industries in the United States," was his view of broadcasting. Was Sykes aware of monopoly allegations and the demands for public service? "I'm not losing any sleep over it." Colonel Harold Brown of Ohio, a slow-moving individual glad for the $10,000-a-year post during a depression, was the soul of caution. A reporter asked what he thought of the relationships between the networks and their affiliates. "I really don't know enough." Did Brown think newspapers should own stations? "I have no fixed policy on that." Did he find anything unethical within the industry? Brown thought hard and long before replying. "I would say . . . they were . . . very exceptional."

Indeed, were it not for the changes in faces one might have assumed the FRC had merely been reincarnated under a new banner. This was understandable since there always had been and would be a clash between the need to exercise governmental power to regulate what had been decided belonged to the public—and was only licensed to private interests—and freedom of speech.

Sarnoff's methods in dealing with the regulatory agency lacked the high drama found in the stories of radio and television's development, but it was of equal importance. It wouldn't be going too far to suggest that had Sarnoff lost the battles with the FCC in the second half of the 1930s, RCA might have lacked the muscle to develop television in the next two decades, or the incentive to do so. So long as NBC remained its centerpiece, RCA's major concerns had to be its defense, preservation, and expansion. In time the FCC would threaten all three, and so the parent corporation itself.

In the late 1930s a perceptive newsman remarked, "The radio industry lives in fear of the FCC and in love with the sponsors of its commercial programs." As with most such quips, this was exaggerated. Attempts on the part of the FCC to exercise its mandate would often be criticized for trying to stifle expressions of opinion, but when the Commission failed to do so accusations of being stooges for the networks would be heard. More often than not in those early FCC years the latter opinion appeared justified. While none of the commissioners who served in the 1930s left to accept posts at the networks, others at the FCC did, and the closeness of the agency to the networks was such that in 1935 the commissioners had to warn employees not to accept gifts of any kind from the industry.

Still, Sarnoff was sensitive to the potential threat posed by the FCC. If headed by activists and backed by an interested and strong President, the agency might exercise more effective control over NBC than GE and Westinghouse ever did. This was one of the reasons Sarnoff became increasingly interested in news and public events broadcasting. Another was his continued fascination with new technologies that might be applied to radio. One of these was a vehicle whereby broadcasting might compete with newspapers, which he called "the electronic newspaper," which would be printed on a device attached to the radio and available on a current and continual basis. This brought RCA and the rest of the industry into conflict with the press.

By the 1930s newspapers had awakened to the potential threat posed by radio. They had been slow in realizing that people might prefer to obtain news and advertisements from radio rather than the press. Shortly after the formation of NBC, Sarnoff created a radio magazine (not unlike the later *TV Guide*) that would take sales from newspapers, but nothing came of this. It appeared that radio and newspapers could coexist, with the former concentrating on entertainment, the latter on news. In the early 1930s NBC had only one prominent newsman, Lowell Thomas, while CBS had two, Edwin C. Hill and H. V. Kaltenborn. In addition, stations utilized announcers as "news readers," and several of these graduated into the commentator and reporter ranks later on. As late as 1933 news and public service accounted for only 2 percent of

NBC's programming, and all of that was nonsustaining. During the next five years much more time was devoted to quiz programs than news on both the Blue and the Red networks.

Even so, the newspapers were wary of any medium that challenged them, especially during a depression. Some retaliated by purchasing stations, a practice that had begun in the 1920s and now became more popular, and several were affiliated with the Blue Network. Others talked of lawsuits, with most of their criticism directed at CBS, which had become more involved with news than was NBC. By 1933 both networks had started to create their own news-gathering teams, which prompted the newspapers to action.

In 1933 the American Newspaper Publishers Association announced that it would bring suits against stations reading newspapers over the air and also brought pressure to bear on the wire services that sold news to the stations and networks. Members of ANPA resolved to cease publishing logs of radio programs as a public service; if the broadcasters wanted listeners to know what was being offered, they would have to pay regular advertising rates.

Although NBC was barely affected, Sarnoff, concerned with reactions from the FRC and with an eye toward the possibilities of a strict new radio act, joined with CBS President William Paley to seek an accord with the Association. Initially the press was adamant in refusing a settlement, which prompted Sarnoff to deliver himself of several speeches about facsimile newspapers sent over the wire to radios in direct competition with conventional newspapers. Perhaps out of fear that NBC would develop this format the Association came to terms. NBC and CBS agreed to disband their budding news-gathering efforts and in return would be permitted two five-minute newscasts per day on a nonsponsored basis. Radio commentators would not use news that was less than twelve hours old.

This arrangement lasted only a few months, however. Independent stations not parties to it expanded their news offerings and so took listeners away from the network affiliates. Offered fees by potential radio advertisers, the wire services risked the loss of newspaper business, and the networks took on additional commentators while failing to leave the local news scene. The Association did not retaliate, perhaps out of a knowledge that it lacked the muscle, but more likely because members feared accusations of violating radio's First Amendment rights at a time when some publisher and editors were troubled that FCC controls over the broadcasters might prompt the extension of them to the press as well.

Early in Roosevelt's second term the FCC became a more activist agency and prepared to investigate network practices. One reason for this was the arrival there in 1937 of Frank McNinch, who served as acting chairman on the death of Chairman Anning Prall.

McNinch seemed an ideal ally for George Henry Payne and the proper person for the task. A Bryan Democrat in 1896 and active in the temperance movement, he had abandoned the party to support Hoover in 1928 because of Al Smith's opposition to prohibition, but he returned in 1932 to work for Roosevelt. Named to the Federal Power Commission the following year, McNinch quickly established himself as an enemy of what he called "financial groups that dominate the electrical group." He was generally credited with having written the "death sentence clause" in the Public Utilities Act of 1935, which barred holding companies in that industry. Roosevelt placed him in charge of the FCC in the hope that he would be able "to put its affairs into order."

Calls for action came from Capitol Hill as well. Rumors persisted that FCC employees had accepted favors in return for granting licenses, and a developing conservative Democrat-Republican coalition in Congress was talking about an investigation that might uncover wrongdoing and embarrass Roosevelt by turning into "a Democratic Teapot Dome" (referring to the Harding scandals).

Talk of an investigation of the FCC continued. A young Democratic congressmen from Texas, William McFarlane, made a series of speeches in 1937 castigating the networks. These came at a time when because of the recession of that year Roosevelt was preparing the most massive antitrust crusade in history, with big business being portrayed as a malevolent force. According to McFarlane, RCA was the cornerstone of Wall Street influence. He ticked off the list of the bankers involved: Harbord (who served on the board of Bankers Trust), Newton Baker (legal advisor to Morgan and Rockefeller banks), Cornelius Bliss (a Bankers Trust director), Bertram Cutler (a director of several Rockefeller companies), and so on. McFarlane called the 1932 consent decree "infamous" and "illegal," charged RCA with rigging receiver prices, and made detailed references to the Philco case. "I sincerely believe that the issue of re-examining the effect of the consent decree is resting squarely on the shoulders of Congress," McFarlane said. "Shall we face the issue or evade it as has been the custom in the past?"

John O'Connor (D, New York) was equally critical, inveighing against industry lobbyists attempting to defuse the situation and prevent an investigation. "You will have difficulty getting through the lobby because of the crowd of radio lobbyists," he told his colleagues, and quoting columnist Drew Pearson, said, "Apparently RCA is worried about a congressional investigation. [It has sent a] high powered publicity agent scurrying around the Halls of Congress to mold public opinion."

For a week or so in 1938 the investigation became the *cause célèbre* of Washington. By then the New Deal coalition was flying apart. Seeking more radical solutions to the depression, reformers felt free to criticize Roosevelt, and they seized upon this issue as a symbol of their discontent. "My concern is to preserve the Democratic party against political scandals which exist in the FCC," O'Connor said. "My misguided Democrats, submit to this pernicious lobby if you will, but I feel you are making a grave mistake."

Chances are that if the Roosevelt-dominated FCC had not investigated the industry a larger and more detailed effort would have been mounted by Congress.

McNinch was wary of the networks in much the same way as the reformers of the 1920s, and under his leadership the FCC did become more efficient and aggressive. In March 1938 the Commission authorized an investigation "to determine what special regulations applicable to radio stations engaged in chain or other broadcasting are required for the public interest, convenience, or necessity." The following month McNinch named a three commissioner subcommittee to supervise the investigation, which one magazine now called "the biggest probe of the industry." By the time the investigation began in November it had expanded to cover a far wider range of subjects, such as network operations, programming, licensing, and ownership. But it had become clear that the focus would be on the networks and their means of conducting business.

The investigation lasted until the following May, with a preliminary report made in June 1940. Then additional evidence was presented before the full committee, and a report and recommendations, known as *Report on Chain Broadcasting,* was released in 1941. This was on the eve of America's entry into World War II, by which time some of the issues that appeared so important in 1938 had faded and new ones had taken their place.

For example, news and public affairs had come to occupy a greater share of programming as a result of the developing world conflict, though FCC supporters would claim the agency was responsible for the shift. The panel had no intention of exploring television in 1938; public policy toward this new medium occupied center stage in discussions toward the end of the sessions.

Those who had thought McNinch would smash the networks as he had the utilities holding companies were disappointed as the hearings degenerated into discussions of programming. It turned out that the Chairman's pet interest was preventing what he deemed smut from findings its way on the air. Dismayed and in any case more concerned with other matters, Roosevelt let McNinch have his way but transferred his hopes to a new member, James Fly.

To some, Fly appeared a younger version of McNinch (he was forty years old when selected), but he had more depth and substance. A Naval Academy graduate, after a brief stint on active duty Fly resigned his commission to enter Harvard Law School where he became an acolyte of Felix Frankfurter. He went on to corporate practice and in 1929 arrived at the Justice Department. Through Frankfurter's intercession, Fly joined the legal staff at the Tennessee

Valley Administration in 1934 where he battled successfully against Commonwealth & Southern, the utility from which TVA had wrested much of its territory. He was an effective litigator, prompting C & S's chief counsel, future Republican presidential candidate Wendell Willkie, to remark, "Fly is the most dangerous man in the United States—to have on the other side."

Tall, lean, with an acerbic sense of humor and a crusader's dedication, Fly was a quintessential New Dealer with a passion for public ownership and regulation. So his arrival at the FCC troubled network leaders, and they were disappointed when he took charge of the subcommittee.

This was the beginning of the struggle between the FCC and the networks led by NBC, during which Fly attempted to overhaul the industry, in the process becoming the first important governmental critic of radio since Hoover. Sarnoff deemed him "irresponsible, dangerous, and socialistic." The last term was one of the most demeaning adjectives in his vocabulary. Sarnoff often utilized it to describe reformers, especially those who were effective.

Fly was hardly a radical, and none of his major proposals was aimed at smashing the networks. Nor was he threatening their freedom of expression, an allegation Sarnoff would make in attempts to rally support. Rather, Fly hoped to use the FCC's licensing powers to oblige the networks to carry *more* public service programs, as well as exploring methods to provide the affiliates with greater freedom.

The first company called to testify was NBC, and Sarnoff arrived to defend it against all charges and plead for self-regulation. McNinch was unimpressed, remarking sharply, "I don't want any after-dinner speeches." Rumors flew that he would demand a breakup of the networks, something hardly possible at that stage of broadcasting's development. But he held back as Fly worked to develop a more realistic approach. Then McNinch fell ill, and when Roosevelt named Fly to succeed him the networks were dismayed.

Over the next three years Fly led the agency in developing a reform stance insofar as network practices and organization were concerned. He wanted the affiliates to have more leeway in deciding which network programs to accept. Several of them complained that they were being dominated by the networks, unable to make plans because of their demands, and they also charged that the networks underpaid them for their time.

Fly pressed the networks to make reforms in their relations with affiliates. This presented NBC with no real difficulties. Since 1935 both Red and Blue had provided options to affiliates, in contrast to CBS, which in its contracts retained the right to co-opt affiliate time as it desired. Few affiliates complained specifically about the lack of options since listeners demanded the more lavish and better-known network shows, especially those aired during the 7:00 P.M. to 10:00 P.M. period, considered prime time. Still, the networks were troubled by the FCC recommendations, viewing them as only the initial step toward a more drastic restructuring.

The rejoinder made by NBC was clear and to the point: "It [The FCC proposal] seeks to compel a drastic revision of business arrangements between network organizations and approximately 500 independent standard broadcast stations, which make possible the nationwide broadcasting service existing in the United States today. It disrupts the present nationwide services and deprives each of these stations of a most valued asset, its present network affiliation." Which of course was a gross exaggeration. "The whole future of this expanding method of mass communication is here at stake. . . . This ill-defined and amorphous power is sought to be grafted upon the licensing power, which is the power of life and death."

The network discoursed on freedom of press and speech and attempted to compare Fly's activities with those of Adolph Hitler. "The fact that Hitler imposed his will upon the German people largely by plenary control of radio amply bears out this recognition. . . ."

A court challenge from the FCC followed, with the networks divided (NBC and CBS vs. Mutual) and two of the seven commissioners coming to their defense. Appeals were heard up to the Supreme Court, which in 1942 decided in favor of the FCC. In the end CBS affiliates did obtain wider options, but the final settlement was along the NBC model. Network critics were delighted at this, but it truly was a meaningless victory.

By then Fly and network officials, including Sarnoff, were clashing openly, a climax of sorts taking place at the National Association of Broadcasters convention in 1941, when the Chairman was seated on the dais and subjected to harangues by network officials while not being permitted time to respond. When a reporter asked him to comment on this, Fly paraphrased John Randolph and said the NAB was "like a mackerel in the moonlight—shining and stinking." Association President Neville Miller tried to apologize, but at the same time indicated he believed Fly was making too much of the matter and had blown it out of proportion. It was somewhat late for reconciliation, and in any case by 1941 the differences between the Chairman and the networks had gone far beyond the options issue.

Fly also wanted the networks to divest themselves of their talent agencies, through which they exercised important control over those performers who appeared on popular programs. Both NBC and CBS conducted such operations, the former getting into the business shortly after being organized. In 1931 NBC had purchased a half interest in Civic Concert Services, which managed concert tours nationwide. By 1937 the company, now a $6 million entity, was vending the services of some 350 artists, making the RCA operation one of the largest in the agency field.

The FCC held that this situation created conflicts of interest, in that the network was supposed to represent the artists while at the same time owning the company with which they negotiated contracts. In its final report a majority of the commissioners sketched the picture of a powerful nexus:

> [The] step-by-step invasion of the phonograph business . . . gave RCA entering wedges into the transcription and talent supply businesses; RCA-Victor artists broadcasted over NBC and made RCA transcriptions, while NBC artists recorded for RCA-Victor. The result was to give RCA and its subsidiaries a marked competitive advantage over other broadcasting companies, other radio manufacturers, and other phonograph and phonograph-record companies. . . . If broadcasters need talent, NBC not only will hire them, but is also glad to manage the artists and act as their agent in the concert as well as the radio field.

This was a more serious problem than network-affiliate relations. If Fly had his way the networks not only would lose profitable operations but would have less control over their artists. Perhaps feeling himself on weak ground in this case, Sarnoff bowed; the NBC Artists Bureau was restructured and in 1941 set loose as the National Concerts and Artists Corporation.

Almost from the day he arrived at the Commission Fly had made clear his intention to force separation of the Blue and Red networks. He noted that in 1927 approximately 7 percent of all stations, or forty-eight, were either owned or affiliated with NBC; ten years later the figure had risen to 161 stations, which came to 25 percent, and it continued to increase.

The two network-NBC presented Fly with an excellent target, being difficult to defend on competitive grounds. It will be recalled that the two networks often shared talent and facilities, creating bookkeeping problems and tension with the affiliates, which might be switched from one network to the other with little warning. This prompted knee-jerk opposition at RCA, so eventually Sarnoff came to terms with what increasingly seemed an inevitable development. Mark Woods, NBC's treasurer, had long argued that the relationship between Red and Blue was awkward. In Woods's view, each network would be better off if operated on an individual basis, and since Red was the stronger of the two, it should be the one retained by NBC. In fact, after lining up outside financing in 1936 Woods and NBC President Nick Trammel had tried to purchase the Blue Network, but at that time Sarnoff was unwilling to part with it; by 1941 he had come to see benefits from such a divestiture.

In any case he had no choice in the matter. On May 2, 1941, the FCC promulgated a series of new regulations, one of which was aimed squarely at NBC: "No license shall be granted to a standard broadcast station affiliated with a network organization which maintains more than one network, *Provided,* that this regulation shall not be applicable if such networks are not operated simultaneously, or if there is no substantial overlap in territory served by the group of stations comprising such network."

The only company to own two networks was NBC. The rule was so narrow that RCA's attornies thought it could be opposed on Constitutional grounds, and there was an appeal. However, the Supreme Court supported the FCC

KEY STATIONS IN THE RED NETWORK IN 1938		KEY STATIONS IN THE BLUE NETWORK IN 1938	
STATION	LOCATION	STATION	LOCATION
WEAF*	New York, N.Y.	WJZ*	New York, N.Y.
WNAC	Boston, Mass.	WBZ	Boston, Mass.
WTIC	Hartford, Conn.	WBZA	Springfield, Mass.
WJAR	Providence, R.I.	WEAN	Providence, R.I.
WTAG	Worcester, Mass.	WICC	Bridgeport, Conn.
WCSH	Portland, Maine	WFIL	Philadelphia, Pa.
KYW	Philadelphia, Pa.	WBAL	Baltimore, Md.
WDEL	Wilmington, Del.	WMAL	Washington, D.C.
WFBR	Baltimore, Md.	WSYR	Syracuse, N.Y.
WRC*	Washington, D.C.	WHAM	Rochester, N.Y.
WGY	Schenectady, N.Y.	WEBR	Buffalo, N.Y.
WBEN	Buffalo, N.Y.	KDKA	Pittsburgh, Pa.
WCAE	Pittsburgh, Pa.	WHK	Cleveland, Ohio
WTAM*	Cleveland, Ohio	WSPD	Toledo, Ohio
WWJ	Detroit, Mich.	WXYZ	Detroit, Mich.
WIRE	Indianapolis, Ind.	WOWO	Fort Wayne, Ind.
WMAQ*	Chicago, Ill.	WENR*	Chicago, Ill.
KSD	St. Louis, Mo.	WLS	Chicago, Ill.
KSTP	Minneapolis, Minn.	KWK	St. Louis, Mo.
WHO	Des Moines, Iowa	KSO*	San Francisco, Cal.
WOW	Omaha, Neb.	WMT	Cedar Rapids, Ia.
WDAF	Kansas City, Mo.	WTCN	Minneapolis, Minn.
WLW**	Cincinnati, Ohio	KSO	Des Moines, Iowa
WCKY**	Cincinnati, Ohio	KOIL	Omaha, Neb.
WSAI**	Cincinnati, Ohio	WREN	Kansas City, Kan.
		WLW**	Cincinnati, Ohio
		WCKY**	Cincinnati, Ohio
		WSAI**	Cincinnati, Ohio

* NBC-owned.
** Used on alternate basis.

position, though providing RCA with sufficient time to make an acceptable sale.

Sarnoff and Woods considered potential purchasers in early 1942, the price being in the $6 million to $12 million range, depending upon what was to be included. More than one hundred prospective buyers appeared, but all thought the price too high, especially when it was learned that by itself the

Blue earned only $66,000 after taxes in 1942. Several months passed, with little happening except that business was picking up. The Blue would earn $1.5 million in 1943—and therefore seem more desirable.

Then the investment banking house of Dillon, Read & Co. offered to form a syndicate to back Woods and buy the Blue for $7,750,000. This would have been accepted were it not for the fact that one of the earlier interested parties, Edward Noble, who had made his fortunes in Life Savers candies and already owned New York radio station WMCA, had joined with publisher James McGraw to offer RCA $8 million for the Blue Network. Part of the agreement was that RCA would sponsor a series of programs on the newly independent network, the price being $1 million, and this eased matters somewhat.

Since the Blue Network owned three stations, the change in ownership required FCC approval. This provided Fly with the opportunity to grill Noble and Woods, and at the same time air the debate regarding the need for greater diversity of opinion on the air. Woods refused to be drawn into discussions of First Amendment rights, insisting repeatedly that "we are in the advertising business, gentlemen, and that business is the business of selling goods to the American people." While a trifle rattled by Fly's intense manner, Noble performed well. "I propose to meet each request for time with an open mind and to consider such requests strictly on their merits and without arbitrary discriminations," he said when questioned as to whether he would refuse to sell time to unions and other "left wing" organizations.

The sale was concluded on October 12, by which time McGraw had dropped out of the syndicate for reasons of health. Noble went ahead on his own, paying RCA $4 million in cash and $4 million in the form of a three-year note. He obtained some of this money the following January by selling an eighth interest in the company to Time Inc. and another eighth to Chester LaRoche, an advertising executive, shares Noble repurchased in 1945, at which time the network's name was changed to the American Broadcasting Company.

That year ABC reported time sales of $40 million, and Noble sold off a minority interest in the network for $15 million, almost twice the price he had paid RCA for the whole operation two years earlier. Clearly he had done well; Sarnoff had badly underestimated the value of the Blue Network. But he had other things on his mind in this period; earlier in 1941, for example, RCA sold its remaining shares in RKO to Atlas Corp. for $6.5 million, bringing the venture into motion pictures to its conclusion. More important, however, were two new challenges: television and American involvement in World War II, both of which would have important effects upon both RCA and Sarnoff.

7

Radio with Pictures

UNLIKE RADIO, AND before it electricity, motion pictures, the automobile, and the airplane, there is no one single individual, inventor or businessman, who typified and came to symbolize television—no Marconi, Edison, or Ford is embedded in the collective consciousness. Instead we have such relatively unknown figures as the Abbé Caselli, Paul Nipkow, Lazare Weiller, Boris Rosing, A. A. Campbell-Swinton, Charles Jenkins, John Baird, Paul Langevin. Not even Vladimir Zworykin and Philo Farnsworth, generally credited with being "the fathers of television," are readily recognizable names. Instead, most Americans would say that the key man in television's early years was David Sarnoff.

In contrast, few consumer-oriented inventions have been so heralded and anticipated. It was written about, discussed, and forecast in the popular press throughout the 1930s. Were it not for the Depression, World War II, and industry conditions, television sets might have appeared in the homes late in that decade. Indeed, millions of Americans saw television displays at the New York World's Fair in 1939 and 1940 and went home dreaming of the time they might see "movies in the living room" or "radio with pictures."

Research on modern television began three quarters of a century earlier. In 1862 the Abbé Caselli attempted to send pictures across telegraph wires, and twenty-two years later Nipkow invented what he called "the electrical telescope," in actuality a crude transmitter and receiver. Weiller, Langevin, Swinton, and other Europeans added to the technology in the next generation.

Americans were also involved. The ubiquitous Alexander Graham Bell took out patents for television devices as early as the 1880s. In 1920 Herbert Ives of Bell Laboratories experimented with what he called "telephoto" transmission and seven years later sent a "pictorialized broadcast" of Secretary Hoover from New York to Washington. Reporting on the event in a front-page headline, *The New York Times* proclaimed, "Far Off Speakers Seen As Well As Heard Here," the subheading adding, "Like A Photo Come To Life."

General Electric established a television project; none other than Ernst Alexanderson became involved in the late 1920s, when experimental programs were broadcast from the Schenectady laboratories. In 1925 Charles Jenkins produced televised images, and the following year Baird did the same in Great Britain. But the key player insofar as practical television was concerned was Vladimir Zworykin, one of Boris Rosing's students before World War I at the St. Petersburg Institute of Technology.

Intrigued with television Zworykin went to France to study under Paul Langevin. He then returned to Russia and conducted some experiments for the Russian Wireless Telegraph & Telephone Company. Caught up in a war and revolution neither of which he felt concerned him, Zworykin immigrated to the United States. He arrived on January 1, 1919, and soon after contacted a countryman, I. E. Mouromtsev, who attempted to locate backers for his experiments. After a short visit to the Soviet Union Zworykin returned to America in August, to learn that Mouromtsev had been unsuccessful. Despite his generally apolitical nature, Zworykin was able to find employment at the Soviet Embassy, where he served as financial agent, remaining there for a year, still seeking a scientific post. One opened at Westinghouse in 1920, at which time Zworykin left Washington to relocate in the East Pittsburgh plant. Unhappy there, he joined the staff of C&C Development Co. of Kansas City, an oil exploration concern, only to return to Westinghouse in 1923, at which time he began work on television.

Late that year Zworykin developed and patented a rudimentary television camera, which he called the "iconoscope." Along with others in the field he perceived how television might become an adjunct to radio and tried to associate himself with Conrad's experiments at KDKA. Zworykin also saw television's possible relationship with motion pictures and for a while considered an offer to create just such a system for Warner Brothers, this of course long before the advent of talking pictures. He developed a second device known as the kinescope, a receiver for images sent by the iconoscope, and he demonstrated both in November of 1929.

By this time AT&T was the leader in the technology, as it was in so many other areas, with Herbert Ives going beyond the others in working on color television, but the corporation realized that much had to be done before the medium could be placed on a paying basis and was therefore uncertain whether it was a proper area of interest. "Purely as a novelty, television might have a vogue and possibly be made remunerative for a limited time," thought AT&T Vice President and Bell Laboratories President Frank Jewett in 1929. "Until, however, we can devise a much better and cheaper scheme than any hitherto proposed, all claims of substantial commercial utilization of television would seem to be fantastic."

The experiments continued. General Electric had held a demonstration in 1928 and Philco three years later. In fact there was hardly a major radio receiver manufacturer that wasn't involved in one way or another during the interwar period.

Naturally, RCA was deeply involved with the new technology. In 1923, perhaps after learning of or even witnessing Zworykin's experiments, Sarnoff sent a memo to his Board predicting a bright future for television, "which is the technical name for seeing instead of hearing by radio." He went on to sketch what must have appeared fantasies for his businessmen readers—seeing and hearing events in London, Buenos Aires, and Tokyo at the same time they occurred, for example. Sarnoff wrote of a linkage with films. "I also believe that transmission and reception of motion pictures by radio will be worked out within the next decade. This would result in important events or interesting dramatic presentations being literally broadcast by radio through the use of appropriate transmitters and, thereafter, received in individual homes or auditoriums, where the original scene will be re-enacted on a screen with much the appearance of present-day motion pictures. . . ."

In a 1924 speech at the University of Missouri, Sarnoff speculated on having "every farmhouse equipped not only with a sound-receiving device but with a screen that would mirror the sights of life." Later he spoke of "a separate theater for every home, although the stage may be only a cabinet and the curtain a screen—that, I believe, is the distinct promise of this era of electrical entertainment."

However, Sarnoff was far too concerned with radio to make a major move in any new direction. In any case he intended to move slowly in this complex and costly area. The creation of RKO would be made without reference to television, even though Sarnoff was one of those who clearly saw the commonality of the three mediums.

In 1929, after the iconoscope-kinescope demonstration, Sarnoff sought out Zworykin to learn more of his work. Impressed, he asked how much money the inventor would need to continue the experiments and how long it would take before they bore fruit. Plucking numbers from the air, Zworykin replied, "$100,000 and a year and a half." Apparently it was the right amount, and the meeting occurred at the right time. Sarnoff already was planning the divorce from GE and Westinghouse, and he intended to take with him all the television experiments. Shortly thereafter he arranged for Zworykin to be transferred to RCA, where he headed what was known as the Electronic Research Group at the Victor site in Camden. In 1930, when RCA acquired GE's radio engineering and manufacturing operations, it also obtained the services of its scientific personnel, who were headed by Elmer Engstrom. They went to Camden as the General Research Group, which also explored television.

The company first commented upon the technology in its 1930 *Annual Report.* "While television during the past two years has been repeatedly demonstrated by wire and by wireless on a laboratory basis, it has remained the conviction of your own Corporation that further research and development must precede the manufacture and sale of television sets on a commercial basis." The following year's report of "Talking Pictures For The Home," looking to the time when "instead of serving some 20,000 public theaters [television] may be able to serve eventually 20,000,000 'little theaters' of the home. . . ." Regular reports followed, all stressing technological progress, but adding that commercial TV was not yet in sight.

In 1931, while radio set sales and network operations were improving and Zworykin's experiments with television proceeded apace, Sarnoff learned of another inventor, Philo Farnsworth, whose work might be more advanced than that being conducted at RCA.

A Utah-born, self-educated scientist with a name right out of the pulp fiction of the time and the personality and appearance of an eccentric, Farnsworth had grasped the rudiments of television in 1922, at which time he was a high school student whose home had only recently been wired for electricity. Farnsworth bounced around the Far West, usually working as a radio repairman, eventually winding up in California. It was there, thanks to financial support of $25,000 from George Everson, an interested advertising man, that he was able to put together a small laboratory, out of which in 1927 came the equivalent of Zworykin's iconoscope and kinetoscope. The first image Farnsworth sent out over the airwaves was a dollar sign.

Other experiments followed; from 1926 to 1929 Farnsworth took $140,000 from his backers and seemed to have come up with a workable system somewhat similar to the one Zworykin was developing. To perfect it he organized Farnsworth Laboratories in 1927, which two years later was reorganized into Farnsworth Television, expected to become a manufacturing company.

Needing additional funds, Farnsworth traveled east where he met with the Philco management, which offered to finance his future efforts. The understanding was that he would work toward creating a commercial product that Philco would manufacture. Farnsworth agreed and shortly thereafter he applied for a patent. This sent shudders through the small television establishment at RCA, which contested his claims.

Farnsworth triumphed in this encounter and in 1930 obtained his patent, which in the eyes of most students of the history of television gives him equal credit with Zworykin for inventing television. At this time, too, he moved his company to Philadelphia to be closer to Philco. By then he had expended $200,000, with still nothing of a commercial nature to show for it.

While Sarnoff viewed Farnsworth as a potential threat, Zworykin managed to remain sanguine regarding the superiority of his system, a feeling reinforced by a visit to Farnsworth's laboratory the following year. Then Farnsworth hired E. A. Nichols, an RCA executive, to manage his company and talked about producing and marketing receivers. Sarnoff didn't take this too seriously; after all, who would buy a set when there was only experimental broadcasting? But he went to see Farnsworth, quickly recognized the similarities between the two technologies, and knew that given RCA's financial muscle it would have little trouble besting the young Farnsworth Television. Would the struggle be worthwhile? For the moment at least Sarnoff was content to monitor the situation.

As it turned out Farnsworth and Nichols had no real talents for management and even with Philco's backing could not establish television as an alternative to radio or motion pictures. The time wasn't right for such an invention.

Think about trying to sell television sets in the mid-1930s, perhaps for $1,000 or so, when that amount represented the annual salary of many middle-class families. Consider too the attitude of the FCC, especially after James Fly took over; the regulators might not have been able to change radio significantly, since the practices there had already been established, but they were eager to rectify perceived errors in judgment with television, and in such a way as to diminish potential profitability.

Finally, radio was doing well in this period. Why attempt a change under such circumstances? Even Sarnoff, ever the optimist, toned down his statements. At the 1935 stockholder's meeting he remarked that while it might be said that "television is here" on an experimental basis the technology was unrefined, and "as a system of sight transmission and reception, comparable in coverage and service to the present nationwide system of sound broadcasting, television is *not* here, nor around the corner."

Nonetheless RCA now started to view Farnsworth as a threat. When Philco filed its legal action against RCA in 1936, alleging conspiracy to steal trade secrets, among the most important of the secrets were those relating to Farnsworth's television experiments. While the matter was settled out of court, within the industry it generally was accepted that RCA had been caught with its hand in the till. Nonetheless Philco cut off its support to Farnsworth soon after though continuing on as his licensee.

Farnsworth next approached Paramount, hoping to interest the motion picture company in bankrolling a marriage of television and movies. But that firm, which had recently emerged from bankruptcy, was in no condition to consider the matter and in any case, as will soon be noted, had already made a small commitment to television through another company.

Obliged either to give up or to go ahead on his own, Farnsworth reorganized his company into Farnsworth Television and Radio, managed to scrape up sufficient funds to purchase the facilities of the moribund Capehart

Corporation, and began turning out radios. These were not well-received, and by 1939 Farnsworth was licensing patents with a free hand, even to RCA, which obtained them as an insurance policy against potential lawsuits. Farnsworth Television was saved by World War II, when it manufactured military communications equipment for the Armed Forces, and after the war tried to continue in this area until the long-anticipated television boom started. But the money ran out, and in 1947 Farnsworth sold his company to IT&T for $1.4 million in common stock.

By then RCA owned or had licensed most of Farnsworth's patents and had no further need for him or his ideas.

There were several other players in the field that hoped to turn out receivers, which RCA either ignored or deflected without much trouble. Hazeltine Electronics, organized by inventor-businessman Louis Hazeltine, developed several key patents, which were licensed to RCA. The smallish Andrea Radio was interested as was GE. A new firm, American Television, intended to enter the market with an economy set.

More important than any of these was a company created by the brash, Brooklyn-born Allen DuMont, a highly talented inventor-engineer-broadcaster-manufacturer-businessman, who had come into contact with television at Westinghouse, organized his own company in 1931, and started turning out cathode ray tubes for use in oscillographs. DuMont soon saw how they could be altered to create the "eye" for television receivers. His was the company in which Paramount made its small investment in 1938, the understanding being that it was for the production of receivers and nothing else.

Months after receiving the Paramount money DuMont brought his first sets to market, a threat RCA brushed aside easily. At the time the only television station broadcasting in the New York area was NBC's W2XBS, which had been inherited from GE. Sarnoff simply ordered it off the air for a while, and since the Dumont receivers were worthless without programs, they went unsold. With this, he left the business until after the war.

DuMont continued inventing and planning for a reentry into the field. In his view RCA was a hidebound giant incapable of moving swiftly into the new technologies. What he had in mind to create was nothing less than an RCA for the television age. It seemed unlikely that he would get very far without the assistance of a major investment bank or corporate godfather.

A far more serious threat was AT&T, all the more so since it had a technological advantage in several key areas and, in its telephone lines, a near-perfect means of transmitting TV signals. These went out in straight lines rather than following the earth's curve, meaning that transmission was limited to localities, making networking a cumbersome and expensive affair. Given the technology of the time, wireless broadcasting seemed out of the question; so the only alternative was to send signals by wire. In February 1936, AT&T

obtained FCC permission to construct a coaxial cable from New York to Philadelphia, this being seen as an initial move to obtain for itself a position in television similar to that it held in radio, namely as the provider of interconnects without which networking would be impossible.

Finally there was CBS, which had emerged as NBC's only real rival. It was headed by William Paley, who had become broadcasting's other major figure besides Sarnoff. Equally imaginative if narrower in range than Sarnoff, he was at least as shrewd a judge of the proper moment to make his move. Paley had established two experimental television stations in 1931, and one of these, known as W2XAB, with an antenna on the Empire State Building, operated for a while in competition with RCA's W2XBS.

Both stations were on the air only a few hours a week, and those intermittently. Indeed, the very fact that they were broadcasting was considered newsworthy. For example, on Election Day, 1932, *The New York Times* proclaimed, "Television set owners, believed to be a few hundred, will catch a glimpse of the future when they see the way Americans will get election returns in the 1940s. W2XAB will televise pictures of the candidates and bulletins, beginning at 8:00 P.M." Apparently it did so, though there is no record of just how the broadcast was mounted or how long it lasted. Two months later W2XAB suspended broadcasting, RCA being unwilling to sustain the losses as the economy dipped lower.

More important in the long run was Paley's interest in the development of color television. In 1936 he acquired the services of a young Hungarian emigré scientist, Peter Goldmark, who had initially applied unsuccessfully for a post at RCA. Goldmark soon established himself as a leader in color television research, and the following year CBS announced a $2 million commitment to television broadcasting. For a while there was talk of some kind of deal with Farnsworth, but none came about. Had Paley and Farnsworth been able to work together the combination might have dominated television, changing the entire history of the medium. As it was CBS remained around two years behind RCA.

Paley's strategy was obvious, especially to Sarnoff. He would conduct research and obtain patents. Then, when the time was right, he would come out with a broadcasting technology superior to anything NBC could create and market color television receivers to compete with RCA's monochrome models.

But when might that be? Television faced the same problems in the late 1930s radio did in the early 1920s, that chicken and egg situation in which consumers wouldn't purchase receivers until there were programs, and programmers weren't interested in broadcasting unless there was a sizable audience.

There was an additional complication, which involved Edwin Armstrong, who was not only one of Sarnoff's closest friends but, by virtue of the sale of the superheterodyne patents, a major shareholder in RCA. The friendship and collaboration continued. At Sarnoff's urging Armstrong attempted to invent a better broadcast technology. The current one, known as "AM," for amplification modulation, put out broadcasts that were plagued by static during even relatively minor atmospheric disturbances. Toward the end of the 1920s it appeared that Armstrong was on the verge of success with an alternate technology, frequency modulation or "FM." Public tests of his new system took place in 1933, and soon after Armstrong received patents on the system.

Sarnoff appeared impressed and pleased. According to Armstrong, he exclaimed, "This is not an invention—it's a revolution!" and pledged RCA's support for additional research.

Encouraged by Sarnoff and supported by RCA, Armstrong constructed a studio in the Empire State Building and continued testing from there. By early 1935 it seemed NBC would soon be able to broadcast FM programs and RCA Victor would devote a portion of its assembly line to FM receivers.

But only a small portion, for Sarnoff was unwilling to stake everything on FM and was having second thoughts on the matter. In the first place, the industry and corporation had too great a stake in AM for it to be replaced, even in the unlikely event the FCC would go along with the transformation, which would make obsolete all existing AM receivers. In addition, for all its virtues FM had technological limitations. Like television the waves went out in straight lines rather than following the earth's curve, which meant that the broadcasting radius would be limited to the horizon of the transmitter, requiring expensive way-stations and perhaps, ultimately, a cable system. Then, too, television was higher on Sarnoff's agenda than FM, and he intended to dedicate RCA's resources to that product. Moreover, there were just so many frequencies on the radio band, and Sarnoff meant for television to have most of what would be available, which meant downplaying FM.

Finally, in FM there was an implicit threat to RCA's core business, broadcasting. Throughout the 1930s critics charged the networks with subverting radio's original promise, that of public service programming free of commercials. It was too late to do much about AM, but in the words of critic Charles Siepman FM represented "Radio's second chance."

Siepman counted for little, but the FCC was another matter. Commissioner Clifford Durr, a strong supporter of Fly's reformist stances, stated that while FM offered superior fidelity and greater freedom from static, this opportunity for a new beginning was even more important. He spoke of "the new spaces which it opens up in the broadcasting spectrum and the opportunities thereby afforded of providing the public with a wider range of program choices." Siepman, Durr, and others looked forward to the time when public service FM programs competed with commercialized AM offerings and appeared to believe that news, classical music, and serious drama would do well against soap operas, variety shows and other top-rated AM programs. For RCA, then, FM represented at least as much of a threat as a challenge.

This was a stormy period for Armstrong. He was engaged in a protracted lawsuit with Lee De Forest over which of them in fact had been responsible for several basic radio inventions. He ultimately lost in court though not in the opinion of a majority of engineers. At the same time he clashed with Sarnoff over the future of FM, coming to realize that he would not receive the kind of financial and technological support he required.

The matter came to a head in May 1935, when Sarnoff indicated his views at the annual stockholders' meeting, at which time he spoke glowingly of television and didn't mention FM. After a loss on operations in 1933 the corporation had returned to profitability in 1934, but given the parlous nature of the economy this seemed hardly the time for endangering an established technology and market. Sarnoff dealt with this by exaggerating the differences between radio and TV. "Let me emphasise that television bears no relation to the present system of sound broadcasting, which provides a continuous source of audible entertainment to the home," he said. "While television promises to supplement the present service of broadcasting by adding sight to sound, it will not supplant nor diminish the importance and usefulness of broadcasting by sound."

This would seem to indicate that radio would remain the centerpiece at NBC, and if this were so, the work with FM might be continued. But a few weeks later NBC notified Armstrong he would have to vacate the Empire State Building installation—which would be converted to television experimentation. Simultaneously Sarnoff revealed that "a field demonstration" of television was being prepared, "as the next practical step."

Angered, Armstrong decided to go it alone. He obtained an FCC license and constructed a powerful 50,000 watt FM station in Alpine, New Jersey, known as W2XMN, selling a large block of his RCA stock to raise funds for the venture. His intentions were clear: Armstrong's station, which broadcast classical music, would create a demand for FM receivers, which in turn would lead manufacturers to meet the demand, in the process purchasing licenses from him.

It didn't work out quite as anticipated. A number of companies, RCA included, manufactured and sold FM radios without benefit of Armstrong's patents, claiming they were using alternate technologies, while royalties from others (Zenith, GE, and Westinghouse) were insufficient for him to turn a profit, or even pay for station upkeep.

A year later Sarnoff approached the estranged Armstrong indirectly, offering him $1 million for his patents. Some said it was a token of friendship, others an attempt on his part to avoid messy and perhaps expensive litigation. Perhaps Sarnoff wanted to wed FM sound to television pictures (this was what ultimately resulted). Still another school of thought holds that he needed the patents in order to kill off FM, clearing the way for television. There might have been elements of truth in all four theories, though the last named was most in the Sarnoff tradition. Whatever the reason, Armstrong spurned the offer.

The new technology did develop and was accepted, to the point where the FCC took what would have become Channel 1 on TV and reassigned it to FM. By early 1940, when the FCC approved FM commercial broadcasting, there were more than 150 applications on file for station licenses, receiver sales were increasing, articles about the reinvention of radio were appearing in magazines and newspapers, and Armstrong appeared to be winning his battle.

But not yet. The war intervened, bringing development to a halt. In addition the FCC granted licenses to FM stations wanting to carry AM programming as well, so they could broadcast simultaneously on both frequencies. This meant the owner of an AM radio wouldn't have to purchase an FM receiver to hear FM programming, which cut into sales.

Armstrong initiated a series of protracted lawsuits against RCA and NBC alleging violation of contracts, which drained him of funds and vitality. Completely estranged from Sarnoff, worn out and frustrated, Armstrong committed suicide in 1954, leaving a note to his wife, ending with, "God keep you and may the Lord have mercy on my soul." Sarnoff was shattered on learning of this, exclaiming to an associate, "I did not kill Armstrong."

The suits continued nonetheless, ending with an out-of-court settlement in which the radio and television industry as a whole paid $10 million to the Armstrong estate. The company's share came to $1 million, or what Sarnoff had originally offered his former friend. In all, it was hardly an edifying experience, and one which to the end of his life appeared to haunt Sarnoff.

Possibly FM might have become the dominant radio technology were it not for the advent of television, the coming of war, and the gradual merging of FM and AM broadcasting via the FCC.

Sarnoff went ahead with his plans for television. He had a threefold objective: under Engstrom's direction he would establish a transmitter on the Empire State Building, and limited number of receivers for use in experiments would be manufactured. Finally, RCA would develop an experimental broadcasting operation at NBC, preferably in Radio City, where the hoards of tourists who visited the place daily would be exposed to it, thus generating free publicity.

Sarnoff, by backing a rival technology, was risking the alienation of the motion picture industry, which licensed RCA patents, and the FCC, which could be counted upon to try to control this new area. He tried to placate Hollywood in much the same way as he did the radio interests, by claiming there was no conflict between motion pictures and television. Putting aside earlier talk of "motion picture theaters in the home," he said:

> The motion picture industry need experience no alarm over the impending advent of television. Transmission of sight by radio will benefit not only the radio industry; it also will prove a welcome stimulant, a pleasant tonic to all the entertainment arts. There will be no conflict between television in the home and motion pictures in the theater. Each is a distinct and separate service. History confirms the fact that the creation of a new service for the public does not result in the elimination of an older service, providing each has something of its own to give.
>
> The telephone did not displace the telegraph. The radio did not displace the cable. The incandescent lamp did not displace the candle; more candles are being sold today than before the creation of the incandescent lamp. And television in the home will not displace the motion picture in the theater.

Whether anyone in the audience took this seriously cannot be known. Sarnoff tried to placate Fly, going so far as to show him the proof of an important advertisement for television in advance of its publication, and he came away from the meeting believing he had the Commissioner's approval.

The announcement came on March 1, 1939, in full-page spreads in local newspapers. The company spoke grandly of the programming and receivers, which were "the initial step in the construction of a television radio relay system as a means of interconnecting television transmitters for simultaneous service to and from other communities." In effect, Sarnoff was telling those who were interested in purchasing receivers that while programming was meager, this soon would change, since NBC intended nothing less than to create a nationwide television network.

By making public pronouncements of this kind, Sarnoff hoped to block further expansion of FM, place a damper on CBS and DuMont, and pressure the FCC for approval. Sarnoff was maneuvering to freeze out all potential rivals.

Not that they were flocking to the new technology. The recently renamed Philco Radio & Television argued that the RCA broadcasting system was deficient, and until a new and better one was devised it would remain on the sidelines. "Reception is not the chief problem confronting television as an industry," said Philco Vice President Sayre Ramsdell. "The real problem is largely in the hands of those concerned with television broadcasting."

Zenith's E. F. McDonald agreed. Claiming its experimental receivers were the best available, Zenith proclaimed in a full-page advertisement in *Radio Today* in May 1939: "Radio Dealers! Zenith has television sets. . . . Zenith is ready—But Television is Not." Not only hadn't the FCC established standards, but there were no programs worthy of the name and none likely in the next few years. "When Zenith believes television is ready for general use in the store and the home... Zenith will supply you with television receivers and not before."

As for CBS, it didn't believe it could operate broadcasting facilities profitably given the conditions at the time. According to Vice President Paul Kestan, "our most optimistic studies of the sale of sets indicate that the broadcaster continued to operate at a cumulative loss until some 30 percent ownership of television sets in the areas in which he is broadcasting is achieved." That would take at least seven years, and under these circumstances CBS was unwilling to do more than experiment.

Clearly, RCA was the leader in the field, as much by virtue of default as by its technological prowess. And in the public mind as well. Visitors flocked to the RCA exhibit at the World's Fair to witness television demonstrations, which Sarnoff opened on April 30, 1939, with a typical flourish. "Now we add sight to sound," he told the large audience, proclaiming that NBC would start broadcasting television programs and that TV sets would be in the stores soon after. "A new art and a new industry, which eventually will provide entertainment and information for millions and new employment for large numbers of men and women, are here. It is with a feeling of humbleness that I come to this moment of announcing the birth, in this country, of a new art so important in its implication that it is bound to affect all society. It is an art which shines like a torch in a troubled world."

At the time there were some 200 receivers in the New York metropolitan area, most of them owned by network executives and the curious rich.

At first everything proceeded according to plan. Station W2XBS continued to broadcast experimental programs—talks, antique movies, and sporting events—while Sarnoff ordered the Victor factory to gear up to produce TV receivers. Soon RCA had four models on sale, at prices ranging from $200 to $1,000. There were sixteen other manufacturers in the summer of 1939, including giants like Philco, GE, and Westinghouse, and minor players such as Pilot, American Television, Andrea, Crosley, and Farnsworth. DuMont took out of inventory some of those sets manufactured the previous year and placed them on the market, while applying for a station license, which was taken as the first step in creating a network.

Sarnoff attempted to win FCC support for television, knowing that to proceed without it risked opposition at some later date that could be detrimental to his activities. But Fly was slow in acting, and deciding to risk his disapproval, Sarnoff determined to go ahead on his own, perhaps counting on public acceptance to sway the FCC to his way of thinking.

The FCC did cooperate in a limited way. In February 1940 Fly allocated eighteen channels to television, but since war loomed, eleven of these were reserved temporarily for the military. Applications for licenses poured in, as scores of radio stations and newcomers viewed this as a repeat of the radio bonanza of the early 1920s. By May twenty-three stations were operating on a limited or "experimental" basis.

While Sarnoff welcomed this move, he was annoyed that the frequency on which the NBC experimental station's offerings were being broadcast was not included in the newly opened channels, this meaning the network would have to make expensive changes that would delay things. But he pressed on and said RCA would target the New York metropolitan area for a sales campaign, offering 25,000 units of a new model at a price of more than $600, which in those days was the cost of a new Chevrolet or Ford.

Given the temper of the time—war preparations, talk of direct American participation, and the pressing needs of the military—it seemed likely that both FM and TV would be placed on hold for the duration. Thus, it would appear that Sarnoff was staking out territory, attempting to make certain RCA had a preeminent position in television after the war, when development would resume.

That summer Fly mounted a campaign of his own. Calling RCA "monopolistic," he ordered Sarnoff to withdraw his television receivers from the market, claiming that they might be worthless since the FCC had yet to decide whether broadcasting would be permitted on a regular basis. The battle was soon joined, with the two men flinging charges and insults at one another.

This was hardly front-page news. Electioneering and the war dominated the headlines that spring. Soon the two parties met to nominate their candidates, with Roosevelt running for a third term and the Republicans selecting Wendell Willkie, Fly's old nemesis, at a dramatic convention in Philadelphia. France fell to the Germans, the Battle of Britain began, and the American arms buildup commenced, while on the periphery Sarnoff and Fly debated the future of television before and for a specialized audience.

In April the FCC permitted seven channels to be opened for television and go on the air, but Fly shifted ground soon after; in early May, in a further attempt to place Sarnoff under constraints, Fly withdrew the limited frequency allocations for television, while the Senate Committee on Interstate Commerce prepared to conduct hearings on the matter. Fly testified that he believed television had a bright future but went on to criticize RCA for what in his view was an attempt to monopolize the medium. Sarnoff charged Fly with having gone far beyond the FCC mandate, intimating that the Chairman had his own political agenda and was not the disinterested party he claimed to be.

Roosevelt attempted to soothe the ruffled tempers, calling Sarnoff with a goodwill gesture. "David, I'll pay for the meal if you and Fly take lunch together and settle the argument." "Mr. President, the problem is not in the stomach but the head," Sarnoff answered, "No useful purpose would be served by a goodwill lunch." Besides, he had other matters to consider. Fly had released the *Report on Chain Broadcasting* on May 2, and now Sarnoff had to busy himself with the sale of the Blue Network and a boomlet for shortwave transmission and receiver sales caused by the desire to hear overseas broadcasts regarding the war. And at the same time he tried to prepare RCA for participation in the mobilization program.

A state of national emergency was declared on May 27, 1940, which all but ended the debate. But giving way under congressional pressure, Fly restored the suspended permits, and on July 1 NBC's experimental W2XBS was transformed into WNBT, the nation's first commercial station. Only 10,000 of the promised 25,000 receivers were manufactured and sold, and these stood idle most of the time, since programming was meager at first and then, with America's entry into the war, nonexistent.

Fly continued to view RCA as the major monopolizer in the broadcasting industry, with CBS in a distinctly secondary role. He also realized that after the war television would be at least as important as radio, if not more so, and was distressed by RCA's huge lead in that field. Invited to a demonstration of the CBS color system in 1940, Fly had indicated his approval to Goldmark. As the scientist put it, the Commissioner "right then and there announced he was a champion of color," meaning the CBS system rather than RCA's monochrome. Putting aside his differences with Paley, in June 1941 he gave that network permission to conduct on-the-air experiments. These amounted to little, however, for by then, as Roosevelt put it, "Dr. New Deal" had been superseded by "Dr. Win-The-War."

In 1941 RCA's major concern was filling war-related contracts, not the future of television or even that of radio.

While military procurement programs languished during the 1920s (total defense spending in 1927 was under $680 million) the War Department continually planned allocations of materials for what was dubbed "M-Day"—mobilization day—which included an important Signal Corps role. In 1930 Secretary Patrick Hurley made public a mobilization day program, but it was hardly noticed. Revisions appeared every three years, the last in 1939, by which time war seemed imminent.

The Navy, which had been most concerned with RCA's expertise during the first war, now did little except lobby for additional ships and higher budgets. For this reason, RCA edged closer to the Signal Corps and away from the Navy during the mid-1930s.

There was yet another, more personal reason for this. In 1924 Sarnoff had applied for and received a commission as lieutenant colonel in the Army Signal Corps Reserve. In 1931 he was promoted to a full colonelcy. Doubtless the influence of General Harbord and memories of having been rejected for a Navy commission in World War I had something to do with this, but Sarnoff's application so soon after the Armistice was unusual. How many other executives in his position took such an action, at a time when it appeared peace was secure and a general revulsion against war had surfaced? Sarnoff was ever a man who wore his patriotism on his sleeve and throughout his life was drawn to the military. That he should make this move was more an indication of his personality than any long-range strategy to obtain additional business for RCA.

Military spending remained a minor part of the national budget in the 1930s; it came to $836 million in 1930, and $1.2 billion in 1938. Appropriations rose as threats of war developed. The figure was $1.4 billion in 1939, and in the following year, $1.8 billion.

In this period RCA had provided the armed forces with a wide variety of gear for the Signal Corps as well as maintaining the wireless operations. For example, in 1934 RCA conducted tests on a new series of powerful transmitters and receivers, by which time it had become one of the leading American developers of radar. These were minor contracts, rarely going beyond the tens of thousands of dollars, and often work was held up because appropriations for several hundred dollars had not been made. The Camden laboratories developed an altimeter under Navy and Signal Corps contracts in 1938 and the following year participated with Western Electric, GE, Westinghouse, and Bendix (the group came to be known as "The Big Five") in an $8 million Signal Corps development contract.

Since much of this early work was in telecommunications, RCA was able to press for its point of view in product areas that had a postwar importance for the commercial market. For example, in 1940 the Signal Corp considered FM for its field radios, while RCA advocated AM—and won its point. Indeed, AM did make more sense in field operations, especially at short distances, but in this instance RCA was able to win military approval for a technology that served its commercial ends.

An Army historian wrote in an official history, "Frequency modulation threatened them [RCA] because it gave promise of reopening commercial broadcasting to competition," implying that in this way RCA was serving its own interests in attempting to block FM in the military.

Sarnoff was one of the first of the important American businessmen to warn against the German threat to peace and to advocate a major arms buildup. His concern was attributed to his religion and his fascination with the military, and perhaps there was something to this. The fact remains, however, that Sarnoff ordered RCA to prepare to convert to military procurement hours after the German and Soviet invasions of Poland in 1939 and was willing to divert resources from more commercial areas for this purpose. He even hoped to participate directly in the mobilization effort, asking for activation of his commission in 1940, being dissuaded by those who convinced him he could do more to further the war effort at RCA than in the field.

Pearl Harbor was attacked on December 7, 1941. RCA's office in Honolulu delivered General Marshall's warning message to the Army's Command at Fort Shafter in a routine manner, not realizing its importance.

Hours later Sarnoff sent a telegram to the President, the tone of which indicates his strong feelings and military inclinations: "All our facilities and personnel are ready and at your instant service. We await your commands."

Telecommunications played a crucial role during the war, especially in the Pacific. RCA maintained its wireless operations, carrying on in the manner expected in 1920. But of equal if not greater importance was the work it engaged in for the Signal Corps. The powerful Office of Scientific Research and Development (OSRD) gave out research contracts to laboratories throughout the war, with the largest portion by far going to Western Electric, followed by a consortium known as the Research Construction Company and then General Electric; RCA came next, in fourth position, followed by Du Pont, Westinghouse, Remington Rand, Eastman Kodak, Monsanto, and Zenith.

Whether Sarnoff planned it this way or not, RCA came out of the war as one of the nation's premier electronics companies, prepared to enter several new areas not even considered in 1939. Yet through much of the war it was one of the smaller participants in the Big Five consortium. Of the $4 billion in total Signal Corps outlays in 1942, Western Electric was in first place, GE in second, followed by Bendix, and Westinghouse; RCA was in last place, with $84 million, and seldom would go much higher in the pecking order.

Less than a month after the Pearl Harbor attack, the OSRD asked the Big Five to come to Washington to discuss Signal Corps procurement policies and problems. Appropriations for the coming year were $498 million. These firms, which were to receive 80 percent of Signal Corp contracts during the war, were asked to expand their facilities as rapidly as possible and divert resources from civilian to military purposes. In March 1942 the Signal Corps estimated that the military services would soon have $4.35 billion available for contract awards in radio and radar. Yet total industrial output of the industry at the time was only $250 million. Clearly major expansion would be required.

Soon RCA received its first war-related order, a $2.4 million contract to expand its Camden facilities, the understanding being that it would be used for the manufacture of military radio and wireless gear. By then the company's conversion to military procurement was well underway. Just how large and rapid the expansion was is difficult to say owing to secrecy restrictions, but the company did end the war with a modern research and manufacturing complex.

In 1940, a year during which RCA's total revenues were $127.8 million, military orders came close to $40 million. So as Sarnoff spoke of television's promise, the military was becoming the corporation's first order of business. Radio receiver sales were cut back severely, as military orders expanded, the peak reached in 1944.

RCA'S DISTRIBUTION OF BUSINESS, 1941–1946

figures in millions of dollars

Year	Manufacturing	Broadcasting	Communications	Other
1941	88.9	48.5	14.0	7.3
1942	122.6	52.6	15.0	7.3
1943	211.4	60.8	18.8	3.5
1944	244.3	60.0	22.7	2.5
1945	193.2	61.3	22.6	2.4
1946	160.0	61.1	20.0	2.4

Source: *RCA Annual Reports,* 1941–1946.

Sarnoff had a particular interest in television-directed weaponry. As early as 1934 Zworykin had prepared a monograph on a "flying torpedo with an electric eye," which could be guided to its target by a crew on land or aboard a ship, and in 1940 Sarnoff said that all military branches should "consider RCA the only presently qualified supplier and the one able to solve remaining problems" in this area.

The OSRD wanted a radio device that could be launched from a plane and send back information, really a missile with a television camera on its nose not unlike Zworykin's flying torpedo, given the code name "Dragon," and this contract went to RCA. The program was never completed, but rather was transformed into a more ambitious one called "Pelican," this too run by RCA. Together with Western Electric, it created for the Navy the "Bat," a target-seeking missile guided by radar. It became a major project, replacing Pelican. Significantly, all of these projects utilized military computers, providing RCA's technicians and scientists with some experience in this area as well.

The corporation also manufactured a wide variety of wireless products, from the ubiquitous walkie-talkies to complex gear used aboard ships. The corporation turned out jamming devices, several of which were to be used to deflect German V-2 rockets toward the end of the war. And there were others, many utilizing expertise developed in radio and television. For example, Zworykin created a night sight, an infrared device attached to rifles enabling snipers to "see" objects in the dark, which was a direct outgrowth of his research in television.

The most important contribution was the manufacture of vacuum tubes, for which it was the acknowledged leader. In 1940, with Navy financing, RCA erected a huge complex in Lancaster, Pennsylvania, which became the prime supplier of tubes—2,000 different types, 20 million in all—for the war effort. Other firms also participated, which created some competition. Sarnoff saw no reason why RCA couldn't turn profits during the war, especially when they came from licensees.

There was an exception to this. By the spring of 1942 the government had been offered licenses, most of them royalty-free, from thirty-seven patent holders, including all of the important licensors of electronic equipment except RCA. Sarnoff held that since RCA already had issued licenses for all of those requesting them and did so at reduced rates (so that it would not make more profit in the war years than in the last year of peace) it should not be required to go any further. In a letter to Major General Roger Colton, in charge of Signal Corps research and development, RCA insisted that "the government should continue to require its suppliers of radio equipment to assume normal and usual responsibilities for infringement by their products, which responsibility can be met by acquiring the necessary patent rights."

General Colton replied, noting that RCA would collect more than $30 million in royalties that year and adding, "We do not believe that even your admittedly great contribution to the war effort warrants a tax of this magnitude, especially since the principal justification for royalties is to pay for continuing research work, and since your own current research, to which you retain the commercial rights, is now being done largely by government contract and on government funds." The corporation challenged this and won a partial victory. It waived royalty payments from ninety licensed manufacturers and gave the government a nonexclusive license to run "during hostilities and for six months thereafter" in return for an additional $4 million annually.

This is not to suggest that RCA behaved in an improper or unpatriotic fashion but rather that like all the other defense contractors, its profits rose substantially during the war.

Sarnoff served on active duty on-and-off throughout the war, always at the

---

SELECTED RCA STATISTICS, 1939–1946

figures in millions of dollars

Year	Revenues	Profits	Earned Surplus
1939	109.8	10.6	20.5
1940	127.8	14.1	23.6
1941	157.7	29.9	28.0
1942	196.0	28.3	33.3
1943	293.3	37.5	41.6
1944	324.8	40.6	43.6
1945	278.3	30.6	49.0
1946	236.1	14.6	54.1

SOURCE: *RCA Annual Reports,* 1939–1946; *Moody's Manual of Investments,* 1942, 1946.

direct request of the military. There were two tours in the summer and autumn of 1942, during which he was given broad powers to rationalize the procurement process. His most important assignment came in 1944, when in March he reported for duty for what turned out to be a major role in the telecommunications area, with special duties in public relations, during the invasion of Normandy.

By then RCA was reaching new production levels each month, and the government feared Sarnoff's absence from the helm might create problems. The reason was clear: Sarnoff had done little to develop managerial talents at RCA, which had one of the weakest second echelon of executives in the industry.

Never particularly interested in the nuts and bolts of everyday operations but now obliged to be so, Sarnoff cast about for an individual to handle all operations. It was an obvious move; he was away from the office on war-related duties and while the company did not require the services of a strategist, it could use individuals capable of smoothing the flow of military products to the armed services.

Sarnoff already was thinking of the postwar RCA and the coming struggle for television. If the corporation were to undergo a smooth transition from military procurement to consumer electronics it would need an ablc operating executive.

The best place to look was in war-related operations, and given his many contacts in Washington Sarnoff had no difficulty assembling a roster of candidates. An old friend, investment banker Lewis Strauss, was then on active duty as a desk-bound admiral, and he recommended Frank Folsom, whom he had known before the war and worked with in the Navy Department.

Folsom was an example of a man whose talents might never have been recognized or developed fully were it not for wartime challenges. Born in Washington state in 1894, he was a natural salesman who soon found a niche in that field. Following an apprenticeship as a buyer at several West Coast department stores Folsom joined the Army in World War I and after his discharge returned to marketing posts. He bounced from one to another in the 1920s, and in 1932, at the age of 38, arrived at Montgomery Ward, the large mail order and retail store complex, where he served as manager for West Coast operations. The following year Folsom moved to Chicago to become marketing vice president for the entire operation.

At the time Montgomery Ward was firmly in the control of Sewell Avery. Realizing he had gone just about as far as he would there, Folsom left in 1940 to accept the executive vice presidency of the Chicago department store Goldblatt Brothers and probably would have gone on to the presidency of that medium-sized establishment were it not for America's entry into the war.

Folsom was one of the hundreds of business executives who arrived in Washington in 1940 to help direct the procurement effort, joining the National Defense Advisory Commission in July to serve as assistant coordinator of purchases. Folsom went back to Goldblatt the following January, but not for long. He returned to Washington after the United States entered the war, this time at the behest of Donald Nelson, formerly of Sears, Roebuck, who soon became the Administration's most important procurement officer. Nelson recalled, "When I came down to Washington and was asked to take the job as director of purchases the first man I asked to come here to help me was Frank." Folsom became chief of the division of purchases at the newly formed Office of Production Management, and from there he went on to become a special assistant to Secretary of the Navy Frank Knox, and it was there he met Lewis Strauss.

Sarnoff and Folsom conferred several times. Sarnoff was impressed with Folsom's credentials in marketing, and Folsom liked the idea of joining RCA. The deal was struck, and with the help of Nelson and Strauss the Navy Department agreed to release Folsom for the sake of the procurement effort. Folsom was permitted to resign in late 1943 to join RCA as a vice president.

Folsom was stationed at the Camden plant, where for the first time he had broad managerial authorities over a major enterprise. He performed well at the post, demonstrating abilities at coordination of efforts and dealing with suppliers. By the spring of 1944, when Sarnoff was helping prepare for the invasion of Europe, Folsom had become important in the RCA hierarchy. "I gave him carte blanche," Sarnoff later said, "and he made good, magnificently, as shown by the volume and profit record of the organization in the years that followed."

Sarnoff remained on duty after the invasion, not returning to the United States until October. Two months later he was elevated to the reserve rank of brigadier general and was discharged on December 28. For the rest of his life Sarnoff rarely would be referred to at RCA as anything other than "The General," or "General Sarnoff." It was a matter of great pride to him, a badge of service and honor. As Eugene Lyons put it, "the general's star he brought back to the fifty-third floor of the RCA Building . . . glowed with an inner light that would not dim or lose luster through familiarity."

It reinforced Sarnoff's fervent patriotism, which took the form of strong anticommunism. In the 1950s he sent hundreds of letters on his Cold War views to politicians, offering suggestions on how best to combat the USSR. To an extent this affected the company; NBC was more willing to cooperate with individuals and groups attempting to blacklist suspected subversives than was CBS, for example. Sarnoff moved even further to the political right during the 1960s, all in the name of patriotism.

It remains to be noted that Sarnoff was hardly a major figure in the war, since his responsibilities were not military but informational, making certain the story got back home quickly and fairly. Sarnoff never claimed anything more and to his credit made certain the corporate public relations office didn't inflate his contributions.

A few days prior to notice of his promotion, at a dinner celebrating the twenty-fifth anniversary of the founding of RCA, at which Army, Navy, and industrial leaders applauded him, the event was capped by a warm letter of congratulations from Roosevelt. By then Sarnoff's reputation as one of the nation's major businessmen had been clearly established, and the wartime service only embellished it. Having said this, one must add that he thoroughly enjoyed the experience.

8

The TV Campaigns

THE CORPORATION EMERGED from the war considerably different from what it had been in the late 1930s. During the Depression RCA had relied upon broadcasting to support its manufacturing business. Then war-related orders came in, and by 1945 RCA's revenue from this sector was almost three times that from broadcasting.

As was the case with all major military suppliers, RCA experienced declines in revenues and profits during the postwar reconversion, though given pent-up demand for many of its consumer products the decline was less onerous than for most. In 1947, the first "normal" year of the postwar period, the corporation posted revenues of $314 million, only a shade below those of its peak in 1944, when war orders alone accounted for close to a quarter of a billion dollars. Three out of every four dollars RCA took in that year were from what would later be known as "consumer electronics." In 1940, the last prewar year, manufacturing had accounted for half of all revenue.

Management had changed too. Frank Folsom had solidified his position at headquarters. This was due at least as much to his abilities as Sarnoff's own development during the war, for like the corporation he had undergone a metamorphosis. Increasingly he liked to portray himself as a combination engineer-visionary-industrial statesman, who would set the direction not only for the company but the industry and even the nation. Already Sarnoff was discussing a tape recorder that might be attached to a TV set to record programs as phonograph records did music, receivers that could be mounted on walls like pictures, or were light enough to carry about like portable radios, and an electronic air conditioner with no moving parts. Sarnoff spoke more often about national and international issues having little or nothing to do with RCA's business and set about collecting awards, honorary degrees, and the like. There would be flashes of the hard-bitten aggressive businessman of the prewar period, but the General was a shade more avuncular, fond of reminiscing about old victories and forecasting the distant future, and relatively uninterested in dealing with many of the tactical problems of the present, the details of which seemed to bore him.

Unsurprisingly, he had little patience with the day-to-day operations of the firm. This was where Folsom was at his best, which is to suggest that while Sarnoff liked setting strategy Folsom proved superb at implementing it.

Perhaps because each had qualities required in the business but lacking in the other, Sarnoff and Folsom worked well together. Sarnoff was a natural aristocrat, at home with artists and musicians. He had a passion for the classics, having created a symphony orchestra for NBC under the direction of Arturo Toscanini and counting among his friends Vladimir Horowitz and Jascha Heifetz. For his part, Folsom preferred Jack Benny and, later on, Milton Berle. Sarnoff was elegant, a man who enjoyed fine Havana cigars lit with book matches encased in a gold holder; Folsom was rumpled, casual, and almost plebeian. Sarnoff remained concerned with Jewish affairs, while Folsom was a prominent Catholic layman, and they shared the experience of having been snubbed for their religion.

"Frank Folsom humanized RCA," concluded an investment banker who watched him in action during the next decade and a half. "Every corporation at some period in its development should have a Folsom directing its affairs." But one RCA executive of the period said, "Folsom was Sarnoff's detail man, and not much more. He was smart enough to know just how far he could and should go, and never crossed the boundary." Sarnoff put it differently. "There are times when I'm away and my secretary, to keep correspondence from piling up, has Folsom answer some of my mail. The same is true when he's obliged to be away." Each man was capable of filling in for the other in the short run. "We have no diagram at home," he told a reporter three years later, as though to say his business relationship with Folsom was something akin to a marriage. "I have never had a happier relationship with any man in my long career."

Finally, the two men were contemporaries; Sarnoff was the elder by less than three years. This meant that Folsom would pose no threat in the area of succession, since he would be too old to take over the chairmanship if and when Sarnoff ever retired.

The General wanted it that way, for even then he was grooming his son, Bobby, for that post. Folsom recognized this and while not lacking in ambition and self-esteem was prepared to accept the situation. He also realized that Sarnoff's towering reputation and formidable presence, with Bobby in the background, discouraged others from entertaining ambitions for high office at RCA.

One of Folsom's major problems was organization. Never much concerned with such matters, Sarnoff had done little to restructure RCA after the GE and Westinghouse departures, and Folsom had no time for it during the war. In 1945, however, he asked Edwin Booz, the head of the management consulting form of Booz, Allen & Hamilton, to conduct a survey of the company, make suggestions for change, and also recommend middle managers to carry out his programs. The mandate, Folsom said, was "one, to get color television off our backs; two, institute a major internal profit improvement program; three, plan where we go from here." Booz immediately realized that Folsom couldn't hope to transform RCA into a major manufacturer of television receivers and electronic gear under the existing setup and so recommended a major overhaul of the firm.

Booz died two years later, but his firm remained on retainer. John Burns, a thirty-eight-year-old multifaceted and unusually talented analyst, now became a key figure there and at RCA. Starting out as an engineer with a doctorate in metallurgy, Burns taught for a while at Harvard but in 1934 resigned to take a job as a common laborer at Republic Steel. Promotions came quickly, and within a few months he was out of the foundry and into the laboratory. From there Burns went on to management. He was given control of a deficit-plagued wire mill and, after having to deal with a strike, turned it into a profitable operation within a year and a half.

It was this combination of talents that won Burns the post at Booz, Allen, where by the late 1940s he was one of its prized consultants as well as a nationally recognized authority on what was then called "management-as-a-science." Burns not only continued the work started by Booz but during the next few years became Folsom's most trusted advisor. It wouldn't be going too far to say that he fashioned the organization Folsom led in transforming RCA from what before the war had been an often indifferent manufacturer of radios and phonographs into the leader in monochrome television and then color receivers.

Along with refashioning the organization Folsom attempted to develop the cadre of line managers. With Burns's help he did so with diligence and intelligence. Folsom liked to say that he always looked for the best person in any field, "because the second-best fellow is too expensive," and he made certain they were well paid and recognized.

The trouble was that this didn't suffice. Simply stated, RCA was not a happy place at which to work. Perhaps it was the experience during the period of GE domination, or it might have been hatched during the maneuvering to enter new businesses and parry the FCC during the 1930s. The show business atmosphere must have had something to do with it. Whatever the reasons, RCA was riddled with cabals, little empires carefully guarded by survivors, who scraped before their superiors and hounded their underlings. Folsom might attract talented individuals to RCA, but he couldn't keep them there once they realized the situation. So they came, learned, attracted the attention of others, received offers, and after a while many of the best of them left.

The rapid growth of television and the intense competition and maneuvering of the time masked a host of such flaws. The first skirmishes in the postwar television wars took place on four fronts simultaneously: broadcasting, receiver design, production and distribution, and the FCC. Upon the results of these battles would hinge not only leadership in the industry but the very shape of television.

In 1946 Sarnoff prepared at last to introduce television to the broad American public. The corporation had great advantages in any contest with CBS and DuMont; not only was it a larger and better funded company but it alone had a significant network-manufacturing combination. Indeed, RCA was positioned to take an even more dominant role in television than in radio, where CBS was a major force in broadcasting, Philco remained the leader in receiver sales, and Westinghouse and GE as well as others were prime manufacturers of transmission equipment.

There had been little by way of telecasting early in the war, with most of it being old films and experiments on DuMont stations in New York and Washington. Short of funds, DuMont closed its stations in 1943. The event wasn't even noted by the entertainment papers. On April 10, 1944, RCA reopened its television studio, and CBS followed on May 5; these developments too went unreported.

By autumn the few receiver owners in the New York area could view occasional sports events and news programs, though there was no way of knowing when they would appear since newspapers didn't have TV logs and the stations themselves were uncertain. At the time NBC was on the air four nights a week, most of the time with a sponsored show, "The Gillette Cavalcade of Sports," while CBS broadcast on two nights, its feature being "Missus Goes A' Shopping," which despite its name was a radio game show, the first of the genre transferred to television. The following year ABC entered broadcasting with a single offering, "King's Record Shop," a half hour offering on Wednesdays. There still was no programming on Saturdays that autumn, and the most lavish program was the unsponsored "NBC Television Theater" broadcast on Sundays between 8:30 and 9:00, which might have been seen by no more than 1,000 viewers.

Just as with radio, RCA initially considered televising programs as a means of sparking receiver sales; without attractive programming, TV sets would be purchased by only the affluent and the curious. Still, as late as the autumn of 1947 there were just twenty stations nationwide, and except for New York which had four and Philadelphia and Washington with three each, no city had more than two, while Detroit, St. Louis, and Boston had only one.

Programming was still meager but had expanded somewhat from what it had been two years earlier. Sporting events (wrestling was a particular favorite) and ancient motion pictures (usually westerns) dominated, but newscasts and discussion programs had become more common. There were some additional transfers from radio—"Author Meets the Critics" and "Meet the Press"—but original shows were made up of a handful of dramas ("Theater Guild Television Theater," "Kraft Television Theater," both on NBC). Live music made its appearance in the spring of 1948, having been held up till then by union difficulties.

By then the NBC network connected New York with cities running from Boston in the north to Philadelphia in the west and went as far south as Washington, but programming still remained irregular—on the average the stations broadcast twenty-two hours per week. Indeed, with only 300,000 sets in operation, and half of these in the New York metropolitan area, it was estimated that only 10 percent of the population had even seen a TV show, and many of these only in public places such as saloons. In other words, it was early in the game, and CBS still had a chance to best RCA.

William Paley's major assets were imagination, vigor—and color. In this area, CBS remained far ahead of RCA and went to great pains to apprise the public of the fact. Sarnoff monitored the CBS system, knowing he and Paley would soon become involved in a major conflict regarding this technology. Before that, however, they battled over talent, the means of luring viewers, and, for RCA, selling receivers.

Sarnoff and Paley held differing views regarding programming, an outgrowth of their respective experiences and proclivities. In radio's early days Sarnoff had devoted himself to political, legal, and strategic matters, believing that relations with Washington, General Electric, and Westinghouse and the marketing of receivers were more important than whatever happened to go out over the airwaves. This isn't to suggest he had no interest in such matters, for as noted Sarnoff took great pride in cultural programs such as operas and symphonies. Rather, he occasionally seemed somewhat embarrassed by the more popular offerings, which were not to his liking. He continued to entertain a generally low opinion of most show-business people. In contrast, Paley, a devotee of café society, was something of a social butterfly whose enthusiasms ran from his excellent news operation to popular singers.

The original radio network Sarnoff created had had a meager cadre of stars, and the payroll was much lower than that of the commercial AT&T operation. This continued after the creation of the Red and Blue, and not even the success of the former and the lagging position of the latter seemed to interest Sarnoff to the point of developing additional talent.

In the post-World War II period, when losses from television were being carried by profits generated from radio broadcasting, the order went out to cut broadcasting costs whenever possible, and this included the talent budget. Gone were many of the sustaining programs, not only at NBC but at CBS and ABC as well. But while Paley and Noble might be able to get away with this, NBC, with more prestigious talent, found itself embroiled in protests.

It began slowly, in 1946, when Bing Crosby asked for the right to record his popular "Kraft Music Hall" radio program for later broadcast so as to have greater control over the finished product. Both NBC and Kraft rejected this, considering that recorded programming wouldn't have the appeal of live broadcasts, but also because Sarnoff viewed this as a loss of power to artists. Crosby was a major star and had no difficulty finding another network, in this case ABC, which gave him a free hand in such matters.

Niles Trammel, who had succeeded Aylesworth in 1940 as President of NBC, accepted this defection with equanimity. He had assumed leadership at a time when the network structure was pretty well established. There had been no great problems during the war and few afterward. An unimaginative administrator, Trammel was out of his depth in a period when stars such as Crosby were demonstrating independence, and he had nothing to contribute regarding the switch to television. In short, NBC had grown lazy and was caught off guard.

Perhaps with this in mind Paley decided to stage a major raid on NBC. The bait was a scheme worked out by CBS lawyers under which each artist would incorporate himself or herself to obtain tax benefits, thus prompting them to accept deals that wouldn't put a huge dent in the CBS payroll.

The first salvo came when one of the most popular radio stars, Jack Benny, announced his defection to CBS, a move that made the front pages in many cities. Sarnoff was upset but unrepentant; after all, he had wooed Benny from CBS before the war. Moreover, while Benny might have been a major force in radio his motion pictures were generally poorly received, leading Sarnoff to conclude that he, along with other great radio personalities, would fail to make the kind of adjustment needed for television. Just as most of the silent movie stars faded with the advent of sound, he reasoned, so radio's most familiar names would be rejected by TV audiences. Sarnoff was betting that Benny would decline in popularity. His replacement in the 7:00 P.M. Sunday slot was the bandleader Horace Heidt, who while having a devoted following was hardly a major talent.

Benny's departure plus Sarnoff's attitude prompted others to leave. Edgar Bergen and Charlie McCarthy, Red Skelton (who later returned), Burns and Allen, and Amos 'n' Andy followed in rapid order. Finally concerned, Sarnoff worked out an arrangement with Bob Hope under which that comedian remained on NBC.

Sarnoff telephoned Paley to complain about the violation of the old arrangement. Asked for an explanation, Paley replied with no little embarrassment that he went after the stars "because I needed them." With this Sarnoff hung up, not to speak with Paley for several months. Yet he did little at the network except replace Trammel with Joseph McConnell, a gregarious former vice president with a talent for smoothing over differences at headquarters. The game of musical chairs at NBC was beginning, as were insecurities that at times bordered on paranoia.

McConnell was able to stanch the flow of talent, but perhaps did too good a job; in 1953 he was offered the presidency of Colgate Palmolive, accepted, and was succeeded by Frank White, a former president of the Mutual Broadcasting System, this an indication of just how thin the talent was at NBC. Then White fell ill, and unable to find anyone who came up to his expectations, Sarnoff filled in as interim president.

Paley did not at first attempt to place his new stars on CBS television, however, partly because he felt the medium wasn't ready for them but more so because he faced opposition from the artists who were wary of exposing themselves to possible failure. Instead, both CBS and NBC concentrated upon developing new talent, which opened the way to a generation of unknowns, retreads from vaudeville and motion pictures, and second-line talent unable to crack big-time radio.

The big change came in 1948. A year earlier NBC and CBS had not even broadcast on Tuesdays, a night during which DuMont offered the likes of "Small Fry Club," "Look Upon A Star," and "Boxing from Park Arena." Now NBC took the lead in making a programming switch. At the time it hardly seemed bold. On May 19, 1948, the William Morris talent agency ran an advertisement in the trade newspaper *Variety* announcing that:

VAUDEVILLE IS BACK

> The Golden Age of variety begins with the premiere of *The Texaco Star Theater* on television. Tuesday, 8:00-9:00 P.M. E.D.T., starting June 8 on NBC and its affiliated stations in New York, Washington, Boston, Philadelphia, Baltimore, Richmond, and Schenectady. WANTED—variety artists from all corners of the globe. Send particulars to the William Morris Agency.

Readers and listeners knew that the "Texaco Star Theater" had been a radio variety show, a genre common to vaudeville that had been transferred to radio in the 1920s by Rudy Vallee and others. Just as the radio program had a host, so would its television version, and the network and sponsor settled on Milton Berle, a veteran vaudeville entertainer who had had indifferent success in radio and films and who was to alternate with other old vaudevillians, including Henny Youngman and Morey Amsterdam.

Of the group Berle made the greatest impact, not only drawing the largest audiences but helping to stimulate receiver sales. What Amos 'n' Andy had been to radio, "The Texaco Star Theater" became to television, namely the program that popularized the medium. Two weeks later CBS responded with its version of the variety show, "Toast of the Town," which utilized newspaper columnist Ed Sullivan as host, hoping he would duplicate Berle's success.

In autumn 1948 all four networks (NBC, CBS, DTN, and ABC) scheduled full prime-time programming weekday nights and network and local offerings on weekends. Most polls indicated that the Berle show was in first place with "Toast of the Town" a distant second and that NBC had by far the largest audience share. Receiver sales, which had reached 179,000 units in 1947, soared to 970,000 in 1948. It was a repeat of the 1922 radio experience; manufacturers were rationing TVs to retailers, the networks raised their fees while advertisers clammered for programs and would-be broadcasters flooded the FCC with license applications. As for RCA, its investment was paying off, as television finally was delivering on that well-publicized $50 million investment in television.

The corporation quickly established a strong lead in receiver manufacture. In 1946 RCA Victor marketed a $375 ten-inch set, which had the official designation of the 630TS. One executive there called this "Television's Model T," forecasting it would have as many sales as that pioneer vehicle. But all hopes for it would be dashed if CBS obtained FCC approval for its color system, since broadcasts made with this technology couldn't be received on the RCA sets. Thus, the owner of an RCA television receiver would be stuck with what surely would be seen as a second-rate system, while his neighbor, with a set capable of obtaining CBS color shows, would be far better off. Or at least this was what appeared to be the situation. In such a struggle RCA would need all the allies it could muster.

In recognition of the problem, Folsom encouraged other manufacturers to apply to RCA for licenses. This was an old company tradition, which started when Sarnoff licensed radio technology for the same reason—to obtain additional revenues—in the late 1920s. Now the General proclaimed, "Radio Corporation of America will continue to make available to its licensees all of its inventions in this new field of television as it has done in other fields of radio and electronics."

In addition, this was deemed a satisfactory way of dealing with what was seen as a potentially dangerous threat from Zenith, one of the few major set manufacturers to refuse to pay for RCA radio patents. Alleging antitrust violations, that company instituted a treble damages suit against the old Radio Group in 1946 that dragged on for eleven years and ended in an out-of-court settlement that was a clear Zenith victory. Thus, while converting his corporation to television Sarnoff had to deal with a suit that possibly could make his patent position in that technology open to competitors. For this reason as well, he was eager to line up the rest of the industry behind RCA. Licensing seemed the best method to do so.

In the summer of 1947 Folsom had invited representatives of those firms interested in going into receiver manufacture to the Camden plant. With Engstrom as his side he gave them a tour of the works, highlighted new technologies, and ended by placing copies of the blueprints for the 630TS table model on a table for each to take. "Television is bigger than any one of us," he beamed.

The invitation was accepted; within a few months GE, Westinghouse, Andrea, and American Television had their new models in the stores, and a year later there were thirty-five firms in the field. According to one industry estimate there were 300,000 sets in operation in the spring of 1948, more than half in public places such as saloons, and a year later 940,000 homes had receivers. Each of these was one more vote for RCA's monochrome system, and all of those using RCA patents paid a royalty. Just how much this was is difficult to say, since the company did not release the figures, but *Electronic Industries* magazine thought RCA received around $100,000 from television licenses in 1947. The figure rose to $1 million the following year, $3.2 million in 1949, and $9.5 million in 1950, when the corporation reported a pretax profit of $78.5 million and posttax of $40.1 million. That licensing was and would remain an important source of income was obvious.

However, RCA would not dominate receiver manufacture the way Sarnoff had hoped it would. In 1947 the company accounted for approximately 80 percent of the market; the following year its share declined to 30 percent, as newcomers such as Admiral and GE took away sales from the leader. Thus, even before the great television boom began, RCA's position in that industry was about where it had been in radio during the late 1920s and early 1930s, when it had lost leadership there.

RCA'S POSITION IN THE TV RECEIVER MARKET, 1946–1956

Year	Est. RCA TV Set Production	Est. RCA TV Gross Revenues	Est. RCA Market Share
1946	10,000	$ 2.5 million	100 percent
1947	200,000	40	80
1948	300,000	53	30
1949	600,000	79	20
1950	900,000	162	12
1951	800,000	150	14
1952	800,000	150	13
1953	900,000	104	12
1954	1,000,000	88	14
1955	1,300,000	104	17

Source: *Electronic Industries,* January 30, 1963, p. 101.

This disappointing showing was due partly to production foul-ups and related problems. For example, the firm was stymied by bottlenecks at its two suppliers of picture tube blanks, Corning Glass and Owens-Illinois Glass. Then too, given the reputations and manufacturing and marketing abilities of several major competitors, this was bound to happen.

There were compensations. The machinery used by almost all the other manufacturers had been created by RCA, and it might be argued that most sets they offered would not have reached the market were it not for RCA parts. Fully half of the company's tube production was sold to others, and these included the finished picture tube, an area in which RCA had a 70-percent market share. And there were those large royalty payments. The corporation remained prepared to license its technology to almost anyone who asked and would pay the fee. In time it would do so for Japanese manufacturers as well.

However, RCA wasn't particularly successful in design and marketing. The company's offerings were on a par with most, but eventually would be deemed inferior in technology and reliability to those turned out by Motorola and Magnavox, for example. To compensate for this, Folsom created a superb service operation. Recognizing the early sets might develop troubles, he established the best and most complete support program in the industry. The fee was modest enough: $55 a year for table models working the way up for the more expensive consoles that had to be serviced in the home. Indications were that RCA didn't show much of a profit on service, but it gathered benefits in the form of sales, customers knowing that 2,200 support personnel were there when their sets failed. Were it not for this RCA might have lost an even more significant market share to rivals.

At the time the first black-and-white sets were offered for sale the FCC still had not ruled on the question of whether television should occupy the very high frequency (VHF) or the relatively unused ultra-high frequency (UHF) segment of the radio spectrum. Before and during the war Sarnoff had managed to obtain channels in the VHF band for television, but the CBS color experiments conducted just prior to America's entry into the war had been done on the UHF segment, and in 1944 Paley had successfully petitioned the FCC to permit colorcasts there.

While this didn't seem particularly interesting to nontechnicians, it was of paramount importance to those within the industry. The 1946 RCA television set had thirteen channels on the dial. Color experiments had been and still were being conducted by CBS on a spectrum that the RCA sets could not receive—specifically channels 14 through 83. If the FCC continued to back CBS, and color broadcasting became the accepted vehicle, all of those thirteen channel sets would be made obsolete.

There was another important dimension. Given only thirteen channels and NBC's established position, it appeared that television broadcasting would be dominated by a relatively small number of companies, probably the old radio networks. There were those who disagreed, citing the inability of VHF waves to follow the earth's curve, and concluding therefore that all stations would have to be local. But in 1946 RCA was planning coaxial cable connections and exploring other technologies to assure coast-to-coast capabilities. That there would be some local programming by independents seemed probable, but these would be minor when set beside those put out by the powerful NBC network and its affiliates.

The situation would be quite different if the industry went to the UHF option. In such a situation the viewer would have his choice of literally dozens of channels. There would be many new networks and even more local stations, all scrambling for a share of the advertising revenues. For this reason, as much if not more than for those of receiver production, Sarnoff placed his chips on VHF.

As public acceptance of television increased, RCA roared ahead with its production of sets, turning them out as fast as possible from its Camden, New Jersey, and Indianapolis, Indiana, facilities. Another plant in Lancaster, Pennsylvania, which had been constructed for RCA by the Navy, was now purchased and converted to the manufacture of television receivers. Even so, RCA's output, which in 1947 was averaging 5,000 sets a week, couldn't keep up with demand.

Sarnoff didn't offer projections for public consumption as he once had for radio, but he did repeat that RCA had already invested $50 million in the technology without a payoff and was prepared to double that. He believed this would not be necessary, however, that profits from receiver sets were on the way, and these could easily support broadcasting costs. The only problem was with the FCC.

The FCC's attitude regarding color and UHF was crucial. When Fly and Sarnoff met during the war, their encounters were polite, but the old enmity remained. Paley, on the other hand, had come to look upon Fly as an ally and perhaps naively expected his support for UHF. But Fly was about to take his leave from government.

In 1944, he received a particularly enticing offer to head the Muzak Corp., which he accepted. At the time and later, RCA officials noted that Sarnoff was close to the Muzak board, and rumor had it that he arranged the offer hoping to get Fly off his back, which cannot be verified. In any event Sarnoff now maneuvered to obtain a more friendly commissioner, or lacking that, one who could be "educated."

World War II continued, and Roosevelt and Sarnoff both had more important matters to attend to than who should take the chairmanship. Nothing happened for more than a year, during which the Commission met only occasionally. The dominant figure seemed to be Paul Porter, a former publicity director for the Democratic Party, who was considered sympathetic to both the CBS color system and UHF. Fortunately for RCA, neither would be discussed so long as the war was on.

Roosevelt died the following year, and the fighting came to an end soon after. Harry Truman prepared for peace by easing out the Old Roosevelt loyalists and replacing them with his own supporters. Not surprisingly he sought a like-thinking individual to head the FCC. Truman had little in common with the New Deal intellectuals and certainly would have clashed with Fly had he been at the FCC. As it was, almost everyone expected him to name Porter to the chairmanship.

However Truman had bigger things in mind for Porter, who was named to replace New Dealer Chester Bowles as head of the Office of Price Administration, and to head the FCC he chose Charles Denny, an amiable, colorless man generally perceived as little more than a timeserver of the type that had dominated the old Federal Radio Commission.

Thirty-two years old at the time of his appointment, Denny had gone from Harvard Law School to the powerful Washington law firm of Covington, Burling, Rublee, Acheson and Shub. He left in 1938 to become an attorney in the Justice Department. The bureaucracy was more to his liking; Denny became assistant to the Attorney General in 1941, moved over to the FCC the following year, and next rose to be assistant general counsel and then general counsel, this hardly deemed an important post during the war. He was elevated to the Commission in 1946 and a few months later was selected to fill in as its acting Chairman.

In his first important decision Denny reallocated FM wavelengths, which at a stroke made all existing receivers obsolete. The FM licensees protested, arguing that it would cost at least $75 million for them to convert and that the changeover would take several years, during which time they would lose their audiences. The FCC would not reconsider, however, and in this way removed one of RCA's more stubborn obstacles.

Paley should have taken this as a sign that Denny was in Sarnoff's pocket, but he seemed to have been oblivious to this. How else might one explain CBS's willingness to withdraw four applications for VHF stations and place all of its chips on UHF?

All the while RCA had been working feverishly on a color system of its own. A private demonstration had been made in 1941, at which time it was deemed decidedly inferior to the CBS version. Now Sarnoff rushed to perfect it, approving a crash program to be headed by Engstrom. Announcing that this version was compatible with monochrome, he started lobbying for it in Washington.

Sarnoff must have realized that his jerry-built technology wouldn't be accepted, but more monochrome sets were being placed every day. In the pre-Fly period the FRC and FCC tended to bend to public and industry pressures. Sarnoff was counting on the same happening now.

Denny rejected the CBS color system in March 1947, refusing to approve either its version or the one submitted by RCA, though indicating a greater interest in the latter. Then, having given Sarnoff a breathing spell, in October Denny resigned the FCC chairmanship to become an RCA vice president and general counsel! Paley and others in the industry cried foul, but rewarding friendly FRC and then FCC personnel with industry jobs had been a fact of life for two decades.

It was at this point that General Harbord decided to relinquish the RCA chairmanship. Harbord had reached the age of 65 in 1931, and little had been expected of him during the decade that followed. In fact Harbord was more a consultant than an executive after RCA was divested by GE and Westinghouse. He had been ailing since the early 1940s and might have left then were it not for Sarnoff's involvement with the war effort. During the early postwar period, when he rarely appeared at headquarters, Harbord became an almost totemic figure, unknown to most of the wartime newcomers.

He stepped down as chairman and CEO in July 1947 and died a month later. Sarnoff now elevated himself to the chairmanship, retaining the chief operating post at NBC and RCA Communications. Folsom, who had been named executive vice president in 1945, would soon become president.

By then, the RCA rumor mill was in high gear. Sarnoff had developed a warm friendship with David Lilienthal, who had become a national figure as head of the Tennessee Valley Administration and an international one in 1946, when he chaired the Atomic Energy Commission. A man of impeccable rectitude, wide learning, and commanding presence, Lilienthal might have provided RCA with the kind of "image" Sarnoff so prized, and in addition he had the scientific background Folsom lacked as well as impressive Washington contacts. Not yet fifty years old when he left government service in 1950, Lilienthal also was young enough to be considered for the succession. Carl Dreher, who had known Sarnoff since the early 1920s, was convinced that Lilienthal had been considered for the presidency while still at the Atomic Energy Commission. Talk of his coming to RCA surfaced soon after, and in fact he did serve as a consultant there for several years.

Lilienthal possessed a happy combination of much that Sarnoff had been and a great deal to which he aspired. Both men were Jewish, but Lilienthal had far wider experience than Sarnoff. He was a man of vast vision; the TVA had been one of the world's great engineering enterprises, while the Atomic Energy Commission of those days spoke airily of the promise of bringing cheap energy to the world, a sort of global TVA. It was the sort of challenge and dream that intrigued Sarnoff so much in those years. In the younger man he saw a vision of what he might have become had he entered government service, which to Sarnoff was a far nobler enterprise than the simple pursuit of profit.

In the early summer of 1951 Sarnoff and Folsom asked Lilienthal to head the color television project, aware of course that simply by being there he might sway the FCC to the RCA version. Lilienthal refused, the most important consideration being monetary; he had decided to parlay his years of government service into a post that paid better than anything RCA could offer at that level. While Sarnoff perceived in Lilienthal a man of high idealism, the former TVA chief hoped to obtain from Sarnoff the secret of making a fortune.

Rumors of Lilienthal's impending arrival persisted, and when Folsom collapsed in December from the strains of the job Sarnoff held some conversations with him, perhaps raising the subject. But Folsom recovered, and while Lilienthal and Sarnoff remained close, it would appear that nothing more was said of the matter.

Folsom's major task was to keep RCA in the point position in TV receiver manufacturing and in addition to monitor the situation at CBS.

For a brief troublesome moment in early 1947, as Folsom struggled to increase production and keep the competition at bay, there was talk of a four-way merger between CBS, Zenith, DuMont, and Paramount. Zenith was of course a longtime Sarnoff adversary. Its major business was the manufacture of high-priced radios and phonographs; President Eugene McDonald had no interest in broadcasting and for that reason perhaps had a different view of television's future. As has been noted, Sarnoff perceived TV as radio with pictures, and while McDonald conceded this made sense, he also believed it could develop into what amounted to motion pictures in the home. Watching current programming, he argued that television would remain mediocre at best unless it could be wedded to films. McDonald talked and wrote of "Phonovision," by which motion pictures would be transmitted via telephone wires to home receivers, with the recipient being billed monthly in his telephone statement. Decades later a variant of this idea would appear as pay television delivered by cable.

Hollywood considered television a minor challenge at that time but also recognized its potential, given decent programming. In addition, the motion picture industry was facing the threat of breakups under the antitrust laws, with the Justice Department insisting it cease anticompetitive practices, specifically that the studios divest themselves of their theaters. If they lost these major outlets, perhaps they could find another in television.

Several studios had already considered means of entering the field. Twentieth Century-Fox produced some shows in 1947 and applied for a license for a Boston station. President Peter Rathvon of RKO announced its willingness to produce special programs for television viewing, predicting that "half of Hollywood's activities may eventually be in television." Metro-Goldwyn-Mayer, the industry's biggest studio, had applied for two stations, and Paramount filed its application for a Boston outlet, later owned KTLA in Los Angeles, and as noted had a stake in DuMont. That there would be some kind of link between television and movies seemed likely, and it could have taken the form of some kind of arrangement between CBS and Paramount, which might include DuMont.

DuMont was the most imaginative and promising factor in the equation. Allen DuMont seemed on the brink of realizing his prewar ambitions. He had actually started receiver production several weeks before the first of RCA's postwar sets made their appearances, and his company turned out and marketed products considered the best in the field, ranging from a $445 tabletop competitor for the RCA model to a $2,495 console that projected TV images on a large screen. Recognizing the seriousness of the DuMont threat in this area, RCA had struck back with its low-priced service contract and an advertising campaign that stressed experience and reliability, this taken as a tacit admission that it couldn't match DuMont in technology. But DuMont rolled on; in 1947 the firm grossed more than $11 million, on which it earned $600,000. It would have been more had not the company lost $900,000 on broadcasting operations.

DuMont had established WABD in New York in 1944, announcing it would be the cornerstone for the DuMont Television Network. A second station was obtained in Washington, and then a third in Philadelphia. Eventually the DTN had twenty-one stations and, at the height of its success in the mid-1950s, over 100 affiliates, which was more than CBS, though not as many as NBC. The DuMont network was popular initially, and though its programming wasn't as sophisticated (and costly) as the other two networks, it won an important audience share.

While producing receivers and expanding his network, DuMont continued with his inventions. One of these was a so-called peanut station, which would broadcast films and operate without a studio; he thought it could be constructed and equipped for around $50,000, and in 1948 one was sold to an initially doubtful but later satisfied customer. DuMont suggested that if ultra-high frequencies were allocated the country could be dotted with these stations, opening programming to an extent that wouldn't be seen until the 1980s.

Finally, DuMont came up with an experimental receiver that could receive both the RCA and the CBS signals; in 1948 he demonstrated it to FCC commissioners. His inclusion in the merger would assure it of a manufacturing base to go along with Zenith, stations to combine with CBS, and a technology as interesting as anything RCA was turning out. The thought of customers watching Paramount color movies broadcast by CBS and DMT on a Zenith or DuMont receiver must have caused Sarnoff nightmares, for at the time NBC lacked a secure TV programming base and had no relationship with a studio.

The merger didn't come about, however. After initial conversations DuMont and McDonald lost interest while Paramount considered it a long shot. Moreover there were hints of FCC disapproval of such a combination. Also, DuMont was having troubles selling its receivers, even though by 1950 it had 2,600 dealers and thirty-six distributors; the company that was the catalyst for the proposed merger was unraveling.

That year DuMont posted sales of $76 million and a profit of $6.9 million, hardly placing it in RCA's league, but respectable nonetheless. Then followed a market glut in 1951, when sales declined to $50.6 million and DuMont showed a loss of $584,000, which were it not for the now-profitable network would have come to $4.5 million. Realizing that it lacked the muscle to make much of a dent in receiver sales, DuMont sold its television manufacturing division to Emerson in 1951. Its network remained competitive for a while but soon showed signs that it too was in trouble.

Sarnoff also toyed with the idea of some relationship with motion pictures, though in a way so as not to disturb RCA's flourishing receiver business. He saw no reason why motion pictures couldn't coexist with TV just as they did with radio, and he believed that the motion picture companies might use television to show coming attractions to lure viewers into the movie houses. Folsom worked with Warner Brothers and Twentieth Century-Fox to develop theater television, the idea being that from one central studio movies might be sent to hundreds of theaters nationwide. But all of this was of secondary interest, for Sarnoff and Paley both knew that color would be the major battleground.

While CBS had lost to RCA in the opening round of this contest it did have a signal victory over RCA in 1948. It concerned an old technology and product: phonograph record systems.

In this period all manufacturers turned out records that played at 78 revolutions per minute, which allowed approximately eight minutes per side on a twelve-inch disc. While this served adequately for popular music, it meant that an opera might require as many as half a dozen discs, with the listener subjected to pauses while changes were being made.

In the 1930s RCA Victor had experimented with other speeds, most significantly 33 1/3 rpm, and from 1933 to 1937 actually produced several discs for sale on adapted phonographs, but the line was discontinued because of public apathy. Next the firm experimented with another speed, 45 rpm, the idea being to record a single popular tune on each side of a seven-inch disc, and work on this system continued sporadically during and immediately after the war.

By 1948 RCA Victor had developed a 45 rpm record and player, known within the company as "Madame X," that could have been introduced at almost any time. The 45s were considered an addition to the line, and not a replacement for the 78s. Ever the one to milk a product and hold back replacements for as long as possible to extract the last drop of profits, Sarnoff saw no reason to go any further than the research and development stage.

In 1938 CBS had purchased the Columbia Phonograph Company. Paley had visions of emulating the RCA organization by entering production. Just as Sarnoff had turned the trick by acquiring Victor, so he would do the same with a smaller, albeit respected operation. But Victor Red Seal remained the leader and most prestigious label, especially in classical music.

Now CBS was developing its own version of the 33 1/3, known as the "long-playing" (LP), which Paley felt would revolutionize the industry. Not only might one record over a half an hour on a single side, but CBS had perfected a new plastic, vinylite, which unlike the standard shellac was unbreakable and offered better tonal fidelity. Paley worked out an arrangement with Philco under which that company would produce LP phonographs, some of which would be sold under the CBS label, and there was some consideration of a merger between the two firms.

He then approached Sarnoff, demonstrated the new records, and offered him a license, which was rejected. Since RCA was a much bigger company than CBS (1948 revenues of $357 million vs. $70 million), Sarnoff must have felt capable of crushing the LP with his own version. He told his staff to ready Madame X for the market. In order to make it appear novel, Sarnoff had them retool the 45 so as to have a larger hole for the spindle, which would require it to be played on a special phonograph, and the phonographs were rushed to the stores to compete with the Philco and CBS machines.

It was a case of too little too late. Almost overnight Columbia won over devotees of classical music who had no trouble recognizing the advantages of the LPs.

Within months the powerful National Association of Music Dealers voted to support the LP system, while Decca, London, and Mercury records went over to that speed, leaving RCA with a sole ally, Capital, which had always emphasized popular recordings. Attempting to salvage something out of this debacle, RCA countered with a rebate scheme tied to a $2 million advertising campaign, to no avail. It seemed nothing could stop the 33 1/3, or help the 45s.

By 1949 phonograph companies were putting out new models that could play all three speeds (the adjustment to the larger 45 rpm hole made via plastic discs one had to insert in the holes, this adding a complication to the matter). Columbia sales soared, while RCA languished. Realizing that unless drastic action were taken he might lose the classical market altogether, Sarnoff hinted that RCA might abandon the 45 rpm field. But he would not turn out 33 1/3s of his own. His company still controlled most of the major classical artists. If the public wanted to hear them, they would have to purchase 78s or 45s. This was Sarnoff's last arrow in the struggle with CBS.

He could not hold out indefinitely. Many RCA artists were unhappy with the 45s, especially when their CBS counterparts were outselling them. According to one source, Toscanini convinced Sarnoff that he would have to go over to the 33 1/3s after hearing a Bruno Walter CBS recording. Reluctantly the General gave in. While the company remained wedded to the 45s for some of its popular songs, it soon after started recording in the 33 1/3 mode, conceding Columbia a major victory.

While this was an important defeat for RCA, it was eclipsed by the explosive growth of television, as receiver sales climbed, applications for stations increased, and the debate over color intensified. Till then progress and evolution had been relatively slow, and the FCC staff was adequate to handle disputes and licenses.

All of this changed in 1948, by which time Wayne Coy had succeeded to the chairmanship. Unlike Fly and Denny, Coy had some broadcasting experience, having managed two radio stations in Washington, D.C. But like them he was a political appointee, a protégé of New Dealer Paul McNutt who had served as a presidential assistant during the war. Dismayed with Denny's performance and his defection to NBC, several senators had questioned Coy harshly during the confirmation hearings, implying, as one of them put it, that he was "the candidate" of that network. Coy vehemently denied this, but the suspicions remained. Citing the massive work load and the need to reexamine standards, Coy suspended the granting of station licenses in September 1948. Rumor had it that he wanted to reopen the entire matter of VHF vs. UHF and color systems, since during the summer of the previous year Paley had petitioned for reconsideration. But RCA had more reason to be pleased than did CBS, since by that time its network already owned the five stations permitted by regulations, while CBS still had applications for three more on file.

Believing it was falling behind in the race and considering that this could become a permanent condition, Paley tried to purchase ABC for $28 million, an offer that was rejected. As long as the freeze was in place CBS was in an inferior position, but Coy indicated the backlog should be completed within a year or less, and Paley had little choice but to wait it out.

The thought that Coy would prove completely pro-RCA was dispelled when he scheduled hearings on color systems in 1949. At that time the FCC held that the CBS system was superior and that commercial colorcasting on that basis could begin in 1950. Now the advantage appeared to turn to Paley. Receiver sales, which came to 2,970,000 in 1949 and 7,355,000 in 1950, dipped to 5,312,000 in 1951, as purchases of monochrome sets leveled off, with customers awaiting the first color receivers. Moreover, there were signs total revenues if not sales were starting to plateau, providing impetus to the move to color. Further erosion of revenues and profits added to this as the decade wore on.

Sarnoff was taken off guard by the FCC decision. At the time there were some 4 million receivers in use, representing an outlay of approximately $1.6 billion, and on its face it seemed the decision would make all of these obsolete once colorcasting became commonplace. Undismayed, Sarnoff mobilized his forces and developed a strategy, thinking of the problem in military terms. "We may have lost the battle," he told an aide, "but we'll win the war."

The General ordered Engstrom to continue work on RCA's own color system, while entering into negotiations to obtain licenses from Paley so as to

TELEVISION'S GROWTH, 1946–1955

YEAR	RECEIVER PRODUCTION (in thousands)	CUMULATIVE TOTAL (in thousands)	AVERAGE PRICE	TOTAL RETAIL VALUE (in millions)
1946	10	10	$500	$ 5
1947	250	260	400	100
1948	1,000	1,260	350	350
1949	3,000	4,260	315	945
1950	7,500	11,760	360	2,700
1951	5,600	17,360	375	2,100
1952	6,300	23,660	375	2,363
1953	7,300	30,960	230	1,679
1954	7,300	38,260	175	1,277
1955	7,800	46,000	160	1,248

Source: *Electronic Industries,* January 30, 1963, p. 101.

have a fallback position in case of failure. Paley had begun searching for companies to acquire that would enable CBS to produce receivers, and he didn't need RCA; so he indicated that the price would be stiff.

Next, Sarnoff contacted other monochrome receiver manufacturers, who were as distressed as he, and suggested the creation of an industry organization to oppose the CBS system. Companies like GE, Sylvania, Hazeltine, and others came along, and with Sarnoff's leadership they joined the new National Television Systems Committee, a lobbying group that swung into action soon after. They agreed not to produce receivers capable of receiving the CBS color signals. In addition, NBC, ABC, and DTN would reject the new technology as long as possible, which is to say until pressures mounted from advertisers and the FCC. (Actually, ABC and DTN lacked funds to make the switch.) Thus, when the time came for commercial telecasting, customers would be able to buy only CBS receivers and receive broadcasts only from that network.

Those considering the purchase of a CBS set also would have to reflect that if the experiment failed they would be stuck with what amounted to a piece of furniture. Such limited access would discourage sponsors and so make Paley's gambit all the more expensive.

Finally, RCA mobilized its battery of lawyers and challenged the FCC decision in the courts. There wasn't much of a basis for the litigation, but Sarnoff's objective was to delay the CBS color system to the point where an overwhelming number of Americans owned monochromes and public pressure for reversal made its impact. Paley had the technology; time was Sarnoff's most important weapon.

Helped by the Korean War, which obliged Coy to delay the introduction of colorcasting, the strategy worked. The cases worked their way through the courts, and all the while additional monochrome receivers were purchased, each a putative vote for RCA. Sarnoff grew more confident with each turn of the calendar.

In the end the Supreme Court upheld the FCC decision, and CBS was free to proceed with colorcasting. But the final decision came in June 1951, by which time there were more than 12 million monochrome sets in use. Thus, CBS was faced with new lawsuits—these from consumer groups and receiver manufacturers—if it decided to proceed with its version of color television.

Perhaps feeling he had gone so far that he couldn't turn back, Paley decided to plunge ahead. The most obvious problem was that no company was turning out CBS-compatible receivers, and no member of the NTSC intended to do so. Because of this Paley decided to enter the field on his own by acquiring for $18 million in stock a manufacturer, Hytron Radio and Electronics, the owner of Air King Products, which was renamed CBS-Columbia. The plan was for CBS to advertise its color programs, in this way creating a demand, which in turn would spur the sales of the CBS-Columbia receivers.

While the strategy was sound, the implementation proved difficult. For one thing, at around $1,000 the receivers were more than twice as costly as monochromes, and in addition were quite complex, often requiring servicing that CBS was slow to provide. Then too, there was very little programming, and since the CBS sets couldn't receive monochrome offerings they were hardly used.

Colorcasting had begun with the usual hoopla on June 25, only days after the FCC decision, when the Air King signs hadn't been replaced by the CBS-Columbia ones. Arthur Godfrey, a CBS star, appeared on an experimental color program that was seen by some 400 invited guests assembled around thirty handcrafted receivers. Sixteen sponsors paid $10,000 each for bragging rights of having been represented on the pioneer show. They were assured that more were on the way.

It seemed a perfect time to bring all that radio talent signed away from NBC to television, and in color. Paley and Frank Stanton talked of Burns and Allen, Jack Benny, and the others going against the NBC lineup. Burns and Allen went on in the fall of 1951, and Benny followed in 1952. Both were in monochrome, however, for by then it had become apparent that the CBS experiment was in deep trouble. The receivers weren't selling, and CBS was having technical difficulties with colorcasting.

The talk within the industry was that Paley was seeking a graceful exit, and he found one in October, less than four months after the Godfrey colorcast, when in his capacity as chairman of the National Production Authority, Defense Secretary Charles Wilson asked CBS to halt colorcasting during the Korean war. The network immediately acceded, simultaneously closing down its manufacturing facility. Later on it was revealed that the project had cost CBS $50 million, which was written down to zero.

Sarnoff felt vindicated, and at Rockefeller Plaza network executives chortled that it was all too transparent. Paley had been Wilson's aide at the NPA and probably wrote the request himself. In any case the CBS system was as good as dead, leaving the way open for approval of the RCA version.

In early July, less than two weeks after CBS initiated colorcasting, Engstrom had announced that "we have refined and put into pilot plant production our tri-color kinescope," which he claimed represented a technology superior to the firm's earlier efforts, and inferentially, the CBS version. "We propose to proceed with careful and extensive field tests on these and other improvements," he said. By autumn he was ready for a demonstration, at which one motion picture executive pronounced it "amazing." Color was ready for introduction, but Sarnoff was not.

The General moved slowly. He could afford to do so, since there was no rival on the horizon, and the monochromes were finally showing a good return on his initial investment. As with the long-playing phonograph, Sarnoff would pioneer with research, but he was always slow to introduce new products until the ones they replaced were clearly unacceptable. His development costs for color would eventually come to around $130 million, and it was imperative that care be taken in the introduction of the RCA version.

Sarnoff began by readying the network for the change. In 1953 he stepped down as interim president of NBC to make way for Sylvester (Pat) Weaver, at the time an NBC vice president and one of the few top managers there willing to accept the post. The reason was obvious: Bobby Sarnoff was also at the network, involved with programming, clearly preparing to take over when the General thought the time ripe. "I knew I was just warming up the seat for Bobby," said Weaver.

In the end the decision for color was forced by congressional action. The House Committee on Interstate and Foreign Commerce opened hearings in March of 1953 to determine what was holding up the introduction of colorcasting. RCA appeared as leader of the NTSC, which by now was made up of twenty manufacturers. What was called the "NTSC process" (not the RCA system) was demonstrated successfully, with CBS indicating it was prepared to colorcast over its network. Stanton conceded it would be "economically foolish" to do otherwise, though to preserve his network's pride he indicated that the "new" system represented an improvement over previous versions. "Perhaps this time it is different, perhaps this time they have found the answer," was the way he put it.

Chairman Charles Wolverton (R, New Jersey) declared, "Color TV is ready for the public; there is no reason for delay." The FCC agreed and on December 17 reversed its 1950 decision and approved the NTSC system. Anticipating this, NBC swung into action and prepared several Christmas colorcasts, including "Amahl and the Night Visitors," and the Rose Bowl Parade, even though there were only a handful of sets capable of receiving the signals.

Under Folsom's direction the Camden factory geared up for color receiver production, only to be beaten to the market by Admiral, which under RCA licenses produced $1,175 sets and had them in stores on December 30. At the same time NBC moved swiftly to convert its programming to color, so that by March there were at least ten colorcasts a week. As with the earlier CBS sets, the RCAs were expensive, and the public was slow to replace serviceable monochrome receivers, which could receive the same programs, with newer models. Only 8,000 color receivers were sold in the first half of 1954, prompting Bob Hope to remark that his color program had a "tremendous" audience—"General Sarnoff and his wife." That he did so on NBC hurt all the more.

The payoff for color was slow in coming. It soon became apparent that even deep price cuts wouldn't convince owners of monochromes to buy another receiver. Westinghouse took this route, and after one month of intensive advertising it sold only thirty sets nationwide, prompting talk that the company would cease production. While CBS continued to convert to colorcasting, ABC and DuMont held back because of the heavy costs involved. In fact both were in bad financial shape, with DuMont to leave the field in 1955 and ABC hanging on precariously.

In late 1954 Sarnoff and Fulton conceded that it would be years before the investment showed profits, while others whispered that in the end RCA would suffer worse losses than had CBS. That year RCA was the only color receiver manufacturer remaining in the field. Zenith's McDonald called the complex RCA tube "a Rube Goldberg contraption," while GE's Ralph Cordiner was only slightly more polite: "If you have a color set, you've almost got to have an engineer living in the house."

In 1955 RCA entered the ranks of billion dollar corporations, a club that at the time was exclusive. In contrast, Zenith reported revenues of $153 million, Philco $373 million, CBS $317 million, ABC $198 million, and DuMont $59 million. Thus, RCA was less than half the size of former parent GE ($3.4 billion) but it was closing in on Westinghouse ($1.4 billion).

All of this had been purchased for a price. The company's cash flow couldn't provide sufficient funds for those new factories, intensive research and development, and the creation of first monochrome and then color television. From 1946 to 1955 revenues rose almost 350 percent and earnings 330 percent. In the same span, however, long-term debt went from $44.6 million to $246.6 million, a rise of more than 450 percent. This was troublesome, but no more than that. Along with IBM and a handful of others, RCA was one of the glamour companies of the 1920s that underwent a rebirth in the postwar years. Not only was there the success of monochrome television, but NBC put in a dazzling performance in the first half of the 1950s, with promise of more to come. There was the long-anticipated payoff from color television; when that arrived profits would soar, and the debt could be shaved. Or at least that was the view at Rockefeller Center.

And on Wall Street too. In 1955 RCA common hit a high of 55⅜, a level not seen in a quarter of a century.

SELECTED RCA STATISTICS, 1944–1945

figures in millions of dollars

Year	Revenues	Net Income	Senior Capital
1944	324.8	10.3	35.0
1945	278.3	11.3	35.0
1946	236.1	11.0	44.6
1947	312.7	18.8	50.6
1948	356.9	24.0	54.6
1949	396.1	25.1	54.6
1950	584.4	46.2	74.6
1951	596.8	31.2	114.6
1952	690.6	32.3	144.6
1953	848.9	35.0	164.6
1954	938.1	40.5	164.6
1955	1,050.7	47.5	264.6

Source: *Moody's Industrials,* 1947, 1949, 1953, 1955.

RCA'S DISTRIBUTION OF BUSINESS, 1944–1954

figures in millions of dollars

Year	Manufacturing	Broadcasting	Communications
1944	244.3	60.0	22.7
1945	193.2	61.3	22.6
1946	152.6	61.1	20.0
1947	233.3	65.7	19.1
1948	270.6	71.0	21.1
1949	308.2	72.9	20.0
1950	476.1	92.4	22.2
1951	440.1	137.1	26.6
1952	507.4	162.5	29.1
1953	645.1	176.0	36.6
1954	709.9	200.4	35.7

Figures differ from totals owing to adjustments for intercompany transactions.
Source: *RCA Annual Reports,* 1941–1946.

As it turned out the public would buy color receivers, but more often than not when replacing their monochromes rather than as a second set. Sarnoff had thought color would be seen as a new product, when in fact it bore a relationship to monochrome not unlike that of FM radio to AM, namely an improved version of an existing technology that while interesting hardly was a pressing need. Advertisers would pay premium rates for color shows, though not until there were sufficient receivers in the hands of potential customers. The breakthrough wouldn't come until 1960, when the combination of lower unit prices and replacements of discarded monochromes with color receivers prompted by more programming had its effect. That year there were some 200,000 color sets in use, compared to 55.5 million monochromes; five years later the number of monochromes had gone to 75 million, but there were 5 million color receivers in American homes.

The company finally broke even on color in 1959, after which profits were substantial. In 1962 RCA had over 70 percent of sales and was supplying tubes to other manufacturers, who as with monochromes and before that radio were catching up rapidly. The Lancaster, Pennsylvania, factory, where its picture tubes were being manufactured, had to ration them to customers, RCA included. "Sometimes I have trouble explaining to the chairman of the board that even after he spent $130 million he still can't have all the tubes he wants," said group executive vice president W. Walter Watts.

MONOCHROME AND COLOR RECEIVER SALES, 1954–1965

in thousands of units and millions of dollars

YEAR	MONOCHROME SALES	REVENUES	COLOR SALES	REVENUES
1954	7,405	$1,040	5	$ 2
1955	7,738	966	20	10
1956	7,351	845	100	46
1957	6,388	752	85	37
1958	5,051	620	80	34
1959	6,278	802	90	37
1960	5,707	746	120	47
1961	6,155	753	147	56
1962	6,558	837	438	154
1963	7,019	823	747	258
1964	8,028	878	1,404	488
1965	8,409	890	2,694	959

Source: Skinner and Rogers, *Manufacturing Policy in the Electronics Industry,* p. 60.

By 1965 RCA's share of the market had fallen to 30 percent, thus repeating the experience with radios and monochromes. It was still the leader and earning more money than ever, but once again dominance would elude Sarnoff's grasp. That year the industry-wide value of color set sales surpassed that of monochromes for the first time ($959 million vs. $890 million), and in 1968 more color sets were sold than monochromes.

Hardly noticed in all of this was another chapter in the UHF struggle. In 1952 the FCC had decided that the VHF band was to be supplanted by seventy additional channels in the UHF spectrum. Eleven years later the next activist Commission chairman, Newton Minnow, obtained congressional backing for a measure to require all receiver manufacturers to equip their sets with tuners so as to enable them to receive the additional channels. This indicated that there would be dozens of new entries into the field, some to challenge the supremacy of the established networks, but little came of this until the 1980s. In the mid-1960s all industry interest was on color and colorcasting, which was hailed as yet another Sarnoff triumph, though not as spectacular as radio and monochrome television.

As it happened it was the last of these, for in the second half of the 1950s the General led RCA into uncharted territories, which resulted in a string of missteps, errors in judgment, and outright blunders.

9

The General Stumbles

THE NEWS CAME in a single paragraph buried in the inside pages of the business press, to be repeated in some of the weekly newsmagazines soon after. Few gave the matter much thought. In October 1951, Folsom announced that RCA would enter the air conditioner business in a small way. The corporation did not intend converting TV assembly lines to this product. Nor would it erect additional factories. The sets would be manufactured for RCA by Fedders-Quigan, one of the largest independents in the industry. Initially they would be the familiar Fedders units, but in time they would be made to RCA's specifications.

What prompted RCA to make this move? Ever since the end of the war Sarnoff had been talking about electronic air conditioners. But this product never appeared. Instead, RCA was about to enter a new product area with conventional offerings. In making the announcement Folsom spoke of giving dealers an opportunity to "round out" their lines by adding air conditioners to radios, television sets, and phonographs, hinting that if it worked out more would follow—refrigerators, ranges, washing machines, the gamut of "white goods."

The idea of expansion into related areas without major capital investment was alluring. By then RCA had become the most important supplier of television sets to Sears, Roebuck, sold under that retailer's Silvertone brand name, while Fedders supplied Sears with air conditioners. Why not acquire Fedders and other, similar, suppliers? Risks would be minimized with an assured market such as Sears, and given this base a new entity might compete favorably with the established leaders.

Nothing came of discussions with Fedders, but during the next three years RCA approached several companies regarding possible mergers and acquisitions. One of these was Whirlpool, which provided washing machines and dryers to Sears to be sold as Kenmores, and another was Seeger-Sunbeam, whose refrigerators were offered as Coldspots. The company approached both, and discussions took place on-and-off in 1952–1954.

An agreement was finally worked out in 1955, under which RCA transferred its kitchen range and air conditioner operations plus $15.7 million in cash to a merged operation comprised of these plus the two other companies' white goods businesses. Out of this came a new Whirlpool Corp., a $280 million firm which had *pro forma* earnings of $32.7 million, with RCA owning 20 percent of the stock.

Since Whirlpool was in good financial shape at the time, RCA was really trading funds plus other assets claimed to be worth $21.6 million for equity worth approximately twice that amount. It was the kind of arrangement at which Sarnoff excelled; the dividends from Whirlpool soon made up the cash outlay, and RCA received consumer exposure, since the white goods sold through retailers other than Sears were labeled "RCA Whirlpool."

Later on this would be seen as a move toward transforming RCA from an electronics-entertainment company into a conglomerate, but it wasn't the intention at the time. Rather, the General was attempting to expand into a related area, and he did so not by acquisition but participation, which spared management involvement and capital infusions.

By then RCA had made its initial entry into electronic data processing, which was more closely related to its core operations.

It wasn't done quietly this time, but with a great deal of ballyhoo, complete with full-page ads in the more important newspapers. Prospects were far more exciting than with air conditioners, and the business itself was as glamorous as television. But as it turned out Sarnoff's foray into computers, which pitted him against International Business Machines CEO Thomas Watson, Jr., must be considered one of the major business blunders of all time. It almost destroyed RCA and certainly tarnished Sarnoff's reputation.

When it was all over many claimed that defeat was inevitable, but Sarnoff's defenders saw this as another case of second-guessing and 20-20 hindsight vision. The latter view is more plausible. The company had many assets in the struggle against IBM. Indeed, during the mid-1960s Watson considered RCA a greater threat to IBM's hegemony in data processing than such well-entrenched firms as Sperry Rand's Univac division. However, the venture was risky from the first.

Start by considering the record of past achievements. In the struggles for the radio market in the 1920s RCA had many advantages, such as patents, the support of two large and powerful parents, and early entry with Radiolas. Yet it soon gave ground to a number of companies, among them Grigsby-Grunow, Atwater Kent, and later on, Philco, Zenith, Magnavox, Motorola, and Crosley. Again, RCA had the first network—two of them, in fact—but gradually lost market share to CBS and to a lesser degree, ABC. Further,

RCA's pioneering work with monochrome television gave it a large lead in that market, but then it slipped, as Zenith, DuMont, GE, and many others gained ground. It would happen the same way with color television. Pioneering paid for RCA, but not as much as might have been expected.

If the company couldn't dominate in areas it knew best and had the most experience, how could it expect to perform well in one in which it had no direct knowledge, after starting late, against a firm that even then was deemed one of the toughest and most astute in the world?

But RCA hardly was a novice in computers and in fact, through its electronics work for the military, could claim to have been in the field since its earliest days. As Arthur Maclarney, the young manager of the defense operations who soon would take over in computers remarked, "In defense work, wherever you look you find a computer."

During World War II Jan Rajchman, an RCA scientist, developed a device to aim large guns automatically, which while not called a computer was just that. Toward the end of the war the RCA laboratories began work to create an analog computer for the Navy known as the Typhoon. It wasn't completed until after the fighting had ended and was delivered in 1947.

By then RCA had become one of the several companies working under government contracts on computers, all of which were designed for military purposes. Several defense firms, among them Bendix, Lockheed, North American Aviation, Raytheon, and General Dynamics, were entering the computer field. That RCA, with more expertise than any of them, should also do so, was not surprising. As Sarnoff put it in 1962, "while fully aware of the entrenched and powerful nature of the competition, we were determined to establish a foothold in this business that is fundamentally electronic in character and therefore closely related to our commercial and military activities."

Generally considered the first large electronic digital computer, ENIAC was created late in World War II with RCA participation, and its creators, J. Presper Eckert and John Mauchly, later observed it could not have been completed without RCA's input in creating ultra-reliable vacuum tubes. Sarnoff had shown a keen interest in that project, and for a while it seemed he might be willing to fund Eckert and Mauchly's efforts after the war, but this didn't transpire.

Sarnoff realized that RCA might play an important role in computers by supplying producers with vacuum tubes and, later on, transistors. The corporation was by far the leading manufacturer of the older products and was rapidly asserting itself in transistors, so that by 1963 it claimed to be "the leading domestic supplier of solid-state semiconductor devices for consumer products," making strong inroads into the computer field in this way.

The company also gained a lead position in a related area, core memories, which differentiated computers from calculators. In 1953 an RCA publication announced, "Recently ferrite materials have been developed which are suitable for use as memory elements for large-scale electronic computers. A memory unit capable of storing ten thousand bits of information has been developed by RCA."

At that time Sarnoff might have elected to take a safer path than attempting to go against Remington Rand and IBM, by funding additional research into electronics, creating at RCA the equivalent of another Texas Instruments, and becoming an important source of components for IBM and other computer makers. It wasn't so farfetched an idea; with far less in the way of resources, Motorola would evolve from a manufacturer of radios and TVs into one of the three or four largest electronic suppliers in the nation. Such an approach wasn't appealing to Sarnoff, who was ever on the prowl for major new projects. Computers could provide him with just such an outlet for his energies.

There would be explorations and additional research, as was in the Sarnoff tradition. In the same tradition was a reluctance to come to market until the situation was ripe—some might say overripe. For by the time RCA was finally prepared to move, Remington Rand and IBM had already carved up the market between them. Even so, RCA might have leaped to third place and remained there had Sarnoff been willing to divert energies from television. That he didn't do so is understandable, given RCA's history, interests, and the relative positions of the two products (television seemed much more promising in 1950).

The company started research on commercial computers in 1950, though in a very small way, and then as an adjunct to its more lucrative work in the military sphere. The rationale at the time was provided by Loren Jones III, an RCA engineer with a mandate to uncover new opportunities for the corporation's technological capabilities. Jones believed computers would become a major product and would attract two kinds of producers: business machine manufacturers hoping to expand their lines and technologically oriented firms seeking outlets for their expertise. In his view IBM was in the former category, along with National Cash Register and Burroughs, while RCA was in the latter. Considering the complexities of the technology, thought Jones, the advantage would go to those firms whose strong suit was technology.

Given RCA's other commitments, any corporate thrust into the computer market would have to be like that into white goods: on the cheap. This meant obtaining military contracts and conducting research at government expense. From the vantage point of the early 1950s, Jones's analysis of the forthcoming industry shape seemed plausible. It seemed that the civilian market would be dominated by IBM, Univac, General Electric, National Cash Register, and Burroughs, while RCA would compete in the military market against Raytheon, Northrop, Lockheed, General Dynamics, and many smaller entities.

Jones convinced the General. "If I approve of this project and submit it to the board, it will be because of the concept that computers will be the next 'estate' in electronics," he told Jones, who wanted $10.6 million to get things started. As was customary, the board agreed, and Jones got his funding.

Of paramount importance in this period was the SAGE (Semi-Automatic Ground Environment) program, geared toward producing a system that could provide an early warning of any Soviet attack. Begun in 1945 at the Massachusetts Institute of Technology, by 1952 it was ready for the design stage. Along with Burroughs, IBM, Remington Rand, and Sylvania, RCA was one of the finalists in the competition. Ultimately, IBM was selected and in this way was able to leap to a lead in the field, since a good deal of the military work had civilian applications.

The RCA program continued, with his scientists convincing Sarnoff that IBM's SAGE computers would be old-fashioned, since they were to be based upon vacuum tubes. The future, they said, rested with the transistor, and with the exception of AT&T's Western Electric, no firm had greater expertise than RCA in this area. In 1952 the firm reported that a "substantial part of [its] Laboratories Division activity . . . was devoted to research on classified Government projects in such fields as electronic computers."

During the next year and a half, while color television remained the central concern at RCA laboratories, several teams worked to convert military expertise in computers to civilian uses, but it wasn't a high priority item. Recall that 1954 was also the first important year for color television, and Sarnoff knew that RCA's future depended upon the reception of this product.

Now consider the nature of the data processing industry. In 1954 IBM's revenues were $461 million, with only a very small part of that derived from computers. In 1954 Whirlpool's revenues came to $282 million, and RCA's, $938 million. Many believed data processing had a bright future, but would it ever be as important as washing machines, electric ranges, refrigerators, dishwashers, and dryers? Or color TV? Not likely. Little wonder, then, that computers occupied a decidedly secondary position in RCA's view of things.

Such was the situation the following year when RCA announced its BIZMAC computer, which was supposed to establish the company in the field and was unveiled in 1956.

BIZMAC was based upon RCA's earlier military-oriented computers, which is to say it was powered by vacuum tubes, not transistors, and so was not the great leap forward many within the industry had expected from the company. Initially advertised to sell at $4 million, it had a smaller memory system than equivalent IBMs and Univacs, and this too was disappointing. Moreover, RCA claimed that BIZMAC was a military computer, which the Army would use for "stock control of replacement parts for military combat and transport vehicles." It would also be used to "provide speedy and accurate information on inventories, to determine in minutes the current supply of any item at any ordnance depot in the nation, and to compute forecasts of future requirements."

The name indicated otherwise. At a time when computers were known more by acronyms than numbers (ATLAS, MIDAC, MANIAC, JOHNIAC, FLAC, ILLIAC, and of course UNIVAC), RCA had opted for BIZMAC. Why? The name BIZMAC clearly stood for Business Machine, but Sarnoff and others at RCA had indicated no intention of entering the business field. Yet a computer used to keep track of military stores might easily do as much for civilian inventories. Did this, combined with the name, mean RCA was about to challenge IBM and Univac?

This was of no little importance, especially for IBM. Thomas Watson, Sr., stepped down in favor of his son in May 1956. Tom Watson, Jr., whose reputation had been erected on the computer program, knew of RCA's resources, but gave little thought to any challenge from that direction mostly because of conversations he had held with Sarnoff.

These concerned John Burns, whose reputation continued to grow in the 1950s, largely owing to his work at RCA. Watson wanted to take him on as a consultant for IBM but would do so only if there was no conflict of interest. If BIZMAC meant that RCA intended to compete with IBM, Watson certainly would not retain Burns's services, for this would give him not only valuable insights into IBM's operations but also knowledge of its plans. Sarnoff assured Watson that RCA had no intention of entering the commercial computer field. Therefore IBM approached Burns with an offer to become one of its consultants.

At the time IBM was attempting to restructure itself in order to deal better with the rapid growth attending the acceptance of computers. During the late spring of 1956 Watson, his chief lieutenants, more than one hundred managers, and Burns met in Williamsburg, Virginia, to plan strategies. Watson was particularly impressed by Burns. "We had a superb sales organization," Watson later said, the credit for which belonged to his father, "but we lacked expert management organization in almost everything else." Clearly this would have to be rectified, and so it was. "We went in a monolith, and we emerged three days later as a modern, reasonably decentralized organization, with divisions with profit responsibility and clear lines of authority."

Hyperbole, perhaps, but Watson was convinced this conference was one of the company's more important turning points, and he credited Burns with having played a key role at it. Had he so desired, the consultant might have had an important position at IBM. But the relatively young Watson was firmly entrenched there, and Burns wanted a shot at a top spot; so he remained at Booz, Allen.

In March 1957 Sarnoff announced Burns's appointment as RCA's president and chief operating officer, with full authority, as Sarnoff put it, "to run the company." Soon after, he organized the Industrial Electronic Products division "to handle RCA's expanding activities related to manufacture of equipment for broadcasting, for industrial and scientific use and electronic data-processing, as well as marine and international communications services." This was to be Burns's cockpit in the battle for the EDP market.

Folsom was elevated to the vice chairmanship and also became chairman of the executive committee. Whether he felt bypassed or demoted cannot be known. At the time Folsom graciously remarked, "You have to stand aside for young men on the rise," and since he considered Burns a protégé, must have derived some pleasure from his success. Moreover at sixty-three he was preparing to step down anyway.

At the Annual Meeting the following year Sarnoff said that one of Burns's more important assignments would be to make the firm a major force in computers. "You have what I regard to be a most experienced, a most intellectual, a most competent administrator and coordinator of a complex technical business," was the way Sarnoff introduced the new president.

There was more to it than that. Color television was still losing money, there were difficulties in the electronic components area, and RCA had lost in the bidding for several government contracts. Except for NBC, which as before the war was now providing RCA with the largest share of its profits, the company seemed stagnant. In replacing Folsom with Burns, Sarnoff was acknowledging the need for fresh blood.

If Folsom took Burns's appointment with a degree of stoicism, Tom Watson was furious. Watson justifiably felt Sarnoff had deceived him, especially when Burns told reporters that RCA was dedicated to the "three Cs—computers, communications, and controls." The order didn't seem accidental.

Watson called a meeting of his sales managers and told them that while placements lost to any competitor might be tolerated (but not accepted) any replacements of IBM machines by RCAs would require careful explanation. In addition a warning went through the company: take great care when speaking with Booz, Allen consultants.

Burns understood what he had inherited. During the previous year RCA had a net profit of $40 million, enough to finance the color television campaign, expand transistor production, and take care of the corporation's other businesses, but insufficient to mount a major, protracted campaign in data processing. During the late 1940s, prior to committing important funds to color TV, RCA generally had operating profit margins of over 10 percent, and in 1950, when the payout for monochrome began, it came to over 16 percent. In 1956 the operating profit margin was 7.3 percent, and in 1957 it declined to 6.8 percent. The reason was clear: RCA was attempting too much for its resources to bear.

With senior capital of more than a third of a billion dollars RCA couldn't afford to borrow substantial amounts. Of paramount importance would be extracting important earnings from color television and streamlining operations further so as to cut back on costs. This done, RCA might double earnings, or even do better than that. Burns's future at RCA rested upon his abilities at squeezing larger profits from existing products and services and holding down costs in the new ones.

"We knew we had to get into the [data processing] field. And we had to come in during the growth period," Burns later reflected. "So we had this dual experience; color not having arrived yet, and data processing taking heavy investments and expenditures. But not getting into the market when it was beginning to move would have been seriously to restrict our own growth." The trouble with this approach was that RCA had to be daring in order to catch IBM but couldn't afford the kind of mistakes such risk-taking involved. There would be a constant struggle for available monies, and given RCA's tradition and interests, television and consumer electronics had a higher priority than data processing. As Arthur Beard, an RCA scientist-manager in the EDP program, later noted, there was a "greater total effort in television from the engineering point of view than there was in the computer." Another said, "The names tell it all. They were International Business Machines, and we were Radio Corporation of America. They were involved in the industry, knew their customers, and we were experts in producing and selling TVs. RCA trying to beat IBM in computers was like IBM attempting to get into the color TV business. The simple fact of the matter was that they were too smart to make such a move and we weren't."

Clearly, IBM was in fighting trim, with Watson willing to commit all of its resources to data processing, and it also had the financial reserves and earning power for the task. Operating profit margin was consistently in the 20-percent range; in 1956 it reported revenues of $734.3 million, but on that earned $68.8 million, which is to say that on 43-percent lower revenues than RCA it earned 45-percent more income. The reason was known throughout the industry, and certainly to Burns: IBM traditionally leased its machines, generating a strong cash flow, and so was able not only to fund a substantial research and development program but also to realize larger net profits than would have been the case with outright sales.

Considering the financial aspect alone, it should have seemed clear to all involved that attempts by any firm except AT&T and GE to compete in data processing against IBM would be extremely difficult. One approach for RCA might have been an alliance or merger with another computer manufacturer in the same situation, and several were considered.

The most promising of these was a proposed partnership with Burroughs. Burroughs President John Coleman was interested, and discussions with

Sarnoff and Burns appeared fruitful. The RCA board approved the idea of a joint venture, and Coleman seemed capable of swaying his board to the idea. Then he died suddenly, and the idea with him. What might have turned out to be the best possible challenger to IBM (and the most sensible method for RCA to enter the field) died with him. So RCA had to go it alone.

To complicate matters, Burns was unhappy with the BIZMAC; it was after all a military machine with modifications and not one designed for the commercial market. So in 1958 RCA's scientists started work on another series of computers, which were to be completely transistorized, this not only to take advantage of RCA's expertise in this area but also to provide customers with a machine superior to anything the competition might offer. These were done to government specifications—once again RCA would create a military product with civilian applications—but this time perceived flaws in BIZMAC would be corrected.

The strategy was both simple and cost effective. The company would offer a complete family of computers and so compete with IBM down the line. "We were seeking to get in on a broad-range basis, to expand in all directions so that whenever business opportunities opened up, RCA would be squarely in the middle of it all," recalled an RCA executive in the early 1970s. "We thought we could set off a big explosion, and blow a hole in the market, and then walk in."

But there was no blitz; RCA proceeded in a cautious fashion. Except for the substitution of transistors for vacuum tubes the company wouldn't attempt to be original. What Burns was seeking were machines that could perform the same functions as their IBM equivalents but cost less and be more reliable. This meant not only that he intended to utilize predatory pricing but that he would be willing to forgo profits in order to obtain market share.

To carry out this mission Burns went into the market for talent, and as might have been expected, hired a number of salesmen and scientists from IBM, which increased Watson's ire. In his view Burns was trading on knowledge gained while a consultant. Watson soon realized Burns was attempting to do nothing less than recreate the RCA data processing operation in the image of IBM.

In 1958, RCA unveiled the first in its new family of computers (and the first of the second generation of machines as well), the 501. A few months later IBM announced its own second generation offerings, the 7000 series, which though more expensive were also more powerful and backed by the IBM reputation.

Unfortunately RCA was unable to provide reliable peripheral equipment; the printer was deemed inadequate by data processing managers. Aided by discounts, RCA's Electronic Data Processing Division claimed forty-one orders by late 1959, but these proved "soft." Indeed, prior to 1960, only three

501s were placed outside of RCA itself, and one of these, to New York Life, racked up unacceptable downtime.

By then the flaws in the peripherals had become obvious. Another RCA product, the RACE random access storage unit, was a technological disaster. The best the EDP Division could report in late 1959 was that it was just "beginning to overcome the major obstacle that plagued us previously; namely, doubts as to RCA's seriousness in the EDP business."

Conditions improved soon after, as ninety-one additional 501s were placed on lease in the next two years, enabling Burns to claim that it was second only to the IBM 7070 in its category. All of this had been achieved at a cost; RCA priced the 501s too low to show a profit. "With two or three more such victories we would have been out of business," commented one RCA engineer.

Still, RCA's earnings were rising now that R & D costs for color television had declined somewhat and receiver sales were picking up. The company might have used some of its higher earnings to beef up the computer operations, especially in the research area, but Sarnoff held back, apparently considering a cleaner balance sheet more important than a larger, broader assault in data processing. In 1959 he called in some of the debt, and the following year an issue of convertible debentures was transformed into common shares, this lowering the debt from $335.9 million to $242.1 million. Given higher earnings and the lower debt-to-equity ratio, RCA might have floated additional debt and so obtained needed financing for computers, but he decided against it. The payoff from computers seemed near, as it would for the next dozen years.

Hopes were now vested in two new machines, the 301 and 601. The former was a small system, the latter a large one that might be used for scientific as well as business purposes. They were announced with great fanfare in 1960. The 301 proved a success, though there were the familiar problems with peripheral equipment, this time the disc files and the printers.

Through the 301 RCA entered the foreign market, for three European companies, Compagnie des Machines Bull (France), International Computers & Tabulators (United Kingdom), and Hitachi (Japan) showed interest in it, and between them they eventually would take over 150 machines. By 1962 RCA was turning out 301s on a six-day-a-week basis and claiming to be leasing them at a rate of $60 million worth a year. Success seemed near; an RCA manager predicted losses would be halved in 1963, and the EDP operations would start showing significant profits the following year, what he called "the end of the rainbow."

The 601 changed all this. Not only was it a flop, but one so large as to almost finish RCA as a factor in the industry.

The 601s were delivered later than promised; the first of the line, which went to Southern Railroad, was contracted for October 1961 but wasn't ready a year later. When RCA asked for another extension, Southern canceled and leased an equivalent IBM computer. Other orders were also wiped from the book. There were large cost overruns, which made the 601 a certain loser even before completion, and the wiring proved deficient. There were constant breakdowns. Edwin McCollister, a vice president at the EDP Division, later recalled that the 601 "cost [RCA] money, from which we received no worthwhile return, both from the manufacturer and the development expense, which was quite substantial, and it also lost us time of engineering people because, while they were working on that product, trying to salvage it within the limits that had been established, they were unable to put their efforts into the design of products that might have had a more important business future."

McCollister went on to say that the 601 embarrassed everyone at the Division and headquarters, and "hurt RCA's reputation very badly, because we placed great public emphasis upon the 601 as a product and its capabilities, and it hurt us with several important customers." He ordered a temporary pause in the sales program; why offer machines that couldn't be delivered? "One unfortunate result [of this] was that skepticism about RCA's intentions developed in the marketplace." Indeed, so severe was the reaction that McCollister said "the company began to look for a way out of the program."

The 601 was finally discarded in 1962; only five of the machines were produced, and of these four were delivered.

This debacle meant the end for John Burns. In December 1961 he stepped down as president and chief operating officer, saying he was doing so for "personal reasons" but would remain as a consultant. Folsom retired at almost the same time, but remained on the board. Five years earlier the General had told the stockholders that "the team is Burns, Folsom, and Sarnoff, and if we can't deliver the goods, get rid of us; don't blame anyone else." Burns and Folsom were gone, but to no one's great surprise, Sarnoff remained.

For his new president Sarnoff selected Elmer Engstrom; he was replacing a management expert with a technician. More important, however, was the fact that in the face of mounting costs ($100 million by 1962) Sarnoff decided to take a more active role himself. Engstrom, who had been at RCA for more than thirty years and was sixty-one years old at the time, was a mild-mannered, soft-spoken, cautious scientist with little in the way of large-scale management experience. When Burns had been elevated to the presidency Engstrom went from executive vice president for research and development to executive vice president, this making him first among equals at that level. Few thought much of it at the time; it appeared a reward of sorts, and recognition of the importance of computer research for the company's future.

Burns had been the kind of person one might want to mount an aggressive campaign of expansion; Engstrom would be willing to take whatever orders Sarnoff gave and carry them out to the best of his abilities. Finally, had Burns succeeded he would have had to be considered for the CEO post, an ambition Engstrom never entertained. So if computers failed, the blame would go to Burns (and to David Sarnoff for having taken him into the firm in the first place). Success—and Sarnoff fully expected it by mid-decade—would be his alone, and this in hand, he could retire in favor of his son.

Yet there was no compelling reason for him to remain in the field. Had RCA decided to ease its way out of computers at that time the damage might not have been too severe. Had the firm's finances been in worse shape Sarnoff might have been obliged to do just that. But color television was paying off nicely. In 1962 RCA reported record profits of $51.5 million, and given the demand for color sets and higher time charges at NBC, it appeared this would continue for quite a while, in what appeared a replay of the radio and monochrome television experiences. The following year's revenues and earnings were even better, the figures being $1.8 billion and $66 million respectively, while the operating profit margin of 7.6 percent was the best showing in more than a decade. The price of the common stock started to rise in mid-year, when it hit a post-1929 high, attributed not only to the success of color television but to the glamour of computers. Under these circumstances, RCA remained in the game.

All of this was achieved at a price. Ever more interested in technology than marketing, Sarnoff did not capitalize upon RCA's long lead in color television as he might have done. He cut back R & D while keeping prices high, and in addition he licensed patents freely, especially to the Japanese. The company's share of the color market declined steadily; what might have been RCA's preserve for decades became a battlefield between it and more aggressive American (and eventually Japanese) firms shortly thereafter.

In the early 1960s Sarnoff believed the color TV campaign had ended, and was shifting resources to the next struggle—electronic data processing. It was then that RCA started to lose its leadership position in television. William Webster, an executive and engineer who worked on both projects, later said, "We shot a whole generation of research and engineering on computers and starved the real cash cow—color television—to do it."

In a letter to stockholders in early 1964 Sarnoff noted the computer-related losses but claimed that deficits in this area would be halved that year and halved again in 1965, after which profits would be generated. Later that year he conceded that "our frontal attempt was obviously overambitious. We had gotten into more turbulent water than we could navigate. Trying to compete all along the line was a kind of overextension of inventory which had to be disposed of at some point. We also ran into the difficulty of any overambitious attempt—the danger that you may neglect the established businesses. So we began a policy and program of selectivity—the rifle instead of the shotgun."

From this one might have assumed he meant cut back on the scope of the EDP program and devote more attention and funds to RCA's more traditional businesses—television, broadcasting, and government work. To those who knew the industry it seemed a sensible enough policy considering IBM's ambitious 360 program. But from what happened next it would appear Sarnoff had no intention of retreating. Instead, he formed additional partnerships with several of his foreign computer contacts—The United Kingdom's International Computers and Tabulators, France's Compagnie des Machines Bull, and Japan's Hitachi—the idea being that RCA would combat IBM overseas in a union with native corporations that presumably knew the markets and might also obtain government assistance.

So RCA remained in the race, with Sarnoff talking grandly of becoming the third largest factor within the foreseeable future. Heavy discounting remained the only path to sales, which meant the probability of ever turning a profit was becoming slimmer all the time. Still, the General's ego was involved as well as the future of the corporation. He was intent on leaving the scene a winner; the man who participated in D-Day could do no less.

The company replaced the 601 with the 3301, which had been planned as a "hold-the-line" machine to keep customers happy until the next main generation was ready. Much to Sarnoff's delight the machine performed well, and though orders were slow in coming it soon became evident that RCA finally had managed to turn out a large machine that might be compared with the IBM, Univac, and other offerings. Hardly a threat to the leaders, but at least RCA remained in the game.

In 1964 IBM announced its 360 program. This was a major undertaking dwarfing anything else ever done in the industry. The 360s not only would use integrated circuits (making the model one of the first of the third generation computers) but would run on new programs incompatible with those utilized by the 7000s and earlier machines, thus making those obsolete. It was a daring move, which if successful would seal its position as industry leader, while failure could cripple IBM to the point of making it an also-ran.

This action on the part of IBM obliged all the other major mainframe manufacturers to respond with third generation machines of their own. Thus, RCA's answer was to lower prices on the 301s and 3301s and rush new machines to completion. The price cuts brought in additional orders, most for outright sales rather than leases, so that in 1964 the EDS Division reported its first operating profit on revenues of more than $100 million. To its earlier overseas partners RCA added the German firm of Siemens & Halske, claiming that "these agreements are expected to develop a multi-million dollar business for RCA."

There now was hope at headquarters, not only because of the black ink on the ledgers but also because Sarnoff and Engstrom turned to yet another strategy, which as it turned out wasn't really new, but instead was akin to the

LIBERATOR program developed by Honeywell for use with its 200 series computers. This program made the computers almost compatible with the popular IBM 1401 mainframes, which is to say they could run some IBM software. Thus, by offering the 200s at lower prices to would-be IBM customers Honeywell might be able to improve sales—and so it did, setting the rest of the industry in a new direction. In effect, Honeywell was conceding a great deal of technological ground to IBM but in the process hoped to pick up many more placements.

It was with this in mind that RCA created its response to the 360s, which would be known as the Spectras. Even the name was an imitation of IBM's—the designation 360 referred to all points on the compass, or spectrum. Company spokesman Beard made no attempt to hide the fact that the Spectra was "aimed primarily at the IBM 360 series range of computers." The machines were generally well-designed and bug-proof, an indication that the 3301 experience had been no fluke.

Moreover the lease and sales terms were eminently satisfactory; RCA claimed a 15–20-percent price/performance advantage. Engstrom initiated what he called the Flexible Accrued Equity Plan (really a sales-lease arrangement) under which a customer might lease a Spectra for six years at rates competitive with those of similar 360s and take possession of the machine at the end of the period. This would not only prove attractive to customers but also provide RCA with substantial tax savings owing to depreciation. In addition there were cut-rate service charges and other perquisites, all of which were proclaimed in full-page newspaper advertisements. "Being easy to switch to makes RCA the only logical alternative to IBM. Giving you features IBM doesn't have makes us a better alternative."

The strategy seemed to work, partly because of Spectra's features, but also because orders for the 360s came in so fast that IBM had to establish a waiting list, causing a number of customers to switch to RCA's mainframes. In 1964 RCA booked $10.9 million worth of new orders in terms of rental value, half of these from the 3301. The figure for the following year was $42 million, the leader now being the Spectra 70/45, and in 1966, $67 million in orders were booked, most for the Spectra series. This caused no little consternation at IBM, where C. E. Frizzell, president of the General Products Division, conceded that the Spectras offered more calculations per dollar than the equivalent 360s but told Watson his unit was "moving rapidly to meet this challenge and expect[ed] to respond effectively in the very near future."

Industry analysts wondered what would happen once IBM mounted its anticipated counterattack. After all, compatibility worked two ways; if IBM customers could switch easily to Spectra's, might not RCA's turn in their mainframes for IBMs if the terms were right?

No matter; the auguries were fine in 1965, when for the first time RCA's revenues topped the $2 billion mark and profits were over $100 million. The dividend was increased, and the price of RCA common went to a fraction under 50; seven years earlier, on an adjusted basis, it had sold for 8. Color television sales were strong, as for the first time consumers spent more money for these than for monochromes. NBC, which had record revenues and earnings, became an "all color network" that year, this in support of the manufacturing operation but also to realize larger advertising revenues. The company noted that some 5 million color sets were in American homes, but the potential market for replacements for monochromes was ten times that amount. The Japanese challenge was still barely on the horizon.

At the same time RCA seemed well entrenched in data processing. According to industry sources, it had only 2.9 percent of the market, which placed it in seventh position, well behind IBM (65.3 percent) and Univac (12.1 percent). Still, the General claimed the business had been profitable for the second year in a row.

Knowing a good exit moment when he saw one, Sarnoff, now aged 75, announced he would step down as CEO (but retain the chairmanship) the following year. Engstrom would remain as vice chairman and chairman of the executive committee and be elevated to chief executive officer. Bob Sarnoff would become RCA's new president, according to the company at Engstrom's recommendation, as a reward for the fine job he had done at NBC, where as expected he had succeeded Weaver as president in 1955. "Under Robert Sarnoff's direction," said Engstrom, "NBC enjoyed its most successful

---

SELECTED RCA STATISTICS, 1955–1965

figures in millions of dollars

Year	Revenues	Net Income	Senior Capital
1955	1,050.7	47.5	264.6
1956	1,121.1	40.0	340.1
1957	1,170.9	38.5	340.1
1958	1,170.7	30.9	340.1
1959	1,388.4	40.1	335.9
1960	1,486.2	35.1	242.1
1961	1,537.9	35.5	325.5
1962	1,742.7	51.5	345.3
1963	1,779.1	66.0	345.2
1964	1,797.0	82.5	274.6
1965	2,042.0	101.2	273.8

Source: *Moody's Handbook of Common Stocks,* 1967 ed.

RCA'S DISTRIBUTION OF BUSINESS, 1955–1965

figures in millions of dollars

Year	Manufacturing Commercial	Manufacturing Government	Broadcasting	Communications	Other
1955	558.3	228.6	246.2	20.8	1.4
1956	575.3	240.2	286.4	23.7	2.2
1957	588.6	267.0	292.2	26.0	2.4
1958	533.4	304.8	308.5	26.4	2.9
1959	568.4	470.4	323.3	30.4	3.1

	Products and Services (including broadcasting)	Government	Other
1960	934.7	551.7	8.4
1961	955.9	582.0	7.8
1962	1,128.0	614.8	9.3
1963	1,218.4	560.6	10.2

	Product Sales	Broadcasting and Communications	Other
1964	1,113.3	683.7	15.5
1965	1,284.9	757.1	15.1

Figures differ from totals owing to adjustments for intercompany transactions.
Source: *RCA Annual Reports,* 1941–1946.

years in terms of service, prestige, and profits. He demonstrated at NBC, as well as in many other important assignments for RCA, those qualities of business and administration judgment and leadership that make him thoroughly qualified to administer the operations of RCA."

That there was some truth in this was discounted within the corporation—but not within earshot of the General or Bob. In fact the network was doing well, but much of the credit within the firm was given to Robert Kintner, its president, who moved into Bob's vacant slot as NBC's chairman. As for the parent firm, it was clear to all that David would be watching over Bob's shoulder and offering guidance whether asked for or not, that Engstrom would continue to take his marching orders from the seventy-five-year-old patriarch. Engstrom might be a trusted associate and Bob his flesh and blood, but RCA was David Sarnoff's true child, and he wasn't going to permit others to direct it so long as he could function.

10

Bobby in Command

GATHERING HIS THOUGHTS after a long discourse dealing with the past quarter of a century at RCA, a veteran of that period groped for an explanation of the corporation's decline in the late 1960s and 1970s. Mention was made of the flawed EDP program, managerial slack, forays into alien territory, the Japanese Challenge, and simple bad luck.

Always he came back to origins of these difficulties in the last years of the David Sarnoff era and the first during which the oldest of his three sons, Bobby, ran the corporation as chairman, president, and CEO. "Maybe it would have been better if he was called Robert instead of Bob or Bobby," he considered before turning to other matters. "After all, no one at Rockefeller Plaza—not even Engstrom or Folsom—called the General 'Davey.'"

That was part of the trouble, but only a symptom of the deeper problem, that of a son inheriting his father's place in any enterprise, be it a neighborhood drugstore or a giant corporation. It is more vexing if the father was celebrated, had strong contacts with the organization, and refused to let go.

The General constantly interfered with his son to the point where the two men wouldn't speak with one another for weeks. He clung to power even after falling ill, refusing to step down as chairman until the end of 1969, when he became too weak to come to the office regularly. Undaunted, he would dispatch commands by telephone and messenger. David Sarnoff would die two years later, but even then Bob wasn't free since industry leaders and the press regularly compared him with his father.

His name indeed was a problem. But had it been Robert Smith he doubtless wouldn't have gone to the top at RCA, or perhaps anywhere else, and everyone (including him) knew it, or at least behaved as though this were so. "It is not always easy for the son to overcome all the roadblocks and difficulties that attach to such situations," David Sarnoff conceded in 1967 when asked about his son. "I am not weeping for him, because I think perhaps there is an advantage or two which might counterbalance these difficulties."

Bob Sarnoff was 48 years old in 1966. He bore a family resemblance to his father but where the General was thickset, with a piercing glance and sharp intelligence, Bob was slightly below average height, a trifle pudgy, often mercurial, and the best that was said of his abilities was that he was a good team player. Michael Dann, the CBS vice president for programming, noted that "Bobby was never the first to say something during a meeting and was often the last. At the end he would deliver a kind of precis of what had been accomplished, like a student doing a book report. He was the best listener I ever saw." "There's no doubt he's boss," one associate observed, "but most decisions are made by consensus." For good reason: not only did Bob want input to reinforce or occasionally challenge his ideas, but he wasn't overjoyed by the prospect of making major decisions on his own, especially while his father (often described as one of the best *speakers* of his time, and not particularly good at listening) was in the wings, and occasionally onstage as well.

A man who knew them both recalled how "years later, when Bobby had been in office for six or seven years and his father was in his grave, someone shouted something to the effect that 'Sarnoff was on his way in,' and I half-expected to see the General burst through the door."

Bob Sarnoff had an altogether respectable apprenticeship. After graduating from Phillips Academy and Harvard (B.A. 1939) he worked for RCA during the summer at the World's Fair and that fall entered Columbia Law School. He didn't relish the idea of practicing law or the alternative—entering RCA and working for his father—so after a year there he obtained a post in Washington at what later would become the Office of Strategic Services. Then Bob obtained a naval commission, was in several Pacific battles, and toward the end of World War II found himself in Washington engaged in liaison work.

Unsurprisingly, all of these posts involved broadcasting, radio, and communications; Bob Sarnoff's superiors simply assumed with that name he must be interested in these areas. As it happened he was, though not in the technical or managerial sides of the business as was David, but rather in public relations. Bob Sarnoff had developed into an engaging, friendly person, capable of understanding problems and possibilities and working out solutions swiftly. All he needed was a situation where he could demonstrate these talents, but there was no escaping that name.

He tried. After the war Bob obtained a post at Cowles Communications as assistant to Gardner Cowles, Jr., who owned and ran several newspapers and radio stations and who had an ego as big as the General's. Bob did well and in 1946 was transferred to *Look* magazine, a Cowles property that was challenging Time Inc.'s *Life* on the newsstands. Although he had a future at *Look* and enjoyed the work, Bob was constantly being lured by RCA, and in 1948 he arrived there to take up an assignment as account executive in the sales department. Before the end of the year he was named assistant to the national program director in the television department and clearly was on the fast track to the presidency. Every person Bob Sarnoff served under in those days knew he was training him to take his place.

Bob Sarnoff demonstrated talents, but so did others who weren't rising so rapidly. In 1953, when he headed the film department, *The New York Times* discussed his progress. The reporter thought he had "won recognition on his own" and no longer was merely "the old man's boy." This was typical; rarely did a story appear on him that directly or obliquely didn't bring up David Sarnoff.

Bob became executive vice president under Pat Weaver in 1953; as indicated, both men knew that when the time was ripe Weaver would move up or out and Bob would take over. This happened in 1955, when Weaver was elevated to the NBC chairmanship and the younger Sarnoff slipped into the presidency. In fact, however, Weaver had become a redundancy. He understood this when on arriving at his first board meeting in his new position, he found the General seated in the chairman's place at the head of the table. Weaver left soon after, and now Bob became chairman.

Bob Sarnoff carried a great deal of baggage into the executive suite, but this was the most burdensome.

The General hired Robert Kintner from ABC to help Bob, this taken as a vote of little confidence in his son. A tough taskmaster who had put in an apprenticeship in print journalism before switching to ABC in 1944, Kintner had gone from the news section to the presidency and along the way had shown a fine ability to make do with little in the way of resources. Now that he was chief operating officer of one of the two major networks, Kintner was expected to attempt to put into play some of the ideas he had dreamed about but couldn't afford at ABC. Which is to say that most in the industry thought the strong, blunt Kintner would really run the show.

As it turned out the two men, called the "Bob and Bob Show" at headquarters, worked well together, sufficiently so for Bob Sarnoff to begin emerging from the General's shadow. He was named to the RCA board (Weaver had not been so honored when he was NBC chairman), in preparation for the next move, which, as noted, came in 1966, when he succeeded to the presidency at RCA—with David there to supervise.

"One of my problems was convincing people outside NBC that I was running things on my own," Bob later remarked. "I guess Tom Watson went through the same thing."

This really wasn't so, largely because of the differences between Tom Watson, Sr., and the IBM he had fashioned and David Sarnoff and RCA. Although never one for self-depreciation, Watson always took care to subordinate himself to the needs of the firm while Sarnoff often looked upon RCA as an extension of himself. Also, unlike Watson, the General refused to take others into his confidence, was loath to share power, as has been seen in the cases of Folsom and Engstrom, and even his own son. Instead, he fashioned a system of cronyism, with favorites shuttled in and out of power with some regularity, that created an atmosphere of corporate paranoia.

Because of this managers tended to be secretive and distrustful of others within the organization. By the 1950s there were many individual fiefdoms, groups insulated against others in the organization, each with its different view of the business and its own culture. What Sarnoff had done was to create an empire of disparate parts with himself as emperor.

While in command David Sarnoff had kept the factions in check, but now, with a weaker leader, they surfaced. In his time no one but the General spoke for RCA; even Harbord remained in the background. Reporters knew that if any pronouncement on corporate policy was needed they would get it from him. But in the late 1960s, those same reporters had dozens of sources within the company, many in the executive suites, always prepared to offer an opinion (especially when it was self-serving) if promised anonymity. Administration by leak began then; a well-placed rumor could cripple a career and even cause changes in corporate policy.

There is a general view that RCA prospered under David Sarnoff's aegis because he kept the company on track, going from radio to monochrome TV to color, that had he been younger he might even have carried off the venture into data processing. "[David] Sarnoff had a plan for RCA, but it was in his head," said board member Andrew Sigler in 1981. "When he died the plan died." It is worth noting that Sigler had not really known David Sarnoff, but probably was repeating what had by then become part of the legend he had played a major role in fashioning.

According to this version, in attempting to achieve greatness on his own, Bob took RCA into a variety of enterprises having little or nothing to do with communications and electronics, transforming the once-healthy high technology enterprise into a conglomerate, which set the stage for its decline. That Bob did acquire a variety of nonrelated companies was certainly true, but the path to conglomeratization was blazed by the General; even here Bob comes off as a follower, and not an originator.

We have seen how David Sarnoff always had an eye toward expansion through acquisition. In the 1920s he had participated in the establishment of RKO and had purchased Victor; in addition the creation of NBC had been made possible by acquiring properties from others. All of this was familiar horizontal integration; the pieces all fit, as David Sarnoff tried to create an entertainment giant.

After the war he brought RCA into the home appliance business through participation in Whirlpool. That company did well, with revenue and profits rising from $368 million and $13.8 million in 1956 to $465.3 million and $18.6 million in 1962. But this was hardly a glamorous or rapidly growing business, and, while RCA profited from its participation, Sarnoff believed the funds invested in Whirlpool could be better used elsewhere. So in 1962 he began selling off the RCA interest, to the point where it had only a token position by the end of 1964. (As it turned out it was a bad moment to sell. Whirlpool's common stock, which went for around $15 a share when RCA disposed of close to a million shares in late 1962, started to climb the following year, and in 1966, when RCA owned only 25,000 shares, it sold for over $50.)

At the time it seemed that RCA had tested the waters of diversification by participation, found them not particularly to its liking, and decided to stick to its traditional business. Still, there were links between Whirlpool's business and RCA's, in that both manufactured consumer durables and each was involved with electricity and employed the newer electronic technologies. The same could not be said for the General's next foray into nontraditional areas, the acquisition of the publishing firm of Random House. With this, RCA took the first clear step toward conglomeratization.

Publishing was considered a glamour industry in the early 1960s, when shares of publicly owned companies in the field were selling at price/earnings multiples usually reserved for computer and drug stocks. Book sales increased by more than 150 percent in the 1950s, this ascribed to the baby-boom and a more creative approach to marketing. In 1965 Americans spent a record $2.5 billion on books of all kinds, from paperbacks to texts, and it appeared new records would be established regularly thereafter.

Such conglomerates as ITT, Litton, and Gulf + Western had already acquired publishers or were in the process of doing so, while old-line houses like Macmillan and McGraw-Hill were conglomeratizing themselves. Industry analysts spoke airily of publishing being transformed into "information gathering and distribution" concerns, the backlog of books serving as data banks with some connection with computers likely in the future. Of course, books had long been wedded to entertainment, their contents serving as raw material for motion pictures. Publishers saw no barrier to getting even closer to this side of the business, television in particular.

The assets of most companies are easy enough to analyze. Not so publishers, for their most important qualities can't be located on a balance sheet. These include reputation, the value of the copyrights, the backlist, authors under contract, and most important, the talents of leading editors. So it might be that a publisher whose net worth was only three or four million dollars might be sold for twenty or thirty times that amount, the understanding being that valuable talent would come into the acquiring company.

All of which might have led RCA into considering the purchase of a publisher involved with scientific subjects (Sarnoff was known to be considering several of these, the most-often mentioned being the American Book Company, a major factor in the textbook market) or one specializing in the kind of popular novels that might easily be transferred to the television. In the end, RCA bought Random House. It wasn't surprising considering Sarnoff's values and temperament. The General put it this way in the 1966 Annual Report: "A change has become increasingly evident in the character of the electronics industry—an advance from its initial concern with communications and entertainment to the role of a basic industry vital to the technological progress of virtually every other industrial activity." Such as book publishing.

Random House was at the same time an exciting and innovative publisher and strong commercial operation, much of this due to the shrewdness of its president, Bennett Cerf, who by virtue of his appearances as a regular panelist on the popular television quiz program "What's My Line?" (which was broadcast on CBS) was perhaps the most famous book publisher America has ever produced. In fact, he was better known and more recognizable than most of the authors in the Random House stable.

That Cerf was a capable publisher and proficient businessman was overshadowed by this celebrity. Even before "What's My Line?" he had been a familiar figure at better-known watering holes and resorts, knew the fashionable people and enjoyed their company (his first wife was motion picture actress Sylvia Sydney), and was a fine and acknowledged raconteur.

Random House was located in a landmark building at 457 Madison Avenue (which it shared with the Roman Catholic Archdiocese of New York) better known as the Villard Houses, designed by architect Stanford White, which had been used as headquarters for the Free French during World War II, and was purchased from Joseph Kennedy through the intercession of the Church—which wanted the publisher as its neighbor.

Random House would not complement any existing RCA operation, not even broadcasting by providing story ideas of the lighter sort. That firm published serious fiction and nonfiction by such as James Joyce, William Faulkner, W. H. Auden, John O'Hara, and Robert Penn Warren, whose works were hardly the kind to have broad appeal on commercial television. Moreover, in 1960 Random House had merged with Alfred A. Knopf, Inc., headed by an individual whose reputation within the industry was greater perhaps than Cerf's was outside of it. Knopf published Thomas Mann, Jean-Paul Sartre, John Hersey, and John Updike. Strange company for a TV operation, but not so if one considers that a union with Random House would burnish the RCA image. In the parlance of the time, it was a class act.

Cerf recognized this. Already a wealthy man, he had no strong personal desire for being acquired, but the gyrations of Random House common gave him pause. The company had gone public in 1959 at $11.25 per share and, in the bull market of the time, rose to over $45. After a 4-3 stock split it was listed on the New York Stock Exchange in 1961, trading at $32.25 (or $43 on an adjusted basis) the first day. The stock then collapsed as the publishing boom waned, declining to $8 the following year. There was a recovery afterward, but in 1965 Random House common was selling for around $15, far below that earlier high.

Believing that he might get a better price for the company then than in the future, Cerf was willing to sell. He let the word out and soon had a few nibbles, from such as Time Inc. and other large firms. Always something was wrong, if not the price the personalities involved, or fear of antitrust prosecution.

In late 1966 Cerf was contacted regarding a takeover by RCA by André Meyer, the senior partner at the investment banking firm of Lazard Freres, at the time deemed one of the three or four most influential financiers in the United States. Meyer had known the General for decades and in addition was a member of the RCA board. Lazard was one of RCA's two investment bankers, the other being Lehman Brothers.

Cerf cooperated, and a courtship began that culminated in an offer of one-half share of RCA for each share of Random House, this being around $19 per share in stock. Negotiations followed, with RCA upping the bid a trifle, and Cerf holding out for more.

Now the General—no longer the CEO, but still clearly in charge—took over. After some heated discussions it appeared neither man would budge. According to Cerf, Sarnoff glowered and said, "You may not realize it, Bennett, but you are dealing with a very arrogant and egotistical man," to which Cerf replied, "General, I'm just as arrogant and egotistical as you are."

After two more weeks the deal was completed on Cerf's terms. The price to RCA was $40 million in stock, for a firm whose net assets were less than $10 million. As noted, this wasn't unusual for publishing firms. Besides, the price was paid in stock, the terms being 0.62 shares of RCA for each share of Random House. As one RCA executive said, "we gave them our overpriced stock for their overpriced stock, so really it wasn't a bad deal." The publishing company became part of RCA on May 19, 1966, with Cerf taking a place on the parent firm's board.

Random House wasn't significant in RCA total operations. It didn't require heavy capital expenditures and never provided more than a small fraction of the corporation's business; in 1966 the publisher accounted for around $30 million of RCA's better than $2 billion in revenues. Its importance was in the symbolism rather than any financial impact. Late in his business life the General indulged his whims. Random House was one of them.

In early 1967 NBC announced the purchase of Arnold Palmer Enterprises. Named after the famous golfer, the firm turned out golfing gear and a line of sports clothes. It was a small deal, hardly noticed during a period when much larger takeovers were being announced on a weekly basis. "Perhaps someone at the network thought it would be a good idea to have Palmer on board in some capacity," thought one executive years later, "or it might have been they wanted to play golf with him. Also, Arnold Palmer was a hell of a better symbol than Nipper the Dog for the 1960s."

Far more important was the acquisition of Hertz Corp. on May 11, 1967, for a bundle of RCA convertible and common shares worth more than $200 million. The nation's leading auto and truck renter, Hertz was more than ten times as large as Random House. In 1966 it reported earnings of $12 million on revenues of $330 million, having doubled in size in four years.

Bob Sarnoff received the credit for making this move, but the purchase would not have been made without André Meyer's persuasive efforts. He knew the elder Sarnoff had little interest in Hertz, and undertook to convince him that not only was it a well-managed company in a growing field available at a reasonable price, but its earnings could be used to finance other RCA programs, such as color TV and computers.

No one doubted that Hertz was a viable entity and valuable property. Also, it had an imaginative leadership, then in the process of expanding into other areas of leasing, from heavy construction equipment to hospital beds. Wall Street's analysts and those at Rockefeller Plaza who by now had learned the special language of conglomeratization spoke and wrote airily of the "synergy" between the two firms. RCA's major new commitment was to computers, most of whose users preferred leasing to outright purchase, and Hertz's experience in this line would be helpful.

The car rental business offered unusual opportunities. Typically Hertz would borrow money to purchase fleets of cars from manufacturers, at what amounted to wholesale prices, and would rent or lease them for periods ranging from days to years, and then offer them for sale at retail. In a period of rising car prices and relatively low interest rates, as was the case in 1967, Hertz might obtain almost as much from the sale of its used car as it had originally paid, and in some cases even more. What this meant was that almost all of the rental and lease revenues minus overhead and labor were pure profit.

But there were risks. Hertz had hundreds of millions of dollars tied up in those cars. It might suffer if public tastes changed abruptly in favor of larger or smaller vehicles, which could diminish the value of its holdings. The firm was always at the mercy of the business cycle, and interest rate changes could enhance or demolish its profits. Notwithstanding all of this, Hertz appeared a fine property in 1967, and the price Sarnoff paid for it was hardly out of line.

Meyer's influence at RCA grew as Sarnoff displayed an increasing interest in diversification. Some at headquarters claimed he had lured Sarnoff into becoming a version of ITT, another firm that utilized his services. "André always looked upon him [Bob Sarnoff] as the General's son," thought Felix Rohatyn, another Lazard partner involved with RCA. "Even when he was chief executive, I don't think André ever really took him seriously."

Meyer left the board in 1969 and was succeeded by Donald Petrie, a Lazard partner who before joining the firm had been involved in several ventures, the most important of which was being Hertz's CEO. Petrie took a direct interest in the management of the firm as well as acquisitions.

Now RCA had two businesses—computers and leasing—that required heavy capital investment (although Hertz financed its auto purchases independently). Still, at first glance the balance sheet seemed strong enough, even after the acquisition, and the company's performance was impressive. Revenues had risen 60 percent and earnings by 130 percent in the five years since 1962. The company's public relations officers noted that the return on investment at Hertz was a respectable 11.5 percent and that borrowing to finance the leasing of additional equipment that threw off that kind of return wasn't the least bit dangerous. This indeed was so. In addition the payoff from color television was such that NBC and RCA were generating a large cash flow, which might be fruitfully invested in Hertz.

Yet there were problems, some of a serious nature. In recent years RCA's financial position had been weakened, with accounts receivable and inventories much higher than they had been earlier in the decade and the cash position weaker.

SELECTED ITEMS FROM THE RCA BALANCE SHEET, 1962 AND 1966

figures in millions of dollars

ASSETS	1962	1966
Cash	108.3	107.9
Short Term Investments	108.9	28.9
Notes and Accounts Receivable	307.8	367.3
Inventories	187.4	372.1
Prepayments	31.5	89.3
Total Current Assets	743.9	965.5
LIABILITIES		
Accounts Payable	231.9	372.4
Accrued Taxes	57.0	69.8
Dividends payable	5.8	12.2
Total Current Liabilities	294.7	454.4

Source: RCA, *Annual Reports,* 1962, 1966.

The assets-to-liabilities ratio, which had been 2.5:1 in 1962, had fallen to 2.1:1 in 1966. In itself this was not dangerous, but the Hertz deal, and talk of other takeovers of companies that might require heavy capital commitments, was troublesome for this reason.

The General became ill soon after the beginning of the Hertz negotiations, and more responsibility fell to Bob, who was showing increased enthusiasm for takeovers. He told a reporter that "it is desirable to broaden our base," signaling that the pace of mergers might quicken. At headquarters there was talk regarding "the changing of the guard," and as David Sarnoff appeared at Rockefeller Center less frequently his son seemed more assured.

There was another sign: he was no longer referred to as "Bobby," but "Bob" and by those astute enough to realize the change had come, "Robert." Change was in the air.

The alterations at the company began in 1966, with a little noted but symbolic divestiture: Bob Sarnoff disposed of the radio marine operations, RCA's original business, and soon after abandoned the electronic microscope and medical electronics fields, two areas the General had entered because he was intrigued with the technologies involved. Bob Sarnoff didn't think they could become profitable.

In 1967 Bob Sarnoff redecorated his office, bringing in several fine pieces of the modern art his father disliked, and gradually most of the other executive suites followed. The General sensed he was witnessing the transformation of what had been his domain into one controlled by his 49-year-old son. He tried to accept it with grace.

Other token alterations followed. That year Sarnoff hired the public relations firm of Lippincott & Margulies to study the firm and come up with recommendations as how best to alter its image to suit what he perceived to be its emerging reality.

After a year and a half the PR firm concluded that many of RCA's most hallowed symbols, even its official name, should go. Radio Corporation of America would become, simply, RCA, which almost from the first had been its common designation. "Radio Corporation of America is no longer right in any case," Sarnoff later said. "Radios are a tiny part of our business, and we sell 12,000 different products and services nearly everywhere in the world." This also was in line with Sarnoff's plans for the company. Radio Corporation of America clearly was involved with radios, while RCA could be in any field it wished, since the name signified nothing in particular.

Sarnoff argued that the old logo, designed in 1922 to be placed on the first Radiolas, was stodgy, "closer in spirit to the Jazz Age than to an era of space exploration." He disliked the art deco initials with a lightning bolt coming out of the letter "A" and the whole surrounded by a circle, believing it conjured up images of the power industry, not electronics, while the circle looked out of place on the rectangular shapes of most products. The old logo was superseded by the squarish letters RCA, on everything from matchbook covers to TV sets to the sign atop the building.

He was even willing to reconsider the motto: "The Most Trusted Name in Electronics," since that ignored Random House and Hertz, and anything else that might be gathered into the conglomerate bosom. The Victor Division became "Consumer Electronics Division," while "Electronics Data Processing" became "Computer Systems Division (CSD)."

Nipper the Dog remained—too many old-timers revolted against his dismissal—but he was played down and all but replaced, while the motto, "His Master's Voice," sensible for phonographs, seemed antiquated and was dropped.

Bob Sarnoff also shook up the headquarters structure and field operations so as to make RCA more the kind of company he thought it should be, but also to correct what he and others perceived as flaws in the old Radio Corporation of America. In the past RCA had pioneered but had always seen its market share decline after others whittled away its lead. Now this would change, Bob Sarnoff implied.

Sarnoff thought a turnaround possible through more concentration upon customer needs and less upon technological feats; he judged success by profit and loss statements, not scientific firsts. Dan Seymour of the advertising firm of J. Walter Thompson believed this derived from his apprenticeship at Cowles and later RCA, as well as his personality. "I think that his days at NBC, which is a consumer-minded company, taught him what has to be done. The networks are continually aware of how people react. I think he's combining this past experience with the manufacturing, research, and development aspects. . . ."

This is not to suggest that Sarnoff ignored production; after becoming president in 1966 he visited each of the firm's many installations, claiming to have flown more than 100,000 miles, and justifiably boasted to have more firsthand knowledge of the facilities than anyone else at the firm. This experience convinced him that there was nothing wrong with RCA that a liberal dose of modern management wouldn't correct.

It was quite a change from David, who rarely made such tours, ruled harshly, and seemed to believe that it was his task to inform consumers of what they required and wanted. Kenneth Bilby, who had been close to both men, attributed the differences in approach to the requirements of their respective eras and visions of their roles. "The General grew up in the era of Henry Ford, [Harvey] Firestone, [Henry Clay] Frick, the great entrepreneurs who created industries from the ground up and ran their own businesses by instinct. Bob is a modern industrial leader who has more appreciation for communications inside the company and for the principles of management." In 1970, when Bob was in full command and David was hospitalized, investment banker John Loeb, who was a family friend, conceded that "many men have difficulty following an important father, but Bobby has done it with grace and style. David has been a great dreamer and idea man, with a stronger immediate personality. Bobby is a quiet mover, a man who gets things done."

Sarnoff began with an infusion of new executives who thought as he did and would be loyal to him and not the General's memory. Since few industries had the reputation of being as consumer conscious as autos, he raided Detroit, Ford in particular, for talent.

To head the new corporate marketing staff came Chase Morsey, Jr., who had worked with Lee Iacocca on the Thunderbird and Mustang, two of the greatest product hits of the decade. Morsey brought along a cadre of market researchers and corporate planners and spoke of the "New RCA." He took a place on the new Policy Committee, comprised of the arrivees plus a group of younger men whom Sarnoff promoted. Soon Morsey was RCA's executive vice president.

Always there were comparisons of RCA with Ford; there was no doubt as to Morsey's intentions. Among other things, he often remarked there was no reason why RCA couldn't play Ford to IBM's General Motors in computers. Ford was only half the size of GM, but it was a thriving concern. At the time IBM had approximately 70 percent of mainframe placements, and RCA was aiming for 10 percent or so. It seemed reasonable enough.

Under this leadership came new raids on IBM, with a steady stream of managers and salesmen coming from Armonk, much to Tom Watson's chagrin. Convinced that through better marketing RCA could achieve that long-dreamed of second place, Morsey went into the market to hire the best salesmen he could find. L. Edwin Donegan arrived from IBM in 1969 to become vice president for sales at CSD, and Joseph Rooney, an IBM branch manager, became vice president for marketing and in 1971 headed the CSD. Clearly Sarnoff intended to instill some of the IBM *élan* at RCA and in the charming, buoyant Donegan thought he had the right man for the task. In time Donegan would bring in some 900 trainees, most young men in whom he hoped to inculcate sentiments of pride and efficiency. What he wound up with by 1971 was a clumsy amalgam of former IBMers in charge, newcomers on the way up, and the old-timers of pre-Donegan years occupying an uneasy middle ground.

Bob Sarnoff concerned himself with almost every aspect of the corporation's business in his early years as CEO, but more time was devoted to EDP than anything else. He obviously saw an analogy between the efforts there and earlier ones with color television. The latter product had taken more than a decade to become a winner, but now it was deemed the General's crowning achievement. Bob Sarnoff expected to base his reputation on CSD.

Bob Sarnoff believed that, with superior marketing and the more modern image, RCA would be able to recapture market share in television receivers, and invigorate Random House and Hertz. More would come. As the conglomerateurs had shown might be done, managerial expertise gained in electronics would be transferred to the new areas. This too was an area that intrigued Sarnoff. By then his intent could not be doubted. In the 1968 *Annual Report* Sarnoff proclaimed, "In its formative years RCA's growth depended primarily upon a single product or service. . . . The word that best characterizes the modern RCA is diversity."

Bob Sarnoff was changing the firm's image, in the process signaling that what once had been his father's company was now his. David Sarnoff must have sensed this, but old and feeble, he did little except watch, perhaps in despair, yet also with some amusement and a sense of *déjà vu,* for he had wanted to do the same many times in the 1920s, when chafing at control by GE and Owen Young. In early 1968, on one of the General's infrequent visits to the offices, he inched his way into the newly refurbished suites, glanced at the logo, and scanned the other changes, with his son at his side. "Well," he said, "even an old girl can appreciate a new dress."

Bob now set about altering RCA's substance as well as the public perception. In the late summer of 1968 rumors circulated that with Lazard's help he was considering several acquisitions candidates.

St. Regis Paper was thc most important of these. With 1967 revenues of $721 million, it was a mid-sized, fully integrated producer in a highly cyclical industry without any of the growth characteristics of RCA, Hertz, or Random House. In spite of the early rumors the mid-October announcement of discussions between the two companies came as somewhat of a surprise to the investment community, and even before terms were considered RCA common stock declined sharply, a clear indication that Wall Street deemed the merger unwise.

Sarnoff was unmoved. "We would rather have a company with a sound growth rate than one of the high flyers," he argued, adding that "some of the latter are showing signs of indigestion." When pressed, he retorted, "It's an excellent deal. The positives far outweigh the negatives."

It was difficult to uncover many positives. St. Regis had no overflowing treasury to fund other RCA ventures and, despite Sarnoff's protestations, had an irregular growth rate rendered more precarious by a burgeoning long-term debt. Industry analysts wondered whether Sarnoff thought a recently completed modernization program meant St. Regis was about to realize important new earnings or whether he might be considering selling off part of the company's 5.7 million acres of land. Economies plus land sales were a vision that had attracted investors to forest products companies for more than a decade. Few of them worked out well.

Bob Sarnoff's views on the takeover were important, to be sure, but it was significant that the negotiations were conducted by the ailing David Sarnoff. The deal fell through in early January 1969, as the parties were unable to agree upon terms. It was all to the good. RCA was in no condition to take over a company with so little present performance or future promise as St. Regis. All that remained was to determine just why the Sarnoffs wanted to purchase so unpromising a property as St. Regis.

Two reasons stood out. A merger with so large an entity as St. Regis would place RCA squarely in the ranks of conglomerates, and so alter its destiny in such a way as to mark that fresh beginning Bob Sarnoff wanted. Also, it would boost RCA to within hailing distance of the top ten American industrial companies in terms of size, and this too would represent the kind of status the General wished the firm to possess.

Bob Sarnoff quickly turned to other candidates. That year he acquired Alaska Communications Systems from the U.S. Air Force for $28.4 million, and this company became part of RCA Global Communications. This new business fit in with the old. Not so the purchase of F. M. Stamper & Co. in March of the following year. One of the nation's leading independent packager of frozen foods, the privately owned company cost RCA 3,850,000 shares of its common shares, valued at $141 million.

Why frozen foods? A company spokesman told reporters that this was a "dynamic rapid-growth industry in the service field which is in line with RCA's activities in the service area," referring perhaps to Hertz. Sarnoff changed the company's name to Banquet Foods, and announced his intention to make it the leader in the industry.

A month later RCA acquired Cushman & Wakefield, a New York-based real estate company, for 1,250,000 shares, which came to slightly less than $44 million in new equity. Again, it was a move toward conglomeratization. This isn't to suggest Bob Sarnoff was out to obtain growth and size for its own sake or at the expense of the main operations. But it was starting to look that way.

In 1970 Sarnoff considered a curious deal that would have drastically altered the situation at RCA, to the point where it might actually have become the subsidiary or partner of a smaller firm. This was Loews, Inc., which the Tisch brothers had transformed from a theater chain into a conglomerate based on hotels, real estate, tobacco, and housebuilding. At the time Loews was cash rich, while RCA's CSD required large amounts of funds. Sarnoff told Meyer he was interested in a merger, and the word was passed to Alan Tisch. Preliminary talks took place and went far enough for a tentative plan to be drawn up, under which Tisch would have become chairman of the merged entity. Did this mean that Loews, not RCA, would be the senior partner? Nothing came of this, for as Tisch put it later on, "We couldn't see that much of a deal for our stockholders."

Also, Tisch could see no future for the Computer Systems Division, and before the talks were broken off he advised Sarnoff to write it off as a loss.

Anyhow, Sarnoff had too much of an emotional commitment to RCA to have followed through, and naturally no wish to appear a loser. Besides, RCA's 1969 performance had been fine. Revenues that year came to a record $3.2 billion and while earnings were down slightly to $151.3 million, they were the second best for the company. Taking the acquisitions into account, said Sarnoff, RCA had developed "a more satisfactory balance . . . between manufacturing and service activities" and was about to embark upon a program of global expansion, with manufacturing facilities construction underway in Belgium, the United Kingdom, Mexico, and Taiwan.

The prospects for color television remained good; more than half of America's homes still had only monochromes, and by now the pattern of replacing them with color sets had become firmly established. Radio sales were at record levels as were those for cassette players, records, and tapes, while on the horizon were videotape recorders, then in the R & D phase.

At the same time, NBC had a banner year, holding the lead among the three networks in revenues, advertisers, and audience share. Sales to government in the defense and space areas were also on the rise. The company was a major contractor in the Apollo program, was active in weather forecasting satellites, and had just received a $253 million Navy contract to develop the new Aegis surface missile system, which Sarnoff thought might eventually bring more than $1 billion of business to the firm. Even the smallish publishing operations were posting new highs—18 percent over the 1968 figures.

Electronic data processing was the exception. The business had posted a loss in 1966 after two profitable years, and the red ink continued to flow for the rest of the decade. In 1969 the new team at CSD appeared convinced it could obtain a 15-percent market share, that this division would become profitable in a shorter period than it took color TV to do so, and perhaps make an even greater contribution to earnings. "By the early Seventies we expect to become second to IBM," Bob Sarnoff flatly predicted, thus going one up on the General, who usually spoke of ambitions for the third position. "And we expect to be profitable."

A quarter of a billion dollars worth of mainframes and peripherals were shipped in 1969, and still RCA was in fifth position. By then RCA's financial commitment came to over $570 million, with almost half of that in the previous three years, and, while the division showed profits in 1968, there were losses again the following year. But RCA continued to follow the chimera of achieving success in electronic data processing.

11

Failure, Drift, and Decay

IN JUNE 1970, as President Nixon carried out his campaign pledge to withdraw from Vietnam, Bob Sarnoff plunged deeper into RCA's version of that conflict by committing additional financial and personnel reserves to electronic data processing.

That month IBM announced its new 370 series machines, claiming the initial offering, the 370/145, would have five times the performance of the 360/40 it was to replace. At the time RCA was considering successors to the Spectras. There was brave talk of a New Technology System (NTS), but nothing was done to implement it; RCA was so far behind that IBM probably would have another generation to offer by the time the new machines came to market.

There followed a period of deep soul-searching at headquarters, with talk of dropping out of the contest or at the very least cutting back to a more modest program.

Sarnoff would hear nothing of this. In the 1970 *Annual Report* he said, "The highest priorities today are the establishment of a profitable computer business and the capture of the domestic industry's No. 2 position. RCA has made a greater investment in this effort than in any prior venture in its history, and we are convinced that the returns will be substantial."

It was an exercise in bravado; even then it should have been clear that CSD had been outgunned by IBM. For one thing, the funds simply were not there. In order to improve cash flow RCA had opted to sell many of its leases at a discount to financial intermediaries such as Transamerica. The company stinted on research and development. In 1970 IBM spent $450 million on R & D, this almost twice the total *revenues* RCA realized from its division. Communications between headquarters and the field was poor; CSD leaders were not elevated to the Board and Policy Committee, where most important decisions regarding its fate were made. Also, despite the rhetoric, Sarnoff didn't give data processing the kind of priority it required. Had he done so, talents and funds wouldn't have been diverted to the acquisitions program.

Edwin McCollister, who it will be recalled had been at CSD almost from the first, felt that some of the newcomers there were part of the problem. For example, Chase Morsey and others from the automobile industry were accustomed to thinking in terms of market share and paid insufficient attention to cost controls and profits. "In other words," he said, "you tend to de-emphasize some of the other important market aspects of running a successful business, and share of market is only one consideration."

Informed by this way of thinking, Sarnoff opted to meet IBM across the board, not with the NTS, but rather with what at first blush seemed an ambitious plan to be known as the RCA series. In September the company announced the RCAs would consist of four small-to-medium sized mainframes. When the specifications were released, computer engineers soon realized that while the RCAs would have new memory systems, they really were little more than revamped Spectra 70s offered at substantially lower prices.

This program fared worse than the 601 debacle. For starters, the RCAs were released in the midst of an economic slowdown that affected the entire data processing industry, leading to fewer than anticipated placements and greater competition. The pricing policy was ill-considered. Realizing they might obtain a better price/performance ratio with the new RCAs than with comparable Spectras, leasors turned in their old mainframes for the newer ones, in this way getting substantially the same results at discounts amounting to around 15 percent. The corporation was in the strange position of having a backlog of RCA orders and a mounting inventory of Spectras, and both pretty much the same machine.

Thus, RCA was becoming something of a joke within the industry. Its mainframes were outdated, while the peripherals seemed poorly put together IBM copies. The company's computer shipments declined by 20 percent in 1970, estimates running that one out of every eight Spectras returned was because of economic tightness, and the others from Spectra-RCA tradeoffs.

Although CSD appears to have just about broken even in 1970, as always headquarters was optimistic. As was customary, CSD prepared its financial report in the fall. The plan projected 1971 revenues of $323 million, a large jump over the previous year's anticipated $259 million, and clearly based upon a best-case scenario, including a strong economic recovery and widespread acceptance of the new lines.

Some of the financial people objected, claiming the projection was overly optimistic, and told Rooney of their feelings. Word of the troubles reached the executive suites, and searching for a way out of the problem, Sarnoff elevated Donegan to the general managership of CSD. Together with Rooney he was given a mandate to undertake a major overhaul of operations.

Donegan and his staff discovered not only discrepancies in projections but accounting errors as well, opening a new can of worms at headquarters. It seemed that CSD's records were so fouled up that it was impossible to make accurate statements about the division's financial condition. Donegan's people labored day and night simply to understand the situation. Revisions were made, and after a long delay the plan projected revenues of $261 million and a loss of $44 million.

This was the first inkling that CSD was out of control. Lease records were kept on a haphazard and even occasional basis, to the point where it was difficult to discover whether a specific machine was making or losing money. Donegan later conceded, "I hadn't seen what was happening. The group financial staff hadn't seen it. The outside accountants who were in our skivvies hadn't seen it."

This was disturbing in itself, but in the process of making changes management discovered $30 million worth of errors of judgment—and $10 million in simple arithmetic! Furthermore, the firm's internal comptrollers told Sarnoff that they had doubts whether the division could ever be viable and asked for reconsideration of its objectives. This came soon after the resignation of executive vice president for finance Howard Letts, a move that appeared to be connected with the embarrassing discoveries.

Things started to come apart in late January 1971, when RCA's auditor, Arthur Young & Co., informed Sarnoff of additional alterations required in the CSD projections. The major problem, according to the crew from Young, was that the Division appeared incapable of generating proper figures. "The basic failure to develop acceptable planning information in the division involved the lack of a reliable information base, principally relating to revenues, from which plans could be developed and current performance measured." The report went on to say that the situation was aggravated by "communications gaps which developed in a period of organizational change."

This was verified later by V. Orville Wright, who headed an internal task force looking into the problem. "RCA was not devoting sufficient attention in engineering a product to the matter of cost," he concluded. "They tended to engineer the product to get it built, but ignored what it might cost to build it after it was engineered." Wright added that RCA's manufacturing costs as a percentage of revenues were 42 percent, against 14-15 percent for IBM and 24 percent for Univac. Reforms were possible; costs could be shaved, but hardly as much as would be required, so deep was the dry rot at CSD. Poor management was to blame, which ultimately meant Bob Sarnoff.

"Perhaps only an individual with engineering knowledge could have developed a strategy for CSD," reflected a veteran of the period in an interview. Characteristically, he declined to be named. "The General wouldn't have made those basic errors." Yet pioneering without regard to costs had long been an RCA tradition, encouraged by David Sarnoff. In the

1960s the company's fabled Princeton labs, considered one of the best research operations in the country, had come to be known within the industry as "The General's own private playpen," and certainly the decision to enter data processing was made without the kind of organizational and structural spadework so important a project demanded.

Bob Sarnoff certainly had other things on his mind while considering the Arthur Young & Co. report. For one thing, NBC had slipped badly in the ratings, and for another he was putting the final touches on his new acquisition, Coronet Industries, a major carpet manufacturer. Martin Seretean, who controlled Coronet, was initially reluctant to consider a takeover, but Sarnoff wooed him assiduously. At a dinner with Sarnoff and Petrie, Seretean said the losses at CSD bothered him. Since Coronet was to be purchased for RCA stock, the red ink might cause their worth to decline. Attempting to reassure him, Sarnoff predicted that CSD would break even in 1971 and by 1975 would be posting pretax earnings of $50 million. "But what if it doesn't turn around?" Seretean asked, to which Sarnoff replied, "My job is on the line," indicating that he considered his fate tied directly to that of the data processing operation.

Somewhat mollified, Seretean agreed to the sale, which was completed on February 24, 1971. In February RCA announced it would pay 6 million shares of common, worth approximately $189 million, with an annual dividend payout of $6 million, at a time when RCA had heavy capital requirements at CSD and Hertz, and more would be required for NBC. Of this Seretean received almost 1.5 million shares, making him the firm's largest noninstitutional stockholder and giving him a seat on the board, from which he carped continuously about the deficits.

The strains were beginning to tell on everyone at the firm, but none more than Bob Sarnoff. That April he suffered what at first seemed a heart attack but turned out to be a bundle-branch block, a serious but not necessarily fatal ailment in which the heartbeat slows and insufficient oxygen reaches the brain. This required the implantation of a pacemaker, and soon thereafter he was back at the office, where the situation had deteriorated further.

By now Seretean and Petrie had started to criticize the handling of the CSD more openly than before. In May Petrie demanded reliable statistics from Morsey, who had to concede he wasn't able to generate them, and discontent grew. The following month a team of accountants from both Arthur Young and RCA drew up a memo stating that "the CSD 1971 loss could deteriorate significantly from the Business Plan levels." Then the estimates were revised to a $37 million loss. The Division's leaders went on to say that additional losses of more than $100 million might be expected within the next two years. An internal memo added that RCA would require an additional billion dollars in new capital by 1976 and that $500 million of that would go to CSD, this in the face of a deteriorating balance sheet.

Seretean exploded. "I can think of two dozen things I would rather spend $500 million on." Soon thereafter Petrie told Sarnoff, "My recommendation is that you get out right now because, in my professional opinion, you can't raise the half billion dollars you will need to finance it."

Sarnoff disagreed, citing RCA's record earnings, for which he might have claimed credit since it had been made possible by the acquisitions program. The companies purchased from 1967 to 1971 were doing far better than the other operations. "Without the diversifications of the past five years," he told the annual stockholders' meeting in May, "we probably would have had virtually no sales growth and substantially lower profits." Sarnoff's troubles were with a division he had inherited but had made his own. Diversification had drawn attention from CSD, which had it commanded more attention might have succeeded. One wonders what might have occurred had Sarnoff devoted the time it took to acquire Hertz and Coronet to finding a partner in data processing to complement his own computer operations.

SELECTED RCA STATISTICS, 1965–1970

figures in millions of dollars

YEAR	REVENUES	NET INCOME	SENIOR CAPITAL
1965	2,042.0	101.2	273.8
1966	2,549.8	132.4	266.4
1967	3,014.0	151.8	686.8
1968	3,106.2	165.6	750.0
1969	3,187.9	161.2	785.7
1970	3,317.2	91.3	973.5

Source: *Moody's Handbook of Common Stocks,* 1973 ed.

There were some bright spots in manufacturing, such as a pickup in color TV receiver sales, but the firm had been severely affected by the recession, a decline in military orders owing to a stretchout of several procurement programs, capital needs at Hertz, the loss of cigarette advertising at NBC resulting from a government-imposed ban, and assorted other problems. Wall Street had taken account of this; RCA common, which in 1967 sold for as high as 65½, was under 20 in the summer of 1970. Early in 1971 it started to rise—often on rumors of cutbacks at CSD or the abandonment of the division.

Sarnoff hinted at disillusionment with the EDP business at the 1971 stockholders' meeting, noting that Honeywell's recent purchase of the GE computer business made that firm a much more serious contender. "We'd still like to be number two in the computer business," he said somewhat ruefully, but "we're more interested in profitability." Of course, there was precious little chance of that.

Some dignified way had to be found to leave the business, preferably in a way so as to avoid undo embarrassment and stigma.

In June, less than a month after the annual meeting, RCA announced that Anthony Conrad would become its president and chief operating officer, thus dividing the top two officers which up to then Sarnoff had been filling. At the time Conrad seemed destined to serve as a latter-day version of Folsom, which is to say a detail man who would free Sarnoff for other tasks just as Folsom did for the General.

Conrad was well equipped for the task. He had arrived at RCA after military service in World War II and was assigned to the Service Department, where he became interested in television. The industry was young, enabling Conrad to move up the ladder with relative ease. As one of RCA's investment bankers put it, he "has since been in the right place at the right time." Conrad managed RCA's satellite operations at Cape Canaveral, rose to the presidency of the Service Company, which was concerned with everything from leasing television sets to hotels and hospitals to running the Ballistic Missile Early Warning Systems, and in 1968 joined the corporate staff as vice president for education systems.

Conrad's wife died that year, after 25 years of marriage, and for a while he was disconsolate. In time he recovered, going on to a second marriage. In 1969 he became executive vice president-services, and from that post was elevated to the presidency.

In contrast with Sarnoff, Conrad was deemed pragmatic if a trifle unimaginative, capable of translating the CEO's dreams into reality, and cleaning up his messes in the bargain. He was as well balanced as Bob was mercurial. Conrad's new wife, Nancy, was vivacious and an excellent hostess. Together they purchased land on Gibson Island on Chesapeake Bay, on which was erected a magnificent weekend house. Conrad was well paid, commuted by limousine to Rockefeller Center from an apartment on East 68th Street, and clearly enjoyed the perquisites of wealth, status, and power.

Within the company and industry this was believed to be a significant promotion. Once considered an important supporter of the Computer Systems program, Conrad had turned negative the previous year though this wasn't generally known at the time. Indeed, a month after taking office he told CSD executives, "We are making a greater investment in the computer business than in any prior venture in our history. This is a measure of our confidence that RCA systems and products will effectively meet competitive challenges in the decade ahead."

During the next month Conrad placed several calls to RCA customers, assuring them the company intended to remain in the EDP business, and in

August he approved the extension of marketing activities to the United Kingdom. The company was advertising its computers heavily; in one ad it boasted, "Virtual Memory Is The Trend Of The Future. RCA's New Computers Have It. IBM's Doesn't." The RCA magazine scheduled for rclease in September was to feature an article on the glowing prospects for computers and RCA's role in the industry. Apparently no one at the ad agency or the magazine had an inkling of what was going on.

However on the basis of reports received from RCA's own accountants and the Young team, both Conrad and Sarnoff were coming to the conclusion they would have to cut their losses. Rumors started circulating on Wall Street, one of the more plausible being that Sarnoff intended to sell CSD to Xerox. Owing to uncertainty RCA common plunged, and trading was suspended, while Sarnoff sent a statement to the Securities and Exchange Commission stating that "RCA has no intention of selling its Computer Division. It has had no discussions with anyone in the past concerning such a sale. There are no discussions currently under way."

This was literally the case, but not the entire truth. Management was making plans to approach all major firms in the industry except IBM and Honeywell, the former for obvious reasons, the latter because as a result of its purchase of GE's computer operations it wasn't believed to be in the market for another acquisition.

The decision for divestiture was made on September 16, at which time the board met to hear Sarnoff and Conrad recommend the sale of the Computer Systems Division. They told the other members that RCA might find itself in financial difficulties should CSD lose the projected $137 to $187 million over the next five years. "It is questionable whether the business would ever attain economic viability," and "continued commitment to computers . . . could lead to severe financing problems for the Company, and may contribute to restricted growth in other operations." To this Morsey added one other item: the firm had miscalculated CSD's capital requirements: $700 million, not $500 million, would be needed over the next five years.

Neither Sarnoff nor Conrad had consulted with Rooney or Donegan before making the recommendation. Nor had the two checked the $700 million figure with CSD's financial vice president, Julius Koppelman. Communications at the top were embarrassingly poor, especially for a company in that field.

Even this figure was unrealistic. The report upon which the decision had been made assumed a "worst-case scenario," so as to conform with changes mandated by the Accounting Principles Board, which demanded far more conservative procedures than previously had been the case when calculating anticipated revenues. The situation at CDS wasn't as bleak as had been portrayed. This was no small matter: the difference between the projection and the reality was an overstatement of the deficit of $100 million.

Wright later claimed the board might not have supported the Sarnoff-Conrad decision had all of the facts been known. Indeed, had these two men fully understood the situation they very well could have concluded that RCA should remain in the business.

This important decision was made with incomplete information and without direct input from those individuals closest to the situation. In all probability the board members were so dismayed by CSD they were prepared to believe the worse—anything, in fact, that would enable the company to abandon data processing. Under the circumstances, the members voted to support the management decision: CSD would go on the block. All agreed to sell. As Conrad later recalled, "it was like the sun rising in the morning. Suddenly the path was pretty clear. . . . I've never seen a decision so osmotically come to pass."

A discreet search for a buyer now began—discreet because once the news broke customers might cancel leases and so make CSD less valuable. But as usual the word leaked, and cancellations began, as old and new leasors, fearful of being stuck with an "orphan computer" that couldn't be serviced, besieged RCA. The company slashed prices, but this only added to the suspicion that RCA was desperate. At one point RCA offered to lease two computers for the price of one, but even this didn't stimulate placements.

Meetings regarding a sale were held with several firms, among them Burroughs, Xerox, Memorex, Mohawk Data Services, and Sperry Rand. All knew of RCA's difficulties and so were unwilling to pay anything but a distress sale price. Gerald Probst, head of Sperry's Univac Division, came up with the best offer: $70.5 million in cash and 15 percent of the revenues from existing placements, the final figure being $127 million.

"A hell of a lot of people disagreed with my father going ahead with color," Sarnoff told a business writer soon after, as he lamely tried to make the best of a bad situation. "It took a certain amount of courage and guts and he stayed with it. There is a kind of parallel in a way. It took courage to get out of computers." After a few months reflection, he added, "It's just like getting married or divorced. You reach the point where it becomes the moment to act, so we did."

The company's final move in data processing was of a piece with most of the earlier ones. The sale proved one of the great bargains of modern business history. The revenue stream from existing rentals over the next three years would be approximately $370 million. Univac had taken over a customer base of some 500 companies and government agencies and a year later was able to report it had retained 90 percent of these, which by itself was worth more than the price paid. In addition Univac had more than 1,000 RCA computers on lease, the initial cost of which was in excess of $900 million.

Finally, Univac acquired a work force of 7,500, but not the requirement to retain it. After interviewing all of them, approximately one third of the employees were rehired, among them some of the finest engineers in the industry. "You could never go out in the open market and get so many people with that type of talent," said a pleased Univac executive. "It's like taking the Eastern Division of the National Football League and saying you can take the top ten guys from each team."

All of this is to suggest that it might well have been that the decision to sell CSD was almost as big a mistake as had been the decision to enter the industry. The following April Sarnoff said, "They're doing better with it than either of us expected," a concession that he might have moved too soon and settled for too low a price.

Afterward RCA released figures indicating just how damaging the venture into EDP had been. From 1958 to 1971 it had lost slightly less than a quarter of a billion dollars on the venture, and in September it was obliged to set up a reserve of $490 million ($250 million after taxes) to cover prospective future losses, this according to generally accepted accounting principles. But like so many other numbers generated by this operation the reserve figure proved out of line, though this time in a pleasing way: In December 1973 it was learned that the disposition of assets had brought in more money than anticipated, and the reserve accordingly was reduced to $412 million.

It was the greatest business disaster since the Ford Edsel. Ironically, several of the Ford people who had come over to RCA had also been involved with that fiasco.

While RCA's computer business was unraveling, David Sarnoff was confined to his home, suffering from mastoid complications. He died there at 11:50 A.M. on December 11, 1971, at the age of 80. Immediately NBC's television and radio programs were interrupted to broadcast the news, and that afternoon memorials were aired. Obituaries were carried on the front page of leading newspapers the following day, and his passing was noted in the major newsmagazines.

All repeated the familiar stories—the immigrant boy who entered the industry when both he and it were young, the *Titanic* messages, the creation of RCA. Recounted were the early days of broadcasting, the difficulties with monochrome television—"Forget everything I said. I honestly didn't think TV would catch on as fast as it did," he was purported to have told a reporter—and the risks and smashing success with color. Only a few analyzed his shortcomings, especially those in management and retaining market share. Most mentioned the failures with computers, but these were attributed to Robert, and not David Sarnoff. The obituaries dwelled on his wartime service; all referred to him as the General.

More than one obituary referred to Sarnoff as a "self-made man." Admiral Lewis Strauss provided the litany. "What Ford did for transportation, Carnegie for steel and the Wrights for aviation, David Sarnoff has contributed to public enlightenment and education through electronics." It was hardly the occasion to analyze this, so none explored how well the General had constructed the myth. What mattered was that in fact he had molded one of the nation's great corporations.

More of the same was to come, and it only augmented the myth. It once was said that if an American president were to be considered great he had to be preceded by a failure and succeeded by disasters, so the historians could say, "Look what he saved us from," and "Consider what happened once he left the scene." David Sarnoff's reputation is based on the fact that no one really came before. And as will be seen, he was succeeded by three failures.

The RCA that emerged from the CSD debacle was a badly crippled firm. The write-off reduced its net worth by almost a quarter; the corporation was in its worst financial shape since the 1930s; prospects were not encouraging.

Those highly visible executives connected with the venture into data processing soon vanished from Rockefeller Plaza. Gone were Morsey and others who had attempted to transform RCA into an aggressive conglomerate, and with them went those who had led CSD. There were rumors Bob Sarnoff would also leave, the board replacing him with Seretean, who was known to want the job. Increasingly outspoken in his criticisms, Seretean told a reporter, "I find it highly unusual that a management can write off $490 million, and no one seems to question whether the same people ought to be running the company today."

For the time being, however, Sarnoff had a clear majority of the members, and his position was secure. This became evident in early 1973 when Seretean resigned from the board and simultaneously stepped aside as CEO of the Coronet subsidiary.

The decision to leave the EDP field came at the bottom of the 1971 recession, so some at headquarters thought conditions would improve with the anticipated economic upturn. The company's semiconductor business, from which so much had been expected, lost $24 million in 1971, and Hertz experienced a 38-percent profit decline. Second place Avis, whose profits increased by 23 percent that year and advertised that "We Try Harder," boasted that it might soon have to develop a new slogan.

Despite all of this, RCA's common stock rose in late 1971 and continued to climb into the next year because of Wall Street's belief that the corporation's fortunes would improve now that it had put the computer business behind it. In fact RCA remained a promising enterprise. The network was still profitable and accounted for an increasing portion of the corporation's earnings in the first half of the 1970s. Hertz could be expected to do better once the recession ended and business travel increased; management had been strengthened, and already there were signs of improvement.

On the other hand, despite additional contracts the defense segment declined in importance. In 1961, when RCA had been the tenth largest prime contractor to the Department of Defense and tops among electronics companies, government contracts accounted for 38 percent of the corporation's revenues; by 1975 the figure was 7 percent and falling.

This wasn't due to a lack of technological expertise or experience; RCA had major contracts in the space and missile fields, had been able to sell its computers to the Air Force and National Aviation and Space Administration, and was a pioneer in weather satellites. But as energies were directed toward the civilian markets (where profit margins were much larger) and conglomeratization, less attention was paid to defense and space. More important, as its dedication to EDP grew RCA had tended to overlook other contracts in the search for those involving computers. The dropping of CSD caused its share of the procurement budget to decline considerably.

Finally, in the General's time concentration upon "the national interest" was of prime importance, not only because of business reasons but also because of his increasingly militant anticommunist position. As his presence at headquarters faded so did the devotion to the military.

Consumer electronics was a problem area, with RCA losing much of its market share in television receivers to Zenith, Magnavox, and Motorola, among others, with little hope of a return to the halcyon years of the mid-1960s. The corporation earned $53.7 million from this segment in 1971, at which time it was RCA's leading segment; by 1974 profits had declined to $11.1 million, less than half that from Hertz.

It was hoped that some recovery would take place when RCA released its initial video recorder systems, work on which had begun under the General and continued under Bob Sarnoff. The technology was based upon tape cartridges, or cassettes, that were tentatively priced at $35 for one capable of recording a half-hour program. Sarnoff considered the price a major obstacle but thought reductions would occur once volume developed and predicted that by 1980 videotapes and hardware sales would be more than $1 billion annually.

Although this hardly placed it in the same league as color television, the videocassette player was a product that at the time appeared to require a far smaller capital investment. This was extremely important. Not only did the corporation lack funds for larger ventures, but it had also lost the heart for major bets on new products and technologies. John Jamison, who replaced Morsey as chief of marketing, said, "There is considerably less willingness to make massive investments that will pay out way off in the future. Now the emphasis is on getting into a new business for as little as possible and making a buck as fast as you can."

Later on, when the dust settled and some perspective was possible, William Webster of the Princeton Labs stated his belief that RCA's decline started with this failure of nerve. "The computer venture probably cost us $2 billion pretax, and it took away RCA's courage to take on major new projects."

After color television RCA would not pioneer with another important consumer electronics product. Jacob Rabinow of the National Bureau of Standards, who knew the company well, reminisced about it in 1980. "He [David] also supported Zworykin, for example, for some twenty years before they developed electronic TV. They did it because David Sarnoff liked the idea. Today's management does not do this; it has to have a pay-off and the administration would never support a man like Zworykin for twenty years because he happens to like him."

In the early post-computer period another executive said that RCA was placing "a lot of half-dollar bets," meaning that investments in the nine digit range were out of the question, and that most in the future would be under $10 million. For example, RCA's first laboratory model videotape recorder required only $8 million to develop. The company would develop a satellite-based global communications system, and it already had a stake in Communications Satellite Corp; neither called for major capital expenditures.

This new prudence also took the form of sales of parts of the business that were money losers, slow growers, or required substantial capital. Five small units, which together accounted for $30 million in revenues, were sold in the year following the Sperry Rand deal. Sarnoff claimed all were involved directly or indirectly with computers and so had no place in RCA's future. One of these clearly belonged in a different category. ServiceAmerica, a pilot program that at one time was designed to become a service network for television and other consumer electronics products, was disbanded because RCA encountered strong opposition from independent dealers, whose goodwill was needed.

There were some minor acquisitions as well. Electronic Industrial Engineering and Ballantine Books, the latter becoming part of Random House, were purchased; together they cost approximately $10 million.

Lost in the postmortems of the CSD debacle was an even more important failure: RCA's inability to retain a dominant position in domestic consumer electronics. The reason it received little attention was that the decline came slowly, and there was no dramatic denouement. Then too, it was a defeat not only for RCA but for the entire industry and should be seen in that light.

By the early 1980s, when Americans made a cottage industry of studying what the Japanese did right and they did wrong, RCA officials conceded that quality control in television declined in the late 1960s and that the corporation had delayed the introduction of transistorized models too long so as to squeeze all it could from tube-powered sales.

There was far more to it than that. In fact, the American consumer electronics industry had made one mistake after another, with RCA being the most culpable. One of the major industry blunders of the postwar period was that of omission—the failure of the American consumer electronics companies to move aggressively into the Japanese market at a time when they might have controlled it, when Matsushita, Sony, and the rest were too small and weak to withstand an American invasion or had not yet been born. This was true in other areas as well, from textiles to steel to automobiles, and many other firms besides RCA ignored the Japanese market. But few cooperated more with the Japanese than did the two Sarnoffs, or provided them with so much assistance.

One might understand the failure to capitalize on the craze for transistorized radios. In 1949 Sony purchased from Bell Laboratories for $25,000 a license to manufacture transistors and two years later brought out its first transistorized portable radio. At AT&T there was no interest in consumer electronics, and at the time other American companies thought transistors wouldn't replace tubes in consumer items but instead would be limited to military and industrial applications. Of course they were wrong and were too long in reacting. So it was that the Japanese firms, which had only 2 percent of the American radio market in 1955, had 93 percent by 1973.

The American manufacturers did not feel threatened. Radio was an old technology, after all, and RCA, Zenith, and the others were concentrating on the new: television. The experience with radio should have alerted the Americans to the Japanese challenge, leading them to adopt more aggressive stances, but for a variety of reasons this didn't happen.

For one thing after a decade and a half of intense, costly competition the industry had settled down. Seemingly, RCA, Zenith, Magnavox, and Motorola had learned to live with one another, and unspoken agreements, advertising gimmicks, and slight modifications in design replaced technological change in the marketplace. The market was still expanding, and there seemed room enough for all.

Apparently few gave much thought to the possibility that the Japanese might invade the American TV market in any meaningful way. The Japanese companies had started selling their TVs in the American market in the early 1960s, when Sony brought over its small, fully transistorized sets. In 1962 Japanese receivers were being sold in the United States for a third less than the same sized RCA models. But they weren't well received, the assumption being at the time that the label "Made in Japan" still connoted inferior workmanship.

Under the guidance of the Ministry of International Trade and Industry the major manufacturers—Hitachi, Matsushita, Sony, and Toshiba—came together to form the Television Export Council and the Television Export Examination Committee. Their idea was to sell TV sets for as low a price as possible, gain market share and force out American competitors, and then raise prices so as to realize profits.

The Japanese made a major breakthrough in 1963, owing largely to RCA's indifference to the threat they posed. As noted Sears, Roebuck and RCA had a long-term, mutually beneficial relationship, whereby RCA and Whirlpool produced white goods sold under the Sears nameplate. The giant retailer now was negotiating for the purchase of color sets under the same arrangement. The General felt strong enough to turn aside the Sears' offers and even refused to sell the large retailer monochromes unless they were offered under the RCA nameplate. He wasn't alone in this; Zenith and other American manufacturers took the same stance, feeling that their position was so dominant they could afford to dictate such terms. Perhaps this made sense in the short term. In 1963 Sarnoff noted, "public demand for color outpaced production capacity. Color became the single most vigorous growth element in the consumer [electronics] market. It accounted for a major share of the earnings from all RCA consumer products."

The American manufacturers were wrong. The Japanese firm Sanyo learned of the situation and offered not only to sell Sears as many sets as it wanted but also to produce them to the retailer's specifications and at a price lower than that which might have been paid RCA. Sears accepted and with this struck RCA a major blow. From 1963 to 1977 Sears purchased 6.5 million Japanese TV sets from Sanyo and later Toshiba, worth more than $700 million. Led by these two companies, the Japanese dominated the market for private-branded monochrome receivers and used this as a beachhead for further expansion into the American market.

Unwittingly, RCA actually assisted the Japanese by selling them whatever technology licenses they required. It was a highly profitable exercise. "Clearly ... Japan was dependent on foreign sources for virtually all of the technology employed even to the stage of color television," wrote James Abegglen, a leading authority on the subject.

At one point RCA was earning almost as much from consumer electronics licenses as from sales of products upon which they were based. It was not alone in this; the entire consumer electronics industry participated in what was one of the most striking technology transfers in history. Of the 236 agreements in the electronics area in 1970, eighty-nine were in tape recorders, players, and related gear and a like amount in semiconductors, tubes, and components utilized directly or indirectly in consumer electronics products. There even were license sales to East Europe; in 1976 RCA and Corning combined to transfer cathode tube technology to Poland in a $124 million deal.

Little wonder, then, that the Japanese spent less than 6 percent as much as the Americans on research as late as 1965.

Several American manufacturers finally retaliated. John Nevin, President of Zenith, filed an antitrust action against the Japanese, charging they were engaged in dumping and illegal price fixing. General Telephone and Electronics, an industry factor through its Sylvania division, lobbied extensively for legislation to protect the domestic manufacturers. But there wasn't a word from RCA—because of all the American consumer electronics firms, no other had cooperated so closely with the Japanese. As Abegglen put it, "RCA licenses made Japanese color television possible."

The American response to the Japanese onslaught took the form of price cutting, and while this resulted in higher sales, profit margins suffered. In 1970 RCA had 22.8 percent of the domestic market for color sets, which gave it a better than two point lead over Zenith, its closest competitor. Yet even with the large-scale promotions—which lifted sales by more than 30 percent—RCA lost market share, though not to Zenith. Rather, Sears, which accounted for 7 percent of sales in 1970, rose to 9 percent in 1971, and of course all of its receivers came from the Japanese. Sales of Japanese sets in the United States that year came to 6 million units, up from 5.5 million in 1969. The Japanese companies, which had less than 1 percent of the American monochrome market in 1960, had a 72-percent share in 1972. And it was that way down the line. In 1963 imports accounted for only 7 percent of all consumer electronics purchases. Eleven years later they took more than 40 percent of the market, and Matsushita, not RCA, was the world leader in the field. In 1974 no American corporation manufactured radios, tape recorders, or monochrome television sets.

Yet there was hope for the next consumer electronics product, videocassettes, which, as noted, RCA had been developing in the 1960s. Even so, the Japanese beat RCA to the starting line—by utilizing technology licensed from other American consumer electronics firms. In 1975 Sony brought out its Betamax machine, a console that incorporated the recorder with a TV set. Priced at $2,500, it utilized a cassette that could tape or play for as much as two hours. The price, combined with the fact that little in the way of motion picture tapes existed, resulted in sluggish sales. Early the following year Sony came out with a new machine that could be attached to existing sets, and this did better.

In March 1977 Matsushita announced that its American subsidiary, Panasonic, would soon offer a videotape machine of its own, utilizing a larger cassette that could carry up to four hours of programming. Placing its own program on hold, RCA became a licensee of Matsushita, while Zenith did the same with Sony.

This set off a war for the market, which saw RCA forge to the lead. While increasingly timid in the aftermath of the EDP failure, the company was still one of the nation's most experienced and successful forces in the home electronics marketing area. Before long it was the leading power in videocassettes. But no one in the industry could forget that Japanese technology made all of this possible. The company had been reduced to becoming an ally of foreign companies. The developing struggle for domination of the market for players would be between Matsushita, Sony, and other Japanese firms and the Dutch electronics firm of Philips, with RCA marketing a machine under its nameplate, but manufactured for it by Hitachi and others.

By 1974 RCA's share of the color TV market had dropped to 20 percent (in part because the company persisted in stressing large, console-type sets whereas the public demanded tabletop receivers), while Zenith's stood at 24 percent. Matsushita had recently purchased Motorola's Quasar unit and was turning it around, demonstrating that lower labor costs were only a small part of the Japanese advantage.

That year Japanese companies accounted for close to 20 percent of the American color TV market, or about as much as RCA itself. By then there were doubts whether they could be stopped. Having relinquished the radio and monochrome markets to the Taiwanese and Koreans, the Japanese had zeroed in on color TV, and there seemed no doubt they would do the same for video-related products and anything else that came along in the consumer electronics area.

The Americans were in trouble at mid-decade, and while RCA had obvious strengths it became the focus of discontent, with Bob Sarnoff coming in for a great deal of criticism. The company tried to regroup. There were cutbacks all along the line, with 10,000 workers laid off companywide. The situation worsened during the next decade, for which the domestic American industry bore much of the blame. Echoing Abegglen in a 1985 interview, Philips Chairman C. J. van der Klugt said that the American firms, headed by RCA, have "forged the bullets used to shoot them."

In the spring of 1975 a glum, somewhat haggard, and obviously troubled Bob Sarnoff told stockholders that "the greatest drop in sales" had already taken place, and improvement would be shown for the rest of the year. But his report was generally bleak. Net profits had declined by 38 percent in 1974, and although part of this resulted from changes in accounting procedures, most of it stemmed from a generally poor showing in consumer and commercial electronics, which included the sales of picture tubes and components to others. Earnings from the consumer area had declined to $11.1 million in 1974, owing to price slashes, while commercial electronics was awash in red ink, indications being 1975 would be worse.

There was hope for new products then being developed, especially videodiscs and videodisc players. This was a revolutionary technology for playing movies and other shows on what resembled a phonograph attachment to television sets, and which remained what it had been when Bob took over: potentially RCA's most important new technology in the consumer electronics field. Sarnoff noted that the system—which was called "SelectaVision"—was demonstrated to a number of U.S. manufacturers and to the Japanese industry, an indication that further licensing was being contemplated.

The near future wasn't as promising as the more distant one. Several of Sarnoff's takeovers turned in poor performances. Banquet Foods was plagued by severe competitive strains, and another acquisition, British food processor Oriel Foods, Ltd., was doing badly. Coronet Industries was hurt by a low level of home construction, which impacted severely upon the carpet business, and Cushman & Wakefield by a weak commercial real estate market. As for the rest, NBC was stable, while archrival CBS was growing. Hertz posted advances, but was losing market share to Avis among others.

RCA REVENUES, 1971–1975

figures in millions of dollars

	1971	1972	1973	1974	1975
Consumer Electronics	968	1,098	1,149	1,130	1,171
Commercial Electronics	476	531	644	671	609
Broadcasting	566	611	684	725	796
Hertz	597	636	677	722	715
Communications	118	137	165	195	234
Government Business	423	396	381	356	355
Other	397	454	581	828	936
	3,545	3,863	4,281	4,627	4,816

RCA NET PROFITS, 1971–1975

figures in millions of dollars

	1971	1972	1973	1974	1975
Consumer Electronics	53.7	57.7	48.0	11.1	25.3
Commercial Electronics	0.2	11.7	25.8	(7.4)	(48.3)
Broadcasting	26.3	36.0	47.7	48.3	52.1
Hertz	10.1	15.4	19.3	23.2	27.4
Communications	11.7	13.6	18.2	25.7	31.2
Government Business	5.0	3.4	3.3	3.7	3.3
Other	21.7	20.3	21.4	8.7	19.0
Extraordinary Charges	(244.5)	—	—	—	—
	(115.9)	158.1	183.7	113.3	110.0

Profit information in the above table is after deduction of allocations to the respective segments of corporate expenses not charged directly to any of the reported segments and excludes discontinued general purpose computer business for the year 1971.

Source: RCA, *1975 Annual Report.*

Sarnoff blamed much of this on "an unprecedented combination of inflation and recession [which] produced a climate unlike any we have experienced in a 55-year corporate history that has known the turbulence of war and depression." Yet RCA's leading competitors were doing well. Zenith's operating profits went from $12 million to $26 million from 1974 to 1975, and CBS's went from $108.6 million to $122.9 million.

The company recovered by autumn, but not as rapidly as the economy, and its share of the color TV market declined to 19 percent, this a new low. The grumblings in the executive suites intensified; the rumor mills were working double shifts. That a revolt against the CEO was brewing was evident, with the question asked not whether Sarnoff could hold, but when and by whom he would be replaced.

12

Intermezzo

AFTER IT WAS all over insiders realized that the first clear sign Sarnoff would be deposed came in September 1975. Without any fanfare RCA announced a restructuring of top management. Thenceforth all operations would come under three business groups: RCA Electronics, RCA Communications, and RCA Diversified Businesses. Howard Hawkins would take charge of Communications, with Edgar Griffiths becoming head of Electronics and, until a proper candidate could be elevated, Diversified as well. Both men were RCA veterans, who together with Sarnoff and Conrad would make up the new office of the chairman.

The move strengthened Conrad's position. As has been seen, he had been willing to cut losses at CSD—late enough to be considered a loyalist to the old regime, sufficiently early to claim prescience. Not a person likely to take many chances, he clearly had a firm hold on his position as well as the confidence of the board.

With this restructuring those divisions generating most of RCA's revenues (that is, all but NBC) reported directly to him, and not Sarnoff. Conrad hinted that major changes were in the work, specifically in the area of day-to-day operations. "We're tailoring the church so that it isn't just filled on Easter Sunday," he said soon after the reorganization.

The elevation of financial and operating executives indicated that these areas, and not technology and acquisitions, would be paramount over the next few years if not longer. This was Conrad's strong suit—and that of the two newcomers as well. Griffiths had earned his reputation at RCA as a cost-cutter impatient with long-term, visionary concepts, while Hawkins was a "company man," willing to go along with what the others wanted. Both were close to Conrad, and Griffiths, the more aggressive of the two, considered him a mentor.

Subtle changes that began after the CSD failure became more evident in 1972–1973. Conrad became increasingly involved with strategic planning and assumed additional responsibilities elsewhere, while Griffiths chopped away at corporate fat, attempting to whip his divisions into shape. Sarnoff tended to concentrate on NBC, where he had begun and the business for which his talents were best suited. In addition he spent more time away from the office, making nonbusiness speeches, accepting awards, collecting Oriental art, and later on wooing Metropolitan Opera diva Anna Moffo, whom he was to marry in November of 1974.

Some at headquarters resented these activities. One was George Fuchs, a vice president and director, who ordered an analysis of expense accounts, purportedly to halt what he deemed excesses in such charges.

Fuchs had become something of a legend at RCA. Involved primarily with industrial relations, he had taken it upon himself to compile dossiers on RCA executives, tracking their expenditures. That Fuchs could so act is an example of the Byzantine nature of the RCA that General Sarnoff had created and his son couldn't control. Now Fuchs felt capable of striking out against a man who not only was his CEO but bore "the name." No clearer indication of just how parlous Bob Sarnoff's position had become could be imagined. Correctly viewing this as a personal attack, Sarnoff came close to demanding Fuchs's dismissal, but he realized that he lacked board support. Sarnoff came out of the episode weakened.

Later some of Sarnoff's associates said his spirit had been crushed by failure, criticism, and health troubles. He had become increasingly moody, with periods of apprehension and gloom alternating with those of ebullience. Sarnoff took a great deal of interest in his wife's career. Anna Moffo was signed to a contract at Victor records, which publicized her as one of the great artists of the day. Sarnoff accompanied her on concert tours, a reprise of his earlier career in public relations, an area in which perhaps he had been happier than in the management of RCA.

In late October 1975, while Sarnoff was accompanying his wife on a three-week concert tour of the Far East, the board met to discuss his future. A majority decided that he had to go. The reasons involved what some called his "absentee leadership" and evidence that he had no clear idea of where the company should be headed.

Most important, however, was the previously discussed steady erosion of profit margins and earnings, especially in the electronics area, which despite acquisitions remained the key to RCA, its *raison d'être* in the public's eye. The corporation had declined steadily after reaching its earnings peak of $183.7 million in 1973. Part of this had to do with the recession, but some at Rockefeller Plaza felt the firm had been doing below par even before the economic decline. There had been some improvement in the third quarter just ended, during which earnings had increased to $32.8 million against $30.2

million for the same period the previous year, but this was due largely to industry-wide increases in TV sales and further technology sales. At that RCA was still not doing as well as its competitors. Moreover, while consumer electronics was recovering, its earnings were less than half of what they had been earlier in the decade.

Commercial electronics remained a disaster area; for 1975 as a whole it would post a loss of $48.3 million, wiping out almost all of NBC's earnings. Griffiths made this his prime concern, arguing that William Hittinger, who headed the division, was moving too slowly in cutting corporate fat. Hittinger was soon relieved of his duties, but the problems persisted, and Griffiths moved to take charge of this area too. Now fully two-thirds of the corporation, everything but communications and NBC, reported directly to him, and he to Conrad.

Griffiths halted production of receiving tubes, taking a $43 million write-off there, and by early 1976 seemed to have turned that troubled division around. But there was much more to be done and additional red ink before the job would be completed. The situation was hardly pleasing to contemplate, but neither was RCA in the kind of trouble it had known in 1971. Recovery was possible, given time and a better economic environment.

As it turned out, Bob Sarnoff was in worse difficulty than the company. He had lost the confidence of the board. When the news broke, several insiders, including representatives of Lazard, claimed to be surprised by what had happened. This might have referred to the timing and not the action itself. Rumors of a switch at RCA had floated through the financial district for almost a year and were partially responsible for a recovery of the price of its stock, which rose from under 10 in December 1974 to almost double that price when the board met. After it was over an "inside source" told a financial writer that "the in-house guys met with outside directors and said, 'We won't take this any more.'"

It was difficult to contemplate RCA without a Sarnoff in command, and the decision wasn't made easily. This was as much in deference to David's ghost as Bob's sensibilities as well as an awareness that interested parties would view this as yet another concession of failure.

Unfortunately Bob Sarnoff couldn't provide RCA with the General's dreams and glamour or deliver financial results. It was perhaps his attempt to do both that made him appear erratic and quirky. "Bobby Sarnoff had an attention span that was fully ninety seconds long," complained an associate, who, as had become traditional, was granted anonymity by the magazine writer who quoted him. "He would take great intuitive leaps from an unwarranted assumption to a foregone conclusion."

Lacking a prophet and visionary (and in any case not wanting one) RCA opted for a manager. With no time or inclination to make an outside search, the board looked to present management for a replacement. There were two obvious candidates: Conrad and Griffiths. The former had seniority and support and was better known to the outside board members. Griffiths, who tended to be blunt and abrasive, would in any case have his hands full in turning around the most troubled parts of the corporation. Later on an RCA executive who was there at the time said, "I suppose the board knew Griffiths was better qualified for the top slot, but that Andy [Conrad] would do well enough as figurehead. In any case, he was a nice guy and wouldn't put up too much of a fight when and if asked to step aside. But from the first many of us thought that under the circumstances Griffiths was the best person for the job."

So Conrad took over, the understanding being that Griffiths would play a major role in his regime and become heir presumptive.

Sarnoff was informed of the decision soon after his return from the Far East by being handed a prewritten letter of resignation. According to leaks, only one director supported Sarnoff, who accepted the situation with as much grace as might be mustered under the circumstances. The meeting to decide his fate lasted for around two hours, and, as was the rule in corporate America, none of the participants talked to the press afterward. Traditionally, however, matters dealing with compensation and related arrangements are discussed at such awkward moments.

The announcement was made on November 5, 1975; in the customary fashion the press release stated he would be leaving "to pursue other interests of a personal nature." The resignation as chairman was to take effect on December 31, but Conrad was immediately named chief executive officer.

After the Sarnoffs, Conrad seemed rather pallid.

As president and chief operating officer Conrad had tended to keep a low profile, but he was generally considered to believe the corporation had become top-heavy, that the headquarters staff had become bloated and divorced from reality, and that line managers should be granted additional responsibilities. For this he was neatly categorized as a "meat-and-potatoes operational man," for whom profits were paramount. The feeling was that given more authority while knowing they would be judged by results, division leaders would perform better. "There was jubilation among the division managers" when they learned of the appointment said one RCA competitor, while another observed that "Conrad knows all the flaws and strengths at headquarters and in the field and can be counted upon to eliminate the former and capitalize on the latter."

That the new CEO had the requisite experience and intelligence to carry out the job was taken for granted, but there was some question about his willingness to make difficult decisions and carry them out. Richard Paget of Cresap, McCormick & Paget, a longtime friend, said, "He can be pretty damned tough if the situation requires it. But he's very fair," adding that one of his virtues was steadiness, a quality lacking at the helm since the General left the scene. "Andy is not the kind of guy who comes in on Thursday and decides on Friday you ought to turn the joint upside down. I think RCA is in good hands." An unfriendly critic, an RCA executive at the time, interpreted these qualities differently, telling a *Fortune* writer that "As for Andy Conrad—well, the next decision he makes will be his first."

After his first few weeks in office it had become transparently clear that Conrad had no master plan to alter RCA. Rather, he would prune selectively, dispose of acquisitions that hadn't worked out as expected, support attempts to make NBC the leader in broadcasting once again, and, most important, work with Griffiths to turn Commercial Electronics around. Hertz was doing well as was the old communications business.

Little more was expected of Conrad than a calm, workmanlike approach and performance. Perhaps no other CEO of a major industrial concern had so unchallenging a set of tasks as those he confronted when taking over at Rockefeller Center. All he had to do to be considered RCA's savior would be to run a tight ship.

Symbolic of what the new team deemed change and reform was an episode at NBC, which was losing market share, not only to CBS but to a resurgent American Broadcasting System as well. Fighting back, NBC opted for a publicity campaign based upon a new logo featuring the letter "N," which was to replace the peacock with its multihued tail. The network and its advertising agency were embarrassed to discover that a similar logo was being used by the Nebraska Educational Television Network. As a result, NBC paid the Nebraska firm $750,000 for the right to the logo, this including a $2,500 fee to its designer—who had created it for the public service station for $100.

What NBC hoped to gain from having a new logo is difficult to fathom. But NBC was last in the ratings by the time the matter was settled.

The new team performed as expected during its first half year in power. Griffiths continued to prune commercial electronics, while expanding manufacturing and technology licensing. A picture tube project entered into jointly with the United Kingdom's Thorn Electrical was discontinued, and the company's outdated manufacturing facility in Elizabeth, New Jersey, was shuttered. At the May 4, 1976, annual meeting Conrad announced that administrative costs per sales dollar had been cut by 6 percent, marketing costs declined by 7 percent, and there had been a 15-percent increase in productivity. Profits for the first quarter had been twice that posted in the previous year, continuing a turnabout that began that autumn, when Sarnoff had still been in command. Conrad told the stockholders that barring an economic reverse, RCA would have "an excellent year."

Would it have been different had Sarnoff remained at the helm? Probably not, but nonetheless it was the right kind of beginning for the new team.

Conrad hadn't put his stamp on the company, but changes were taking place. He was negotiating for the sale of Cushman & Wakefield and several foreign food operations, including Oriel Foods and Morris & David Jones Ltd., and it seemed every one of the Sarnoff acquisitions except Hertz would be sold if the proper price could be obtained.

On June 2, 1976, the Board announced that Conrad would become chairman as well as president, chief executive, and chief operating officer, and as a token of support he was given a new three-year contract upping his compensation from $275,000 to $300,000.

No news of consequence came from the company during the next three months. Earnings continued to move upward; for the quarter ended June 30 they came to $53.7 million, more than doubling the figure for the same period in 1975. Revenues were $1.32 billion, and indications were the annual figure would top the $5 billion mark for the first time, with earnings setting a new record. The Cushman & Wakefield operation was sold, and Griffiths continued his restructuring and cost-cutting at Commercial Electronics. Profit margins were rising. Conrad shared the credit for this.

In late August RCA announced it would make a secondary public offering (its first) of 5 million newly issued shares of common stock to bring in around $150 million, a portion of which presumably would be used to finance the introduction of videodiscs. It appeared RCA had settled down to an orderly, if not dull, existence.

On Monday, September 13, Conrad notified several Board members of a problem that called for immediate attention. A special meeting was called for 11:00 A.M. on Thursday, with all the members present except Atlantic Richfield's President Thornton Bradshaw, an outside director, who was on a vacation cruise. The members broke for lunch at around noon, and then all except Conrad reassembled for discussions that continued until 7:00 P.M. The press had been notified that an announcement would be made, and there were the usual rumors, the most persistent and plausible being that a merger, financed by the underwriting, had been arranged.

No one was really prepared for what followed. That morning Conrad had notified the Board that he had failed to file his personal federal income taxes for 1971 and after. The matter had been discussed in the afternoon, when the board announced that Conrad's resignation had been accepted, though this was another one of those euphemisms; in reality, he had been forced from office. "We did what we had to do," said one director, "and we did it promptly." Another said, "It was a case of a board working at its best. I'm very proud of it." "It's a personal tragedy," said Edgar Griffiths, who as expected was immediately named president and chief executive officer. "I feel very sorry for him." Griffiths spoke of the "shock within the organization" and indicated that there would be no sharp change in direction under his leadership.

Tax evasion was hardly new in corporate history, but this wasn't exactly a case of deliberate, premeditated criminal activities. Conrad's tax liability for this period was $704,292, of which $684,618 had been deducted from his salary, which meant he had a federal liability of less than $20,000. In his press release Conrad stressed that RCA was in no way involved, and he denied receipt of improper payments.

Nonetheless the company was affected; for the second time in less than a year its CEO had been forced from office, and this hardly contributed to confidence on Wall Street and elsewhere. Its common stock declined on the news, and the company was obliged to withdraw the secondary offering.

The affair was baffling. Conrad appeared to be claiming that he simply forgot or neglected to file his personal return, and it was reported that way in the newspapers and on television. But the general feeling was that something was being hidden, that serious criminal charges would follow. None came. Everything was just as Conrad had said it was. For failing to do for five Aprils something quite simple—turn over papers to an accountant, sign them, and have them sent along with what to him would have been a relatively small amount of money to the government—Conrad suffered public humiliation, saw his career wrecked, and of course left a post that paid $300,000 per year and gave up stock options worth an additional $160,000.

Further information was leaked to the press during the next few weeks. The situation had been uncovered when the Internal Revenue Service conducted a routine examination of the corporation and discovered the omissions—Conrad had been caught by a computer. One of RCA's board members said that Conrad had suggested he step aside temporarily while the matter was investigated, but this option was rejected.

The reaction was diverse, but no one claimed to have had any clue as to motives. Bob Sarnoff was "flabbergasted," and several executives wondered whether the omission was caused by business stress. Conrad had always lived within his means and apparently wasn't under any form of financial pressure. Proxy statements showed he owned 8,000 shares of RCA common, worth around a quarter of a million dollars, and his Gibson Island home might easily have fetched a million dollars.

"He never impressed me as being money-hungry in all the years I knew him," said an RCA associate. "In all the time I was his boss, he never even asked for a raise." His brother Charles, a geologist and oil engineer who dabbled in investments, tried to get him interested in putting some money into oil leases, which offered excellent tax advantages. As a lawyer who knew both men recalled, he would have nothing to do with them. "I don't think Andy ever got into any of Charles's deals. He didn't understand the oil business and he didn't want any part of it."

Little was heard from Conrad thereafter. He worked out a compensation program with the board, made a settlement with the IRS and state and city tax offices, and dropped from sight. Conrad's death in 1984 was barely noted at Rockefeller Plaza.

13

The Griffiths Aegis

ONE OF EDGAR Griffiths's first acts as CEO was to order the return of Nipper as part of the RCA advertising program. It will be recalled that Bob Sarnoff played down the terrier as part of his program to create a new, modern image for the firm. Now Nipper was back, and one who was there at the time recalled, "It was one of Griffiths's better ideas, like when Gerald Ford took over and said, 'Our long national nightmare is over.' We really expected things to settle down after that period of uncertainty."

It wasn't to be. Before he was through at RCA, Griffiths would become involved in some of the most curious and damaging pyrotechnics that ever befell a major American corporation. This was unexpected as stability was supposed to have been one of his strengths.

Griffiths had started out twenty-eight years before as a $53-a-week bill collector at RCA Service, rose to its presidency, and then went on to higher things. He maintained strong and close relations with field managers and drove his executives with a firm hand. To business journalists he seemed a latter-day version of Harold Geneen, the hard-bitten CEO who had made ITT a multibillion dollar conglomerate. But he lacked Geneen's flair. As chairman of RCA, "a company source" told *Business Week,* "he's a klutz."

Another more telling comparison to a different CEO was made. A heavyset man with a firm jaw and frightening scowl, Griffiths bore more than a slight physical resemblance to General Sarnoff. This seemed fitting. In some respects the corporation was situated as it had been in the mid-1930s when Sarnoff cut back so as to preserve his core business. In both periods broadcasting was the corporation's big money-maker; in 1975 this segment contributed almost half of RCA's total profits while accounting for less than one-sixth its revenues.

But that minor physical resemblance was about as far as it went. Where

Sarnoff delighted in being portrayed as a poet and philosopher of technology and capitalism, Griffiths possessed the soul of an accountant. Much of the time he appeared to have a bunker mentality, more concerned with preservation than expansion. He once said, "What has bedevilled this company for years is a feeling that we had to have something new and different all the time, and we had to go from one technological accomplishment to another, never mastering the prior one and never realizing a proper return on the bottom line." Always the bottom line, one of Griffiths's favorite phrases.

To outsiders Griffiths seemed the kind of person who not only preferred financial and operating stability but also insisted upon it. The story is told that when a Hertz manager reported difficulties in collecting a large bill from a major customer, Griffiths demanded that he go to his office and refuse to move until paid. This he did, and the funds were collected.

In contrast, Griffiths blew hot and cold when it came to executives. Personally introverted and withdrawn, he nonetheless could and did explode in anger at what he interpreted as incompetence and would fire even longtime associates. In 1977, for example, Hertz CEO Robert Stone spoke with Griffiths about the possibilities of being named to the RCA board. It wasn't an unreasonable request, considering that Hertz had performed so well under his leadership. Angered at what he deemed audacity, Griffiths rejected the notion out of hand. Both men had short fuses, and an argument ensued. Soon after Stone was out, replaced by the more complacent Frank Olson. Other executives followed Stone, and by 1980 Griffiths was known as the Red Queen—who in *Alice in Wonderland* screamed, "Off with his head!" quite regularly.

From the first Griffiths operated under a cloud: the open knowledge that he hadn't been the first choice for the job. The board could have named him as Bob Sarnoff's successor, and he had made it clear at the time that he wanted the post, but Griffiths was rejected instead in favor of Anthony Conrad. Now the talk was that had the board had sufficient time to consider alternatives and not been pressured by the sudden news of Conrad's income tax problems, Griffiths might have been passed over for the second time in two years.

There was justification for this view. Vice President Peter Hoffman observed, "You had a situation where the board felt it had to act within the company." Said another associate, "Griffiths was a good line manager. He ran a tight ship, and he had a lot of success in running his divisions." But he added, "Griffiths was never the top choice of the board. He was a compromise candidate."

"Bob Sarnoff and Conrad were like family members," said a former RCA executive, adding that "most board members felt affection for them, and were truly distressed at the way they left." Griffiths was different. "He occupied a position akin to a person's accountant or lawyer. You might like him, but one bad screw-up and out he goes."

After a few months in office Griffiths told a reporter that his priorities were "to create a period of stability and reliability of profit. Then technical innovation in the field of consumer electronics." But not if it were too expensive and meant a period of poor earnings. Later he would claim to have had a carefully worked out strategy in mind while CEO, nurtured for more than a decade while he dreamed of having the chance to command RCA. There would be four, possibly five, operating units. Electronics and communications would be at the heart of his RCA, with broadcasting, Hertz, and possibly another cash cow feeding earnings into the first two. That Griffiths considered this long-term planning indicates just how unimportant he considered it to be worth.

Little that Griffiths did or said, especially in those first few years, indicated that any thought was given to corporate strategy, which distressed the board. According to one source, almost from the first members asked for long-term plans, and Griffiths refused to comply, preferring instead to talk about matters such as next quarter's earnings. A colleague said of him: "Ed believes in running a company month by month. Put three of those months together and that's a quarter. And that's how you run it." "Long-range planning at RCA meant, 'What are we doing after lunch?'" he added. "The Soviet Union has a five-year plan," began one inside joke at Rockefeller Plaza. "Have you heard about Griffiths's five-week plan?"

There were differences of opinion regarding his dedication to research. "Griffiths starved it," said an industry expert, referring to RCA's Solid State Division, one of the industry's ten largest producers of semiconductors. In fact, "RCA's capital spending-to-sales ratio was only one-third to one-half that of the industry average," said Roy Pollack, in charge of the solid-state electronics projects. On the other hand William Webster, who by then had become head of the Princeton Laboratories, recalled being pleasantly surprised when he met Griffiths shortly after he took command. When Webster informed him that overall research and development spending had fallen to 3.9 percent of sales, Griffiths asked, "What do you want?" Webster asked for a 20-percent increase, and he got it. Within four years the R&D budget had risen from $112 million to $197 million. "Not since the 1950s had the labs been given all they needed," White added. This, from a person who supposedly rejected such expenditures in favor of immediate results. "With a bottom-line fiend at the top we thought research might dry up completely," said an engineer at the Princeton facility on learning Griffiths had taken charge. "But it simply wasn't so."

All of which suggests that perhaps Griffith penurious reputation was exaggerated. But it existed nonetheless. This was partially the result of a sharp alteration in the tone emanating from Rockefeller Plaza, where talk often masqueraded for action.

Finally, Griffiths was a booster by nature, at least insofar as the firm was concerned, and this represented quite a change from the mercurial Bob

Sarnoff and the diffident Anthony Conrad. It had been no secret that Conrad and Griffiths had clashed over the need for the 5 million share secondary, the latter arguing that given the proper management and disposing of losers, RCA could post record earnings and so would not need the money. Under Conrad there had been talk of a major acquisition; Griffiths indicated that for the time being he would be content to go with what he had inherited.

Griffiths came to office at a time when earnings were rising. For 1976 commercial electronics posted earnings of $7.5 million against a deficit of $48.3 million the previous year, this credited to the economies he had brought about while in charge of the division. Broadcasting profits rose from $52.1 million to $57.5 million, and consumer electronics to $41.8 million from $25.3 million, in part owing to the success of the new ColorTrak line of receivers.

The 1976 *Annual Report* featured a nonelectronics or abstract motif on its cover for the first time—a Hertz airport shuttle bus, taking smiling customers from the terminal to their cars. Perhaps nothing better indicated the new direction Griffiths intended to take, or the way he measured success. Hertz's pretax profits that year came to $92.6 million, almost twice what it had been in 1974. What Hertz lacked in glamour and sparkle it more than made up for in this vital statistic. That cover along with the return of Nipper was Griffiths's declaration of independence from the Sarnoffs and a clear indication of his values.

Griffiths continued development work on videodiscs, the kind of product RCA traditionally excelled in developing and then marketing to the American people. It certainly seemed promising. While videocassette units were more flexible in that one might record from television or even make videocassette home movies, videodiscs could only play prerecorded programs, presumably movies, but the technology did have advantages. The company planned to have the disc players come to market at $400, less than half the price videocassette units cost in 1975, and the records would also be far less expensive than either the Betamax or Matsushita tapes.

The videocassette was seen as an adjunct to the TV set, expanding its range, while videodiscs might be considered an expansion of the phonograph, enabling individuals to see as well as hear at a reasonably low price. Customers wanting to accumulate a library of classic films might well prefer the discs. Other possible uses were bandied about—putting the Sears catalogue on discs instead of in book form was one. In any case, RCA's engineers and marketing people saw no reason why the two technologies couldn't be complementary. They looked to the time when most middle-class homes would have both a videodisc and a videocassette machine, both carrying the RCA logo.

But Griffiths had his doubts about the product. In late 1976 he commissioned a new study, the results of which indicated that the player Conrad had planned to introduce in 1978 would meet with a poor reception owing to its price and competition from cassette players. Griffiths ordered a stretchout beyond 1978, intending to use the time to develop a machine that could be sold for well under $400. Additional delays followed; technological and economic reasons were always found for putting off the introduction, as though the project was an embarrassment. It was as if Griffiths feared the verdict of the marketplace and so delayed it as long as he could.

Aided by a recovering economy RCA turned in outstanding performances in 1977 and 1978, and Griffiths received much of the credit, though by rights some belonged to Bob Sarnoff and Conrad since the turnabout really began in 1975. The company had reported earnings of $110 million on revenues of $4.8 billion in 1975; for 1978 earnings came in at $278 million, while revenues were $6.6 billion, both of which were records. Yet RCA's total employment rose only modestly, from 113,000 to 118,000, and this was the result of economies instituted by Conrad but for which Griffiths had primary responsibility. But Griffiths received the credit—and more, for in 1978 he was elected to the chairmanship.

On a 43-percent increase in revenues RCA had experienced a 146-percent increase in profits. Its return on equity went from 9.5 percent to a dazzling 18.4 percent, only a shade below IBM's. And for this, too, Griffiths was applauded. His reputation had been built upon an ability to turn profits quickly, and in early 1979, it appeared he had succeeded better than expected.

Yet the picture wasn't as bright as it appeared. At a time when other electronics companies were expanding in the face of increased demand, Griffiths was cutting back. He held down capital spending as part of his cost-cutting program—$302 million in 1975, $277 million in 1978. In this period RCA's greatest expenditures were for Hertz's car and truck fleet; they went from $149 million in 1975 to $428 million in 1978.

Revenues from licensing continued to climb; in 1978 these reached $70 million, or a quarter of total income, and inflated the return on equity and the figures for consumer and commercial electronics. In order to preserve its present, RCA was auctioning off its future. Industry figures told the story graphically. In 1979 Japanese and other foreign color sets accounted for over a quarter of sales. Among U.S. firms RCA was back in first place with 21 percent, but many of these sets were produced overseas or by others. Significantly, when digital recording, the next major move in consumer electronics, arrived in 1985, RCA not only didn't have a nameplate but was completely absent from a field that by the end of the decade may make all other forms of recording obsolete.

Griffiths's clear disdain for uncertain new ventures did not mean he had no interest in acquisitions. In 1978 it became known in investment banking circles that RCA would like to purchase a financial services company, perhaps an insurance operation, that would fit in with Hertz and become a

RCA REVENUES, 1974–1978

figures in millions of dollars

	1974	1975	1976	1977	1978
Consumer Electronics	1,136	1,169	1,376	1,500	1,725
Commercial Electronics	646	601	671	760	839
Broadcasting	725	796	955	1,098	1,215
Hertz	722	715	781	838	938
Communications	195	234	259	289	324
Government Business	362	352	364	443	524
Other	828	936	942	984	1,059
Total	4,614	4,803	5,348	5,912	6,624

RCA PROFITS (PRE-TAX), 1974–1978

figures in millions of dollars

	1974	1975	1976	1977	1978
Consumer Electronics	80.2	78.1	142.0	156.6	164.6
Commercial Electronics	19.0	(19.3)	52.6	71.2	87.4
Broadcasting	94.2	106.9	120.4	152.6	122.1
Hertz	54.1	63.3	92.6	131.3	153.6
Communications	48.9	62.0	52.5	49.9	65.5
Government Business	9.6	8.3	10.8	18.1	21.9
Other	34.0	43.7	33.6	59.8	78.7
Total	340.0	343.0	504.5	641.5	693.8
Interest Expense (other than Hertz)	(55.6)	(62.0)	(61.0)	(58.1)	(63.8)
Corporate Admin. Expenses	(48.9)	(50.3)	(53.2)	(54.7)	(58.6)
Corporate Research Costs	(42.3)	(42.5)	(46.7)	(52.0)	(63.0)
Other Income (expense)	8.5	0.4	(0.5)	(6.3)	6.2
Pre-Tax Income	201.7	188.6	343.1	470.4	514.6
After Tax Income	113.3	110.0	177.4	247.0	278.4

Source: RCA, *1978 Annual Report.*

source of earnings to be invested elsewhere in the corporation. As will soon be seen, Griffiths was also concerned with boosting NBC's ratings, and this would require considerable investment. Perhaps he was taking his cue from

ITT, which had acquired Hartford Insurance, or Avco with Paul Revere. Indeed, during the early 1970s many large insurance companies were taken over with this in mind.

Griffiths prepared the way in early 1979, announcing that RCA Alaska Communications would be sold to a subsidiary of Pacific Power & Light for approximately $200 million in cash. This was not only a sign of rejection of Bob Sarnoff's acquisitions philosophy but also an indication that one of Anthony Conrad's fondest dreams, to make RCA the leader in global communications, was being abandoned. The deal was concluded that June, with PP&L paying $208.9 million, which resulted in an after-tax gain for RCA of $23.3 million.

By then Griffiths had concluded arrangements for the purchase of his financial services company: RCA would acquire CIT Financial for $1.4 billion. There was some talk that Griffiths wanted CIT because he would feel comfortable with its CEO, Walter Holmes. An old RCA hand, Holmes had once been Griffiths's boss.

An old and distinguished name in American business, CIT had been founded in 1908 as Commercial Credit and Investment Company. As the name indicates, it supplied credit to businessmen, mostly retailers, usually on a short-term basis. Over the years CIT expanded into other financial areas, including banking, and had purchased several nonrelated companies, including Picker Corp. (medical equipment), Gibson Greeting Cards, All-Steel (office furniture), and Raco (electrical supplies), but it remained an essentially credit operation. Generally speaking, CIT would borrow from banks to lend to customers, making profits on the spread between the rates. This meant that, along with a large portfolio of loans, CIT would be heavily indebted to its banks. At the time of the takeover CIT's debt came to $4.7 billion. This meant that the rise of one percent in short-term rates might eventually be translated into a charge of $47 million to the company.

Financial analysts immediately questioned the wisdom of the purchase. They regarded CIT as a sleepy company, and Griffiths was paying more than $400 million over its stated book value. The "package" consisted of $670 million in cash, much of which was raised through the sale of commercial paper, and preferred stock. At the going interest rate of 15 percent, and a 40-percent tax rate, the after-tax cost of this portion would come to $60 million a year. The preferred stock would cost RCA $63 million a year in dividends. The total in interest and dividends, then, came to around $123 million.

At the time of its purchase CIT had assets of more than $5 billion and had just achieved earnings of $107.3 million, both records. The numbers didn't make sense, and the fact that the board approved of this takeover and the price was a source of amazement. "There's no synergy for RCA," said an analyst who followed both firms. "For all that Griffiths was supposed to be a financial man, he wasn't sophisticated. He was a controller. He knew cost-cutting, he knew tightening up operations. But sophisticated financial planning or maneuvers? Nonsense. The board ought to be asked where it was when it let him buy it."

Wall Street bankers were also skeptical about the move, but they conceded that it made sense assuming three developments. Under ideal circumstances RCA would sell off the nonrelated companies and use the money to pay off part of the short-term borrowings. Secondly, CIT's earnings would continue to climb as those rate spreads remained large. Finally, and in a related fashion, interest rates would have to remain low so as to keep charges on the short-term debt at an affordable level. If everything worked out as planned, RCA would be able not only to pare the debt but also to generate sufficient additional funds to plow into other operations. Thus CIT would pay for itself and, as Griffiths saw it, do so fairly quickly.

The boards of both companies approved the merger in September, and it went into effect in January 1980.

CIT was to operate as an unconsolidated subsidiary, which meant it would be more independent than NBC, the electronics operation, and the publishing ventures. This was decided upon because of the nature of the business. If RCA's credit declined it would impact severely upon subsidiaries that had to go to the capital markets regularly, as did CIT. To preserve its AA credit rating RCA pledged not to draw dividends of more than 50 percent of CIT's profits. This straightjacket meant that CIT's ability to serve as a source of financing for the electronics business was limited, especially in bad years.

If all went well, the CIT takeover held promise of being one of Griffiths's most important accomplishments. He needed one, for by the time it was completed he appeared to have failed in another area: television.

It was obvious that NBC was in decline. Morale there was low as were profits, which had gone from a pretax net of $152.6 million in 1977 to $122.1 million the following year, this being $50 million less than CBS. In the 1977 *Annual Report* Griffiths spoke of the "steady erosion" at NBC. The network continued to have difficulties in the intense competition for national television audiences not only in prime evening time but in other parts of the program schedule as well. Griffiths promised a turnaround, knowing that unless he could bring one about, his position at Rockefeller Plaza too would be eroded.

He set about doing this in his customary fashion—by cutting costs. But it didn't work at NBC, where important artists could go elsewhere unless their demands were met—something General Sarnoff had learned in the 1930s when CBS wooed and won Jack Benny and Burns and Allen. This time it was Barbara Walters, who in 1976 left for a better paying post at ABC. She was followed by others. Walters's defection caused a stir within the industry and placed pressure upon NBC's leaders.

For years the network had been headed by men who were rather dull by industry standards. Julian Goodman, who had been president until 1974 when he was kicked upstairs to the chairmanship, was deemed competent but unimaginative as were most of the other managers. Programming executive John McMahon, who arrived there from ABC in 1972, said, "It was like walking into the Bank of America. It seemed so solemn. Nobody was pressing to be number one."

Goodman's replacement, Herbert Schlosser, was a successful lawyer-turned broadcaster, who till then had been a West Coast programming executive. Schlosser was brought in to reinvigorate the company but had indifferent success and by 1976 was known more for his penchant for hiring and quickly firing executives than for any accomplishments. In 1975 Marvin Antonowsky was placed in charge of programming; nine months later he was ejected to make way for Irwin Selegstein, who had worked with Fred Silverman at ABC. It was a telling commentary of the time that virtually anyone who could claim to have worked closely with Silverman could obtain a high-paid, influential post at any of the networks, for in the mid-1970s, Silverman was considered TV's golden boy. Schlosser would have dearly loved to obtain his services for NBC; the next best thing was to bring on board one of his protégés.

Schlosser appeared to be attempting to shuck the stodgy image by introducting innovations—more specials and additional offerings modeled after the successful "Tonight" show. Among these were "Tomorrow" and "Saturday Night Live," both of which did well for a while. Schlosser had lost out in the bidding for the 1976 Olympic Games and vowed that NBC would win the contract for the 1980 Moscow Olympics.

For the shorter term, Schlosser was determined to win leadership in the nightly news area in a way that would have appealed to Silverman's darker side. His plan: to replace John Chancellor as anchor with Tom Snyder, an affable "personality" without much in the way of professional credentials, known within the industry for his on-camera, often crude practical jokes. This unusual plan was blocked by news chief Richard Wald.

The network was still mired in last place. Other firings followed; Schlosser got rid of NBC-TV President Robert Howard and replaced him with Robert Mulholland, who then brought in Paul Klein to take Selegstein's place as head of programming. In October 1977 Schlosser fired Wald, replaced him with the more pliant Les Crystal, and announced that Chancellor would be replaced by a team of Tom Brokaw and Snyder. This plan was vetoed by Goodman and Griffiths.

By then one joke around NBC was that an executive told his secretary, "If my boss calls, get his name." The network was receiving bad press, which increased when it announced that there would be a cutback of 300 employees. This prompted a new joke. "What is the difference between NBC and the *Titanic*? The *Titanic* had an orchestra."

Klein opted to experiment with a new concept: blanket programming of specials and miniseries. This was an expensive idea, but Klein managed to convince Schlosser and Griffiths that it would push NBC into second and then first place. It didn't, and in November Griffiths ordered the plan discontinued, as Klein started to pack.

Now Griffiths decided upon a desperate step. He contacted Jane Cahill Pfeiffer, an IBM vice president for corporate communications who also served as a consultant to RCA, and asked her to approach Fred Silverman to learn whether he would be interested in a post at NBC. He was, and Griffiths met with Silverman in December 1977 to offer him not a programming job but the NBC presidency itself. After some quibbling over salary (Griffiths's initial offer was for less than Silverman was receiving at ABC), they agreed on terms. Now Schlosser was out, promoted out of NBC into an executive vice presidency at RCA, and Silverman in.

The fast-talking, glib son of a television repairman, Silverman appeared to be fashioned after the image of a TV programmer that was etched on the public mind by trashy novels and sensationalist tabloid features. A paunchy, thirty-nine-year-old dynamo who worked sixteen hours a day while smoking three packs of cigarettes and watching three television programs simultaneously, Silverman also put one in mind of the entrepreneurs who originated motion pictures in that he was intuitive and ever ready to reinvent the industry.

Known as "the man with the golden gut," Silverman first had been praised for having made CBS the industry's leader with such shows as "All in the Family" and "M*A*S*H." He then repeated his success at ABC, where he brought "Roots" to the tube, receiving credit for inventing the miniseries as well as helping fashion one of the medium's greatest popular successes. Silverman also was responsible for such critically blasted but well-received programs as "Love Boat," "Fantasy Island," "Charlie's Angels," and "Three's Company."

That he was successful and even brilliant at what he did was undeniable. Silverman had the knack of anticipating (and in a sense helping to mold) the public taste in programs running from Americanized versions of the best imports from the United Kingdom to puerile offerings designed for the proverbial twelve-year-old mind. Silverman seemed to have an unerring instinct for the common denominator, which is to say that his programs had mass appeal. One critic observed that Silverman was living proof that Mark Twain was right when he said that no one ever went broke underestimating the taste of the American people.

The announcement of Silverman's switch to NBC was made in late January 1978; Wall Street reacted by pushing ABC's stock down 1¾ points while RCA advanced by 1¼. Yet there were many in the industry who questioned the move. That Silverman wanted to lead a major network was no secret; having been at CBS and ABC, it seemed inevitable he would also want to make a clean sweep of all the networks. Up till then, however, he had never worked in a structured environment or had to direct the efforts of more than a handful of staffers. Silverman was known for his creative abilities, not executive qualities. Of course there were individuals in show business who managed to combine both, but Silverman was mercurial and a difficult person with whom to work.

Griffiths knew this but went ahead anyway. Later he said that he hired Silverman to get "the most outstanding program man in the country" and had offered him the top post at NBC because "that was the only way we could entice him to come here."

He was taking quite a chance. The network was a billion dollar corporation, and its $152.6 million in pretax earnings accounted for almost a third of the RCA total. It was the kind of operation that required the services of an experienced, sophisticated executive, not a novice. But the lure of what success could mean outweighed the risks involved. If Silverman could boost ratings by bringing NBC up to the number two position those profits could soar. In such a case his hiring could be seen as a crowning achievement of the Griffiths years. Together with Hertz and CIT, NBC could provide more than enough funds to bankroll the commercial electronics operations and the costly introduction of the videodisc machines and records.

Silverman's contract with ABC wouldn't run out until June 1978. That network refused to release him before then, so Silverman didn't arrive at NBC until the summer. In the interim he planned his strategy, which to everyone's surprise included turning his back on much of what he had accomplished at ABC. Silverman now talked of being "highly selective," praised the NBC staff as "the best team in the business," and talked of quality programming. Silverman also announced that Jane Pfeiffer would accompany him as a consultant. Shortly thereafter she left IBM to replace Goodman as NBC's chairman.

The network had only recently settled a class-action suit alleging discrimination against women, so at the time several industry observers thought Pfeiffer was brought in as "window dressing." In addition, Pfeiffer's image might counteract some of the criticisms of pandering to the masses that followed in the wake of the Silverman announcement.

Perhaps so, but there was more to it than that. Griffiths knew that NBC was riddled with strife, divided into warring factions, and generally demoralized as a result of Schlosser's activities. This was hardly unusual in the industry; the same problems existed at ABC and CBS (the latter would have five presidents in nine years). But those networks were doing considerably better than NBC, and Griffiths looked upon the disarray as something RCA could not afford. Pfeiffer was there to end or at least mitigate all of this and also to provide the executive qualities Silverman lacked; she was to run the network while Silverman concentrated on programming.

Jane Pfeiffer had risen through the ranks and, after twenty years at IBM, was considered one of the nation's most successful female executives. She was well-respected, known for her outgoing and friendly approach and her cool and reasoned decisions. Dealing as she did with network and newspaper executives, reporters, and programmers, she knew the industry well and seemed tolerant of its quirks and standards.

Pfeiffer proved to have ideas of her own on programming. She insisted that NBC not carry programs exploiting female pulchritude, which in the lexicon of the industry meant "no more T & A [tits and ass] shows." That this did not endear her to industry veterans was obvious. Soon Pfeiffer, who as a young woman had spent six months in a convent, came to be known—behind her back of course—as "Atilla the Nun," and old acquaintances wondered what had happened to transform that relatively easygoing IBMer into the scourge of bad taste at NBC.

Griffiths also had reason to feel uneasy about her. Uncovering petty corrupt practices, Pfeiffer dismissed six unit managers, several of whom went on trial later on for tax evasion. While pleased that Pfeiffer had unearthed waste, Griffiths had hoped this might have been done with little or no publicity and certainly without involving outside authorities. Undoubtedly, NBC had gotten rid of a few executives who were skimming some funds from the company, but the costs of the investigation in terms of money were much more than any savings realized, and of course the further loss of prestige was immeasurable. "Where there are abuses, you handle them quietly," said one observer. "You don't conduct a public purge like Jane did. You don't call in the U.S. Attorney's office the way she did. You could put all your TV and radio licenses in jeopardy."

Although he arrived too late to do much about programming for the autumn of 1978, Silverman did put on some shows of his own, and most were debacles. The most famous of these was a program called "Supertrain," which failed soon after its February 1979 debut, posting a loss of $12 million. Other missteps followed, leavened only slightly by such Silverman hits as "Diff'rent Strokes." In his first half year at the network Silverman canceled eight prime-time programs and developed seventy new ones at an expense of $50 million, most of them comedies, few of which made it to the tube.

The network was still in third place at the close of the 1978–1979 season, and Silverman's reputation was suffering, while Pfeiffer's investigations were destroying whatever morale remained.

Not surprisingly, she feuded with Silverman though their differences were exaggerated by most commentators. Silverman did not attempt to lead NBC, realizing early that he would have a major job in the programming area. "Have you seen NBC's new motto?" asked Johnny Carson on "The Tonight Show," one of the network's most important properties. "It says, 'Proud as a Peacock.' Well, I suppose its better than 'Dead as a Duck.'"

The audience laughed while executives at NBC writhed. And so did the affiliates, as an exodus of them from NBC to CBS and ABC began.

It quickly became evident to everyone with whom he came into contact that Silverman lacked the talents, interest, and temperament to direct NBC. In discussing Silverman, an associate said, "He's the only top executive in our business who's gotten his way by holding his breath and turning blue." As time wore on Silverman came to realize that there was some truth to such cracks, and he sought to free himself from day-to-day administrative work by placing his protégés in important posts. Brandon Tartikoff, whom he had brought to the network, became president of NBC Entertainment, while Selegstein was appointed to the new post of president of NBC Television, which carried a mandate to take over as much administrative authority as possible. "I needed him to clear my desk once and for all so I could act like a chief executive," said Silverman, who proved it by considering just how to dump Jane Pfeiffer.

By then Griffiths was shuttling back and forth between RCA and NBC, attempting to keep both on an even keel. At the same time he worried about rising interest rates, which were jeopardizing CIT, and America's new love affair with compact cars caused by the energy crises, which meant that Hertz was having trouble selling its eight-cylinder cars when they came off rentals and leases.

The board kept demanding that Griffiths produce a long-term strategic plan while maintaining short-term profits and also that he beef up his administration. Veteran director Donald Smiley, who until recently had been Macy's CEO and was taking a stronger interest in RCA, was particularly insistent that Griffiths, now fifty-nine years old, provide for an orderly succession by taking on and training an individual who could succeed him. Griffiths argued that a corporation as complex as RCA really needed an office of the chairman, a five or six person body to direct both executive and operating functions, but he was overruled.

The presidency had been vacant ever since Griffiths moved up to the chairmanship in 1978. Even before then, however, there had been a search for a new president and chief operating officer. Insiders, especially the group vice presidents, were considered, but in the eyes of the board none possessed the requisite abilities or promise, a sorry commentary on the firm. So with the aid of the executive placement firm of Heidrick & Struggles, RCA sought an outsider. At least 50 candidates were identified and twelve were proposed—GE's Executive Vice President Thomas Vanderslice and Pillsbury Vice Chairman Thomas Wyman (who went on to become chairman, president, and CEO of CBS) were on the list—but all either were rejected by the board or were not interested in the post.

In the fall of 1979 Heidrick & Struggles recommended Maurice Valente, a member of the office of the chief executive at ITT. A fourteen-year veteran there, Valente was ITT's executive vice president in charge of consumer goods and before that president of ITT-Europe. A sophisticated, cosmopolitan executive, he had wide experience at a firm known for its broad scope and diverse interest groups. Valente dealt effectively with rival French, Belgian, German, and British factions at ITT-Europe, which might stand him in good stead at RCA.

Moreover, his smooth personality would complement Griffiths's rather dour one. Donald Smiley meant it as a compliment when observing, "Griffiths has never gone through the mill with the social interchange part of the job—going out to dinners and all that. You need a guy as CEO who can run the business and develop people, not someone who is good at representing the company in public or issuing press releases." Echoing this, another director who gave Griffiths a "C– or worse" grade for public relations, observed that under Conrad and Bob Sarnoff "our external communications were superb and our operations mismanaged. It's the other way around now."

The most appealing thing about Valente, in the mind of some on the board, was that he was supposed to be able to do both—help operate the company while providing it with the kind of public image they felt would be useful in a company involved with entertainment. He even had experience in the financial area, which might endear him to Griffiths. Moreover, Valente had worked for many years with Harold Geneen, a man Griffiths appeared to emulate, and this too suggested he would do well at RCA.

Valente was interested. "Being president of RCA with the prospect of becoming the company's chief executive officer seemed like an opportunity to move to the top faster than I could at ITT," he explained. The meetings with Griffiths went well. George Fuchs, still RCA's most knowledgeable insider, was impressed with both the man and his credentials. Griffiths was pleased at the prospect. "He thought Valente was the cat's pajamas," recalled one RCA executive.

Negotiations proceeded smoothly. In November Valente signed a three-year contract providing a salary of $400,000 a year plus a $200,000 bonus, and he arrived to take his position on January 1, 1978.

Valente had troubles from the first. He soon discovered that RCA's internal divisions were far deeper than those at ITT. It was one thing to try to balance French research teams against their German counterparts, but at least they were separated from one another by several hundred miles. At RCA rival factions rubbed against each other on a daily basis, jockeying for position. Moreover there were several senior vice presidents who resented him, feeling they should have been tapped for the presidency, and they did little to make his tasks easier.

Had Valente been a stronger man he might have been able to overcome these problems, but he seemed unable to adjust to the circumstances at RCA. His inability to grasp immediately the complexities of its many power groups was interpreted as weakness. Troubled, he cast about for allies but found none in a company ever suspicious of newcomers and by then accustomed to seeing executives condemned and removed with little fanfare. He had little help from Griffiths, who generally supported old associates against his new chief operating officer.

After a few weeks Valente and Griffiths clashed. Any thought that the two men would complement one another evaporated when it became evident that Griffiths was irritated by what he considered Valente's easygoing style and went so far as to accuse him of what amounted to petty theft. On one occasion he berated Valente for having used a company car to take a member of his family to the dentist, and on another, for using a company plane to visit his mother in Chicago and his son in South Bend, Indiana. Valente's explanation, that this was after attending a company function in Indianapolis, Griffiths considered unacceptable. It had been quite different with Geneen, who didn't care much about such matters so long as the job was done; RCA was a different kind of company, and Griffiths a different breed of CEO.

So it went for five months. "It was almost instantly apparent that, with the complicated issues going on at RCA today, Valente couldn't take over the company," said an anonymous source there—one of many who leaked stories on a daily basis to the press. "He couldn't deal with his managers, and he couldn't deal with the board."

Valente later claimed the problems with Griffiths and the board derived from differences of opinion regarding his proposals for RCA and the Chairman's unwillingness to relinquish even a particle of his authority to any single individual. "RCA was not ready for a president," said Valente, who conceded that some of the trouble was his. "I should have apprised myself of the history of RCA's executive suite, of the situations related to the promotion and dismissal of Robert Sarnoff and Anthony Conrad. And I should have known more about the history of the company generally—about its operations and discipline and controls. If I'd done more checking on the politics and history, I wouldn't have gone to RCA."

It strains credulity to think that he hadn't done just that kind of checking; he certainly knew of the Sarnoff dismissal, which had been the talk of the business world. But then, how could Fuchs and Griffiths have been so utterly mistaken in their enthusiasm for the man? Perhaps Fuchs's passion for dossiers was overcome by Griffiths's impatience to finally fill the position. Still, one might have expected them to have done the kind of spadework required before making Valente the offer. In light of how things were going at RCA, however, perhaps the simplest explanation is the best: everyone blundered.

In mid-April Griffiths and two operating vice presidents told the board—in Valente's absence—that they were having problems dealing with him.

Other meetings followed, and a month later the board decided that Valente had to be eased out of office, with as little publicity as possible.

As with so many things at RCA, this too was handled clumsily. Valente related what happened at the meeting where he learned of the decision. "His [Griffiths's] explanation was that he didn't feel our future together would be effective. He pointed out that I hadn't had good communication with the operating managers. That was certainly true because he'd let them continue reporting to him. But it was contrary to what he'd told me all along about taking my time, about learning the company first."

The two men discussed the wording of a press release announcing the departure, and Valente stated that vague words suggesting that "both sides had agreed to disagree" be employed. It didn't come out that way. In late June Griffiths told reporters, "It was the board's unanimous decision that Mr. Valente's performance over nearly six months did not meet expectations." Later he added, "Why keep a man on as Number Two if it's obvious he can never be Number One?"

After he left there was a steady stream of leaks to the press denigrating Valente. One held that there was a woman on the flight in question who was not his wife, something Valente vehemently denied. There was talk that he had been about to be fired at ITT because of the poor performance of consumer goods in Europe during his stewardship of ITT operations there, which simply wasn't so. Another claimed that Valente was always overrated. While it was true that the European operations did poorly under his stewardship, this was due to political and other factors beyond his control as well as the recession of 1974. But the backbiting continued. An anonymous source said, "RCA had good operating people, and you can't hide from the troops for 30 seconds the fact that someone doesn't know the business and can't manage it." Others claimed that he didn't put in the kind of hours the job demanded, when it was fairly common knowledge that most weeks he worked a twelve-hour day.

Valente received a substantial settlement: $1.15 million. But his reputation had been crippled by the way he had been dismissed, and the whispering campaign that continued for months thereafter. "It was a traumatic experience," he said. "I received a lot of phone calls and letters of condolence. Many people were generally sympathetic, but many also combined sympathy with curiosity. . . . It takes three or four months for it to sink in. Then you begin to seriously question your abilities."

Valente went on to start his own telecommunications concern, but he never fully recovered from the RCA experience. Slightly more than three years after being forced out Valente committed suicide.

Valente out of the way, Griffiths was able to get what he wanted from the first: an office of the chairman such as that which existed during Bob Sarnoff's last months. Five executive vice presidents—Fuchs, William Hittinger, Julius Koppelman, Roy Pollack, and Frank Olson were selected as members along with Griffiths. The betting was that one of them would also become heir apparent; after the Valente episode RCA was in no mood to begin recruiting from the outside. Yet whoever received the designation would know that, like Griffiths himself, he had been passed over at least once, when the original search for a president had been made.

As always rumors were rife, and cabals formed around the favorites. Pollack, who had continued the turnaround in manufacturing started by Griffiths, was one, while Olson, in charge of the well-performing Hertz, was another. They rotated in popularity, while talk was that board member Donald Smiley was prepared to step in if the others eliminated each other, and indeed that this was his plan from the first. In fact Smiley obtained a $250,000 consulting fee, supposedly to "supervise operations," but his assignment wasn't quite clear.

Troubles mounted while all of this was going on, and for once little of it was due to RCA's missteps. An RCA Satcom III communications satellite simply disappeared in space in December 1979, and higher interest rates were savaging CIT. The biggest blow came when, in order to punish the U.S.S.R. for its invasion of Afghanistan, President Carter banned American participation in the Olympics. NBC had won the bidding to televise the games, and had been counting upon them to boost its languishing ratings; now that hope was gone.

Silverman and those growing increasingly critical of him pondered the meaning of the 1979–1980 TV season. The network was still in third place, with an overall rating of 17.4, while CBS and ABC battled it out for leadership, with 19.6 and 19.5 respectively. There was some progress; the gap between NBC and the second-place finisher had been reduced from 4.1 points to 2.2 points, and the network had three of the top twenty rated shows against one of the previous season. Further improvements were in store. "Shogun" was the hit of the early 1980–1981 season, and a rerun of another miniseries, "Centennial," did quite respectfully . There was talk of how NBC might benefit from videodiscs, rumors of the purchase of a motion picture studio to provide products for the network, and other similar matters.

These dreams were counterbalanced by a harsh reality. Revenues were down, and six major affiliates had defected to other networks since Silverman had arrived. As always NBC claimed to have a stable of blockbusters in the wings, but morale remained low, and around the water coolers junior executives placed bets on how long he would last.

"Reach out and fire someone" had become the motto at NBC as well as RCA, recalled one network executive of the time, and he blamed much of this on Jane Pfeiffer, who was becoming increasingly austere and impatient with the slightest sign of failure or the barest hint of corruption. "Many of our key people were dispensed with by Mrs. Pfeiffer," said Griffiths, who now urged Silverman to find some quiet way to ease her out. There seemed more than a little justification of the growing suspicion that the way Griffiths conducted policy was to fire and hire. As another of those anonymous RCA executives told a *Fortune* reporter, "Griffiths tries to solve problems by firing people."

So it was that in early July NBC officials leaked stories to the press that Pfeiffer was about to be eased out. *The New York Times* lead on July 9, 1980, was "NBC Chairman Relieved of Duties Following Refusal to Quit." Embarrassed, Pfeiffer issued a denial. "Nobody has asked for my resignation, and I have not offered it. It is apparent that there are some who are trying to use the media to get me to quit. . . . I won't quit. If anyone wants to terminate my employment contract, I am available to anyone who wants to see me." Now the reporters descended upon Silverman, who made a statement of his own: Pfeiffer had been relieved of "all responsibilities, and, effective immediately, her organization will report to me."

All well and good; firings were *de rigueur* at RCA, but they were being done in an unnecessarily harsh and demeaning manner, as with Valente only a month earlier. It turned out that Silverman spoke with the press without having informed Pfeiffer in advance that she had been dismissed. Now she made another statement: "Yesterday Fred Silverman told me there was no way we could both stay and he wanted his contract renewed now, and for that to happen, I had to make a decision and implement it. He did not ask for my resignation then or ever." She then went on to strike a blow against Silverman and RCA. "He simply stated that RCA people play hardball, and that he would probably follow me out the door in six months. This afternoon through the media I learned that he had relieved me of my duties as chairman."

Now Silverman released to the press a note he sent to Pfeiffer, wishing her "all success" in "future endeavors." An ABC executive observed that "Silverman not only programs comedies, he lives them," to which the Dean of the School of Public Communications at Boston University added that it was a case of life imitating art. "If you can't resolve the problem in a half-hour script, you shoot someone."

This wasn't the end of the matter. Pfeiffer settled her employment contract for $705,000, even though she was entitled to $753,000. Griffiths went before the board to tell it of the terms and boasted of how he had managed to cut the figure by $48,000. Once again his words found their way into the press, making him seem a tactless boor. "We didn't intentionally set out to make ourselves look like fools," mused Silverman when it was all over. By then, however, RCA looked more than ever like a brutal, uncaring corporation on the ropes.

All of this might have been forgiven had Griffiths managed to maintain the earnings momentum generated in his first years in office. But there was a decided slowdown starting in 1979, largely because of problems already alluded to, such as interest rates and the Hertz car fleet. While consumer electronics sales continue upward, the result largely of replacement of early color TVs and success in videocassette recorders, despite Griffiths's willingness to plow additional sums into the operations, commercial electronics remained an industry laggard.

RCA REVENUES, 1978–1980

figures in millions of dollars

	1978	1979	1980
Consumer Electronics	1,725	1,756	1,916
Commercial Electronics	839	1,113	1,281
Broadcasting	1,215	1,368	1,522
Hertz	938	1,122	1,290
Communications	324	282	254
Government Business	524	660	768
Other	1,059	1,154	982
Total	6,624	7,455	8,013

RCA PROFITS (PRETAX), 1978–1980

figures in millions of dollars

	1978	1979	1980
Consumer Electronics	164.6	97.0	99.6
Commercial Electronics	87.4	97.1	95.7
Broadcasting	122.1	105.6	75.3
Hertz	153.6	146.8	127.2
Communications	65.5	68.0	90.9
Government Business	21.9	39.6	50.9
Financial Services	—	9.9	177.4
Other	78.7	66.3	33.3
Total	693.8	630.3	750.3
After-Tax Income	278.4	283.8	315.3
Earnings Per Share	$3.62	$3.72	$3.35

Source: RCA, *1978–80 Annual Reports.*

While the 1979 earnings rose slightly as did earnings per share, this increase was made possible by the $23.3 million profit realized from the sale of Alascom, which worked out to $0.31 per share, and RCA also benefited from lower tax rates. In addition, the company included in its 1979 figures $9 million of CIT's profits, even though the CIT didn't become part of RCA until the following year. Without these special items, RCA would have experienced an earnings decline of $27 million from the previous year, the first of the Griffiths administration.

After-tax income rose by more than 11 percent in 1980, to a record $315.3 million. Once again, this was due to additional special items—$19.8 million from insurance proceeds on the lost Satcom III satellite and the cancellation of the Olympics broadcasts, profits of $11 million from the sale that year of Random House, and a $21 million upward revaluation of CIT's assets, which came to almost $0.70 per share. Without the special items RCA's per share earnings for 1980 would have been around $2.65, which was only $0.30 more than they had been in 1976.

The company's operating profit margin in 1980 was 6 percent; in 1976 it had been 8.8 percent. Moreover, RCA's debt had more than doubled in the 1978–1981 period and was now $2.9 billion. Standard & Poors and Moody's were known to be eyeing the company with a mind toward lowering its credit rating.

The network was in bad shape, as Silverman not only proved incapable of managing the operation but appeared to have lost his touch as a programmer as well. What could one make of "Pink Lady and Jeff," which featured two Japanese singers? NBC went through the entire drill, ordering scripts, obtaining a producer, initiating the publicity, and even placing the show in the fall lineup, before learning the two pink ladies, who were sensations in Japan, couldn't speak English! "Pink Lady and Jeff" was scrapped, and Silverman's days in office were numbered. "The Silverman years were a half-billion dollar mistake," said one broadcast executive, in obvious exaggeration. But if NBC had managed to equal its 1977 earnings in the following three years, the pretax profits would have been $246 million higher.

Hertz was another problem; Robert Stone seemed to have taken the magic with him when he departed. Pretax earnings rose in 1978 but declined in 1979 and fell in 1980 to $127.2 million, the lowest since 1976.

In contrast, CIT turned in excellent results in 1980, posting $177.4 million in pretax earnings. The figure was inflated, however, since part of that represented nonrecurring gains through the sale of loans. Now it appeared that this was what Griffiths had in mind when he took over the finance company. "The CIT acquisition was to gloss over what was bound to be a down year in 1980," recalled one associate later on. "That's how nervous Ed was about the numbers."

As he well might have been. Griffiths appeared to be losing his touch in generating profits. Still there was some hope. The long-awaited videodisc players finally appeared ready to be marketed. Given success in this area, which some within the industry now thought might eventually be an $8 billion segment, he might have recouped all that had been lost. Several journalists thought such success would paper over some of the malaise that had developed.

But RCA was too far gone. It was a company gyrating out of control, where instability had become a way of life. Eleven of the twenty-five top RCA officers there when Griffiths took over had left, as had five of the company's twelve directors. The Valente and Pfeiffer dismissals were still reverberating through the firm in the summer of 1980, when some of the outside members on the board started to discuss the possibility of disposing of Griffiths. "Six months ago we knew that Ed had to go," said one of them. "We just had to work out and how and when."

The board announced that it would organize a search committee to find a new president, but in fact it was for Griffiths's replacement. Donald Smiley was a key figure in all of this, an indication that his consulting fee was being paid for these services. Whatever hopes Griffiths might have had of survival were dispelled when, in November, Smiley approached him with a new employment contract under which he would be paid $250,000 a year for five years to be a consultant following his resignation. "We had to get him under contract and control," said a member. All that remained was to locate the proper replacement and then attempt to ease Griffiths out gracefully, an exercise at which RCA was hardly expert.

The search committee didn't look very far, for by then it had settled on its candidate—one of the veteran outsiders on the board, Thornton Bradshaw of Atlantic Richfield.

14

The Search for Stability

THERE WAS SOMETHING familiar about the way Thornton Bradshaw was asked to consider the chairmanship at RCA. As when Bob Sarnoff had been replaced by Conrad, there were clandestine board meetings to plan just how the old chairman would be removed and who was to succeed him. Maneuvering and jockeying for position intensified while the ax was being sharpened, this accompanied by the rumors and leaks.

Yet there were important differences as well. The board had gone outside of the corporation for leadership; for the first time in its history RCA would be headed by a man who had not put in an apprenticeship at the firm. So there were no disappointed executives who felt unjustly passed over for a less-qualified rival within the organization.

If Bradshaw lacked a cadre of allies, he also had few if any enemies. Most at RCA—even the staff at Rockefeller Plaza—would barely have recognized him had they met in a corridor. He was in the happy position of knowing RCA (in terms of service he was the senior outside director) while not having been embroiled in any of the factional disputes of the period. He had been unable to attend the meeting at which Conrad resigned and so had had no part in selecting Griffiths.

Sixty-three years of age and having recently undergone open heart surgery, Bradshaw had the look of an interim CEO whose major task would be to provide RCA with some stability, attempt to mute if not end some of the internal dissension, and most important, locate and train a successor. If this could be done there could be an orderly transition for the first time since Bob Sarnoff took over. Bradshaw would be the fourth chief executive in six years, and he knew that the firm's morale had been shattered.

He seemed up to the task. Bradshaw was looked upon as a man of breadth and substance, an intellectual who had earned a doctorate from the Harvard

Business School, had been a professor there, and was regularly considered for university presidencies. In addition, he had had a highly successful business career. Bradshaw left Harvard in 1952 to become a consultant and achieved a reputation as one of the pioneers in long-range business planning. Four years later he joined the Atlantic Refining Co. as an assistant general manager, rose quickly, and in 1964 became its president under Chairman Robert Anderson.

They made one of the most impressive, successful, and eclectic teams in the petroleum industry. Anderson was a major patron of the arts, while Bradshaw wrote and spoke on a wide variety of topics, from business ethics to foreign policy to the need for greater coordination of efforts in the executive suites. Together they engineered the acquisitions of Richfield Oil, Sinclair Oil, and Anaconda and parlayed an investment in a drilling operation on Alaska's north slope into the greatest North American oil find since the glory years in Texas and California. In the process Anderson and Bradshaw transformed what had been a small regional refiner into the eighth largest factor in the industry. Meanwhile Bradshaw served on presidential commissions and the boards of several other corporations, joining RCA's in 1972.

That Bradshaw intended to retire from Atlantic Richfield was well known, and he had no burning ambition for a second career at RCA. There was talk of the books he intended to write and a possible position in Washington; Bradshaw was a natural diplomat, an eloquent speaker, and an inspirational leader. But given the turmoil at Rockefeller Plaza and the respect he engendered, it perhaps was inevitable that he would be asked to replace Griffiths.

The outside directors had been considering Griffiths's removal for most of 1980 and late in the year had concluded both that the time for a change had arrived and that Bradshaw would be his successor.

Everything was in place when in late January 1981 Smiley informed Griffiths of the decision. An inside source told *Business Week,* "We couldn't let it go any longer, because we wanted to file proxy material before the annual meeting, so we decided to announce it at the board meeting on February 4."

Hewing to the RCA tradition, the plan went awry. For one thing, Griffiths's impending departure was hardly a secret, and for another, Bradshaw announced his resignation as Arco's president on January 26, and even those few business reporters who were not privy to leaks could see that this was a prelude to his move to RCA. Finally, disgusted with the situation and the atmosphere at headquarters, Griffiths called in reporters and beat the others at their own game by informing them in January of his departure. "I'm tired," Griffiths told the reporters. "It has been a long and very taxing career. I started thirty-three years ago in a very humble position. I don't think I've missed ten days in thirty-three years."

As had become customary, the settlement with Griffiths was generous. He would remain on as chairman of a new finance committee for two years, after which his consultantship would begin. One journalist figured that the severance arrangements at RCA and NBC during the last years of the Griffiths chairmanship cost the corporation $4.7 million.

When it was all over many wondered just where it was that Griffiths failed, the consensus being that his bottom line figures were decaying, he had failed to name and train a successor, the videodisc project had been mishandled, and the CIT acquisition was a mistake. Moreover he had given RCA a bad image with all those dismissals, and of course the situation at NBC was serious. But the CIT purchase had been approved by the board, as was the hiring of Fred Silverman, and the directors had put up with everything else throughout the Griffiths's regime.

Indeed, the situation only served to point up the board's deficiencies. Fuchs, who kept such careful dossiers, had not foreseen the problems that would develop with Silverman, Pfeiffer, and Valente. What had Smiley done to earn his $250,000 a year retainer? His major accomplishments seemed to have been to negotiate the generous severance contract with Griffiths and turn to his fellow-director, Bradshaw, as his successor, and with the others on the board give him a five-year $938,500-a-year contract plus stock options. Others had also gone to the RCA well; Lehman Bros. Kuhn Loeb would garner $2 million in fees for financial services. If Griffiths had faults, so did those who hired and then fired him.

"In many ways, Griffiths played the role of the master mechanic during his reign at RCA," wrote *Fortune,* in an article entitled "A Peacemaker Comes to RCA" that appeared in the May 4, 1981, issue. Its author, Walter Nutly, clearly based his conclusions on leaks from the board, and it reflected the beliefs of several members. "He [Griffiths] tuned the engine, lubricated the power train, put many of the moving parts in sound working order." If so—and this assessment is largely reflective of reality—why make the change? "Bradshaw is left the task of mapping the vehicle's future course." So it would appear that the new CEO was there to give the firm a strategy and then initiate its implementation.

It wasn't that simple. The contrast between Griffiths and Bradshaw couldn't have been starker. Griffiths was a grim workaholic, who insisted upon always knowing exactly what was happening in every part of the corporation at all times. He was temperamental, intolerant toward those who opposed him, and obsessed with the short term. In the parlance of the time, Griffiths was the epitomy of "hands-on management." Bradshaw, on the other hand, was an easygoing, affable man who could spend the entire night with associates without once mentioning business. At Arco he tended to seek the right man for a job, make certain he was capable, and then leave him pretty much to his own devices, observing carefully but not interfering unless a serious breach was about to be made.

Bradshaw took account of human frailties, moved slowly, rarely concerned with quarter-to-quarter comparisons. For this reason some thought him lackadaisical, when in fact he usually knew exactly what was happening. He accepted criticism with grace and humor. There were those who thought Griffiths a strong, forceful leader, when at times he would vacillate and often appeared incapable of making strategic decisions, as was particularly apparent in his inability to select a successor. The opposite was the case with Bradshaw, who appeared slow and cautious when in fact he was deliberate and prudent.

News that Bradshaw would take over was well-received at headquarters where executives unburdened themselves of thoughts regarding Griffiths to reporters. "He tended to pressure the board at the last minute into doing things his way," one of them recalled. "He's a bully and a tyrant." Another said, "RCA has been convulsing for a decade. It may not be over, but I think Thornton Bradshaw represents stability." A third added, "In a company that has been sorely lacking it, Bradshaw has class."

All spoke anonymously. To end such talk and practice would be one of Bradshaw's more important tasks. He indicated as much from the start, telling reporters of the need to install a "meritocracy" at RCA, which translated into an intention to stop cloakroom wheeling and dealing. "That begins with an openness with people in the company and with the press," Bradshaw said.

Griffiths was due to step down on June 30, 1981, but by speaking out as he did he ended his effectiveness. For the next five months, although Griffiths occupied the CEO's position and office, Bradshaw was really in charge. This meant that from February RCA had a CEO who would not effectively be in control and a CEO-elect without authority. Griffiths attended to housekeeping but almost everything else was on hold, the one exception being the videodisc program, finally about to be launched at a time when the corporation seemed adrift. Bradshaw took an office in Arco's headquarters a few blocks away, calling in executives from Rockefeller Plaza and the field, attempting to get a firm grasp of what was going on at the company while at the same time sizing up key individuals and trying to instill in them a sense of loyalty to the incoming administration.

The announcement of Bradshaw's appointment sparked many new rumors, one of which held that the CEO-designate was an ill man, who came aboard only upon assurances that he would not be called upon to perform any onerous tasks. Those who accepted this point of view believed Smiley was exercising power behind the scene, either individually or as part of a group.

A second rumor was that Bradshaw would preside over the disembowelment of RCA. The company's parts were worth more than the whole, and business writers and reporters had a field day calculating just how much each would bring. That CIT and/or Hertz would be sold to pay off part of the burgeoning debt was taken as a matter of course, but there were those who thought other parts of RCA might also be on the block.

As if to confirm this rumor, Bradshaw called in management consultants Booz, Allen & Hamilton to assist in the planning. He was not overly sanguine regarding the future. "We've got to select the areas where we have strength and the capability to grow faster and better than others," he told a reporter after a month in office. "We have an enormous variety of opportunities with lessened capital," he added, while making it known that portions of the company were on the block for the right price. "We are choking off capital expenditures that we want very much to make. We'd like to spend more on our production lines to bring them up to the Japanese level of investment, and a lot more in semiconductors." Time and again he would reiterate this theme: "I am anxious to get back to the roots of this company."

Since Standard & Poors and Moody's had lowered RCA's credit rating, reducing the debt would have high priority. "We are pressing the upper limits of our borrowing capacity with triple-B credit," Bradshaw said. When asked if RCA could regain its old stature, Bradshaw candidly replied, "I don't think so." Referring to David Sarnoff, he added, "The emergence of the new technologies—radio and TV—created a galaxy of products that were sparked by a genius. What we have now are advances on old, existing technology."

The partial liquidation of Bob Sarnoff's conglomerate and the nonfinancial segments of CIT had begun in the waning days of the Griffiths administration. Banquet Foods had been sold in November 1980, and in the first quarter of 1981 it was joined by Avionica Systems, Oriel Foods, Picker, and Raco, while negotiations began with a private group headed by former Treasury Secretary William Simon to dispose of Gibson Greeting Cards. Out went Mobile Communications and some of the foreign interests of RCA Records. The company sold CIT's headquarters building for a profit of over $28 million.

Coronet was on the block, and in the 1981 *Annual Report,* Bradshaw said ". . . we are considering selling Hertz and other of our nonelectronic subsidiaries." Not only might Hertz bring a decent price—perhaps over half a billion dollars—but "the sale of Hertz would remove its $1.4 billion of debt from RCA's consolidated balance sheet" and perhaps nudge the rating agencies into reassessing the company's credit worthiness. Bradshaw specifically excluded CIT from the list of companies to be sold, but no one took this seriously. During the next year it became obvious that RCA would accept an offer in the vicinity of $1.2 billion for the property.

In addition to these sales RCA set up a reserve fund of $230 million for "the restructuring of operations and revaluation of assets," which included $34 million in shows Silverman had planned that now would be scrapped, $130 million for some ailing, failing picture tube operations, and $59 million for Hertz, stuck with a fleet of cars that were doing poorly on the resale market and abandoning a venture in truck leasing. What all of this meant was that in his first half year Bradshaw was wiping the slate as clean as he could, not an uncommon exercise when a new administration takes over. Following the script, once the dross was removed what remained would perform well, enabling the company to blame the losses on the old administration, while crediting the new with the gains.

Of course there was talk of impending dismissals in all of the divisions, with most attention concentrated upon NBC, where Silverman was an obvious target. When asked about this, Bradshaw replied, "Silverman will be on board July 1 unless he chooses otherwise. And I have no indication he will choose otherwise."

Bradshaw was misinformed, uninformed, or dissembling. Silverman jumped before he could be pushed, resigning on June 30, the day before Griffiths officially stepped down. He was immediately replaced by Grant Tinker, the former head of MTM Productions, who had a reputation for possessing managerial skills and hewing to budgets. Tinker was no stranger to NBC, having arrived there as a management trainee in 1949. He was director of West Coast programming in the 1960s. Robert Mulholland became NBC's president while Irwin Selegstein was bumped into the post of vice chairman. Brandon Tartikoff remained in place as president of the entertainment division. These retentions were considered significant. The departure of Selegstein or Tartikoff, or both, might have been taken as an indication that yet another purge was in the works. That they and others from the Silverman era remained meant that Tinker intended to bring the same measure of stability to NBC that Bradshaw was striving to create at RCA. The changes and retentions were applauded though there was a cloud; the swiftness of the move indicated that it was in the works all the while.

The new Tinker-Mulholland team soon made it clear that the period of high spending that characterized the Silverman years was over. A calm, genial individual who like his predecessor was known for his work on situation comedies, Tinker was far more conventional a programmer and was well known for his ability to work within a budget. Ironically, Griffiths, known for his devotion to such matters, had brought Silverman to NBC while Bradshaw, who had bankrolled Arco's Alaska crude oil crapshoot, turned to Tinker.

When all the numbers were toted up RCA reported a net profit of $54 million in 1981 on revenues of $8 billion. In 1980 earnings had been $315 million on a like amount of revenues. After allowing for the preferred stock dividends, RCA lost $0.19 per share in 1981 compared with a profit of $3.35 in 1980. The quarterly dividend, which Griffiths had boosted to $0.45 in his last year, was retained, but in early 1981 it was obvious the payout couldn't be maintained and in fact would be halved in March.

Toward the end of 1981 RCA common was selling for under 17 and before the annual meeting would decline to 15¾, a low not seen since the time Bob Sarnoff threw in the towel on the data processing program. At that price RCA seemed an enticing target for some arbitrageur, who could make a tender offer, acquire the company, and then carve it up into pieces to be offered to the highest bidders. Failing this, units might be organized as separate companies, the feeling being the markets would value them individually more than in the aggregate. After all, argued those who thought this likely, it wouldn't be very much different from what Bradshaw was trying to do. Assuming a price of $25 per share, it would have taken slightly more than $2 billion to acquire all of the common shares. In 1982 RCA had a vastly understated book value of over $20 per share. Far more than $2 billion could have been realized from the sales of NBC, Hertz, and CIT alone, and the owner then would have the entire electronics complex and ancillary operations for a huge profit.

William Agee, the contentious young CEO of Bendix Corp., was one of those who recognized this and acted. In late 1981 Agee decided to make a major takeover. In his treasury was $2 billion in cash and short-term investments, part of which was used to nibble at RCA. In September he met with Bradshaw at Rockefeller Plaza to feel him out on the idea, which was promptly rejected. The following March Agee announced that he had purchased 5 percent of RCA stock on the open market "for investment only," which had become a cliche meaning just the opposite but in this case might have had some substance. Other companies were circling RCA, where Bradshaw and his staff were hastily erecting defenses.

The most important of these was already in place, however; any change in ownership of radio and TV stations would require approval of the FCC, and hearings on such matters could drag on for years. Matters could be eased, however, if the acquisition was friendly, and Agee wooed Bradshaw assiduously during the winter and spring of 1982.

Bradshaw would not be budged, however, and was assisted by sensationalist news out of Bendix. In October Vice President Mary Cunningham was obliged to resign amid rumors that she and Agee were lovers. When Agee made a takeover proposal to RCA, Bradshaw called in the press and told them, "Mr. Agee has not demonstrated the ability to manage his affairs, let alone someone else's." Little could be done without Bradshaw's cooperation, so Agee turned elsewhere. Later that summer he started accumulating shares of Martin Marietta, setting off the most spectacular merger episode of the period. By then RCA common was over 25, and talk of a takeover, friendly or otherwise, diminished. But it didn't disappear entirely. Rumors of dissolution or merger could continue to reemerge.

In early 1984 it appeared that raider Irwin Jacobs was preparing to move in on the company with a tender offer and if successful would break up RCA and sell off the pieces. As was by then customary in such matters, Jacobs would neither confirm nor deny that he had started accumulating RCA common, but later it was disclosed that he had purchased some 1–4 percent of the outstanding stock.

The board reacted in March, announcing it would propose antitakeover measures at the next stockholders' meeting. Specifically, would-be raiders would be forbidden from utilizing a device known as "two-tier pricing," by which they offered one price in the tender and then, when they had control, offered a lower price for the remainder of the stock. The measure was adopted, but talk of a takeover continued, accelerating in 1985 when ABC was purchased by Capital Cities Broadcasting and Atlanta broadcaster-entrepreneur Ted Turner made a bid for CBS. Bradshaw affirmed that RCA would not sell NBC, and after a brief flurry of rumors regarding a move against RCA there was little further discussion of the matter.

Meanwhile Bradshaw concerned himself with the matter of succession. Initially it appeared that either Frank Olson of Hertz or Roy Pollack of Electronics might be tapped for the presidency, but it soon became apparent the next RCA president and chief operating officer would come from outside the firm. Bradshaw employed the services of Heidrick & Struggles (which, it will be recalled, had brought Valente to RCA), and the search went on through the spring and summer of 1982. Gerard Roche of H&S put together an initial list of seventy-five prospects, which was soon pared to five or six.

Roche had a clear idea of what he was to find: unsurprisingly, he sought a younger version of Bradshaw. "Mature, experienced, low-key, nonflamboyant, but with a high energy level: those were the characteristics we were looking for," said Roche. "We didn't want some star-fire executive with a big ego who would knock down the structure Brad was working hard to build." Of course, it would be nice if the candidate had experience at a firm somewhat similar to RCA, but the other qualities were more important. Bradshaw demanded the reality as well as the appearance of stability.

In September 1982 RCA announced the selection: Robert Frederick, at the time GE's fifty-six-year-old executive vice president in charge of international operations. He had arrived there as a trainee when he was twenty-two years old. At the time Bradshaw said, "It's the most important decision I've made since I've been here." So a half century after Owen Young left RCA another GE executive arrived to take a prominent leadership position.

The medium-sized, stocky, and balding Frederick seemed a logical choice. He had served in several divisions at GE and spent some time in consumer goods, credit, and strategic planning, all of which would serve him well at RCA. Considered an intense, hard-working man, Frederick had a reputation for being a good team player, which probably was one of the qualities that impressed Bradshaw—and might have worked against him at GE, where the scramble for the succession to CEO John Welch had become heated. As a former GE executive who understood the situation there remarked, "Welch has a number of tigers coming up—dynamic, high-energy people who'd be giving Frederick a real run for his money."

Frederick knew that this was so and, in addition, considered his age would work against him there. He had just about decided to retire at age sixty when the invitation came to meet with Bradshaw. He later conceded "I knew GE wasn't going to promote me. That was my top-out job. But the issue was: do I leave a company that had been good to me for thirty-four years for a company that had, you might say, an uneven performance and a reputation for chewing up management?"

There was another side to it. In the first place, like others in his position Frederick had long hoped to become CEO of a major corporation, and this probably would be his only chance. Then, too, he respected and trusted Bradshaw, knowing that given his age and health there was no question of his trying to stay on past the period of apprenticeship. In their conversations Bradshaw told Frederick just how he viewed RCA's future, of his desire to concentrate upon the core businesses of broadcasting and consumer and commercial electronics, which was not very much different from much of what Frederick knew at GE. Bradshaw took note of the morale problem at RCA and the high executive turnover and indicated that he wanted to change this. Frederick was told that the new president would be chairman and CEO-apparent, but *his* successor would be someone from within the company. He wanted the new person to bring to RCA the kind of stability and career development that Frederick had experienced at GE.

The hard-working Frederick would mesh well with the easygoing Bradshaw. "Bob's background was exactly what RCA needed," Roche said. "He was a strategic thinker without being too think-tanky or eggheady, and he had run the international sector, which cut across all GE product lines. RCA needed a strong manager who wasn't going to try to upstage Brad or push him out and take over."

As expected Frederick worked well with Bradshaw, and most problems that surfaced could be traced to the fact that neither had come up through the ranks at RCA. While their strategic planning was sound, tactical problems remained. One did not erect alliances easily at RCA. Frederick recognized the dimensions of the problem. He soon won the respect of top executives for his abilities, capacity for work, and—to the surprise of those who had heard he had a quick temper—coolness and fairness. "Nothing that RCA has done has his fingerprint on it," said securities analyst James Magid, who followed RCA for L. F. Rothschild, Unterberg, Towbin. "I can think of no higher praise for Frederick than that statement. The role of a senior executive is to preside over success, rather than get a lot of personal credit for things. This is a guy who doesn't need credit, and that's a far cry from RCA's past, when there was blame and credit and undue egotism."

Frederick expressed surprise over the baroque atmosphere he found at RCA. "There was a survival mentality. They would remove people on very short-term result failures. It was manifested in that people worked to keep quiet the bad news, in the hope they could fix things, because they didn't want to be reprimanded or fired."

Perhaps he had the videodisc situation in mind, which as many had anticipated, wasn't turning out well. In fact, videodiscs turned out to be a major product disaster, second only to that of data processing. If the videodisc failure was not as scarring to the corporate ego, it was because by the 1980s expectations were no longer very inflated.

As noted, the original videodisc concept was to offer a low-priced unit that might sway customers from videocassette machines, or failing that, find its own niche in the home. Perhaps videodiscs would have been viable had they been introduced in the early 1970s, before the nation became hooked on the videocassette units. In 1976 the output of videocassette players came to less than 300,000; by 1983 the number was up to 18 million, and in the same span the price dropped from over $2,000 to under $500. Each videocassette player purchase meant one less potential customer for videodiscs. To further complicate matters, Philips and MCA developed a rival disc technology that employed optical scanning rather than the stylus used in the RCA version. Then other companies joined one camp or the other. On the RCA team were Zenith, CBS, and Matsushita, while Magnavox and IBM came in on the Philips-MCA side.

Magnavox came to the market first, in 1980, with a $775 MagnaVision unit. Sales were poor, which was one of several reasons Griffiths held back, asking his production teams to try to come up with a lower-priced model. Later that year RCA demonstrated a prototype designed to sell for $400. Some within the industry claimed this would result in large losses until volume rose to the point where economies of scale could be realized, while others thought the players themselves would never be money-makers. Profits would come from the discs. A motion picture that might retail for $80 on tape could be sold for $10-$20 in disc form, and it was from this market that RCA hoped to reap its rewards.

The SelectaVision VideoDisc players and an initial selection of discs were finally introduced in March 1981, when Griffiths was winding down his administration and Bradshaw preparing to move in, hardly a time when full corporate attention could be devoted to the new product. Executives predicted first-year sales of over 400,000 units, and were disappointed when only 225,000 of them (65,000 with the RCA logo) were sold.

Trying to put the best face on this showing, Bradshaw noted that in 1955, the first full year of television receiver sales, only 35,000 were sold, and videocassette recorders didn't do much better in their first year, 1976, when sales barely reached 30,000. In early 1982 RCA announced that a stereo version of the player would soon be introduced, with a retail price of $349.95.

Sales rose, but not to levels where deficits could be shaved to a manageable level. Some 130,000 SelectaVisions were purchased in 1982, a year during which 2 million videocassette players were sold. By the end of 1983 RCA could boast that over 500,000 players had been purchased during the past three years and that disc sales were stronger than anticipated. Still, the company revealed that it had lost a total of $303.4 million on the product since its introduction. When pre-1981 charges were added, the total came to more than $400 million.

When Bradshaw took over, the situation was worse than anyone imagined it could be. Videocassette players clearly had the edge over discs in flexibility if not in the price of the "software," but the rapid development of video rental outlets made the price of cassettes irrelevant. Just about all of the players could tape programs from television, which as noted could not be done with videodisc players. By 1983 RCA (which sold more cassette units than disc players) was talking of the possibilities of selling disc units to complement rather than supplant cassette units, and the price of a basic player was lowered to $200. In March 1983 Frederick said that "under no foreseeable circumstances" would RCA abandon videodiscs. "Clearly, the business has taken a turn upward. . . . We will push ahead." But by then it was evident that RCA was looking for a graceful way to drop the product.

This came on April 4, 1984, when RCA announced a sharp increase in the first quarter's revenues and earnings. At the same time, stating that it had lost more than $500 million on the project, RCA gave up on videodiscs. The major reasons for the failure, Bradshaw said, were the "enormous growth in videocassette recorders, the rapid development of a rental market in videocassettes, and the loss of control over videodisc software," the last referring to the inability to present customers with as wide a selection of movies as were available on cassettes. It was a "technological success but a commercial failure."

Other than this, RCA was doing nicely, especially in arranging the CIT divestiture. For the past two years industry analysts wondered just how much of a loss the company would take on this property, but conditions had changed drastically, in such ways as to make CIT a more attractive company than it appeared in 1981. For one thing, lower interest rates meant that would-be purchasers would have an easier time financing an acquisition, while the economic upturn increased CIT's profitability. Also important was the atmosphere of deregulation, which fostered the development of "financial supermarkets." By itself CIT was attractive enough, but as a jigsaw puzzle piece for a company trying to put together an entity capable of providing a wide variety of services it was irresistible.

In October Bradshaw announced that CIT would be sold to Manufacturers Hanover Bank for $1.51 billion, of which $460 million would be in cash, the rest in notes and securities carrying an initial average interest rate of 11.7 percent. Two insurance companies with a book value of some $250 million would be excluded from the transaction (one of these was sold soon after, and the other placed on the block). The acquisition of CIT had cost RCA $1.4 billion, $662 in cash, the rest in preferred stock paying less than 4 percent. The sale, together with the imputed value of the two insurance companies and additional sums realized from the earlier sale of CIT's New York headquarters building, indicated that RCA had realized a substantial profit on the deal. The cash would enable RCA to bolster its weakened financial situation, while interest on the rest, which would be approximately $123 million per annum, would more than compensate for the loss of CIT's contribution to RCA's earnings, which in 1982 were $107 million of total net profits of $222.6 million.

The takeover made sense for Manufacturers Hanover too; CEO John McGillicuddy, who initiated discussions with Bradshaw, said CIT would provide a "substantial shot in the arm" for his company's ambitious expansion program, while Bradshaw told a reporter that "our financial flexibility will increase by a quantum leap."

As would the company's credit rating. On March 26, as final preparations for the sale were being made, Moody's noted that "RCA is making impressive progress in reorganization so that its operations are more integrated and profitable. At the same time the company is strengthening its balance sheet." With this, the agency raised its ratings on RCA's senior debt from Baa-2 to A-3, on subordinated debt from Baa-3 to Baa-1, and on the company's preference stock from Baa-3 to Baa-2. The formal transfer took place a week later, leaving RCA in its strongest financial shape in a generation.

More significant even than the CIT sale was the revival at NBC. Little happened at first, as Grant Tinker hewed to his policy of moving slowly and creating an atmosphere of stability. "I thought we could do just a little fixing and achieve parity with the other networks," he later remarked. "But we have not made [the kind of] progress . . . I thought we would."

Ratings rose slowly, though the kind of programming failures that had marked the Silverman era did not end. The 1983–1984 season was a particular disaster, with nine of Tartikoff's programs canceled due to poor ratings. But NBC also had successes. In 1983–1984 "The A-Team" and "Miami Vice" captured large audiences, and the following year Tartikoff had a major winner in "The Cosby Show," which after being turned down by ABC went to NBC, where it quickly became the most popular evening half-hour program.

In 1984 Robert Igiel of Ayer & Co., one of the more important time buyers, said that Tinker had brought "a stability of thought to NBC," which was the consensus within the industry and one that Tinker shared. "[I] inherited a company whose byword was: 'What God-awful thing is going to happen to us today?' With no false modesty, all I did was calm down the apprehension and political intrigue at NBC and persuade everyone to start pulling in one direction."

Even so, the NBC doors continued to revolve. That year Tinker brought in Lawrence Grossman to replace Reuven Frank as head of NBC News. Formerly the head of the Public Broadcasting Service, Grossman had wide experience but had never been a reporter or editor. "He is a bright guy and he has been around his medium," said Tinker defending the selection, but this was one of the issues that led Mulholland to resign in protest. This was a loss, since Mulholland was considered one of the brightest stars at the network, but it also indicated that Tinker had a solid grip on his job, for Mulholland would not have gone had he believed he had a chance to succeed to the chairmanship in a reasonable amount of time.

As a result of higher time charges all of the networks showed generally increasing profits from 1981 on, but none performed better than NBC. Tinker received a good deal of credit for the upswing, which together with the sale of CIT made RCA more viable financially than ever.

On May 1, 1984, Bradshaw announced his intention to step down as CEO (but not chairman) sometime before the company's next annual meeting the following spring. As anticipated, Frederick was designated his successor.

Bradshaw wrote his valedictory in the 1984 *Annual Report*:

> When your Chairman assumed his position in July of 1981, four objectives were established: to refocus the company on its three core businesses—electronics, communications, and entertainment—to strengthen the balance sheet, to restructure management, and to provide for succession. These objectives have been accomplished, and the company has been set firmly on the path of long-term growth. At this natural turning point, I am stepping aside as Chief Executive Officer but staying on as Chairman of the Board, and your President is assuming the position of Chief Executive Officer.

RCA REVENUES, 1981–1985

figures in millions of dollars

	1981	1982	1983	1984	1985
Consumer Electronics	2,318	2,102	2,402	2,188	1,992
Records and Video	—	—	—	622	758
Commercial Electronics	1,196	1,204	1,140	1,312	1,262
Government Business	896	1,048	1,299	1,442	1,597
Broadcasting	1,619	1,786	2,094	2,371	2,648
Hertz	1,428	1,555	1,372	1,440	—
Communications	270	319	377	417	425
Other	277	223	294	319	291
Total	8,004	8,237	8,978	10,111	8,973

Source: RCA, *Annual Reports,* 1981–1985.

RCA PROFITS (PRETAX), 1981–1985

figures in millions of dollars

	1981	1982	1983	1984	1985
Consumer Electronics	132.2	87.4	122.6	20.8	146.8
Records and Video	—	—	—	31.5	43.4
Commercial Electronics	(55.7)	16.6	(16.5)	73.8	(93.8)
Government Business	64.6	80.0	95.6	104.5	124.9
Broadcasting	48.1	107.9	156.2	218.1	333.2
Hertz	35.8	66.4	68.6	50.0	—
Communications	83.1	143.3	92.5	107.0	57.2
Financial Services	168.3	191.5	212.0	—	—
Other	9.5	(6.6)	14.0	14.1	10.0
Total	485.9	686.5	745.0	619.8	621.7
After-Tax Income	54.0	222.6	240.8	341.0	369.5
Earnings Per Share	($0.19)	$2.03	$2.10	$3.20	$3.79

Source: RCA, *Annual Reports,* 1981–1985.

The board voted to approve the change on March 6, 1985; this was the first time in almost twenty years that the transfer of power was made without the CEO being fired, pushed out, or bought off. Soon after, Bradshaw observed, "I think the major matter Mr. Frederick has to come to grips with—he's 59 and only has six years here—is the preparation of the people who will be the next generation of managers, and the preparation of the corporation for those people. But he knows that as well as I do."

As part of his legacy Frederick received an ongoing negotiation with UAL, the large Chicago-based airline and hotel company, which was interested in purchasing Hertz. A $6.2 billion operation, UAL was the nation's largest air carrier, and in April had agreed to acquire Pan Am's Pacific division for $750 million. In June came the announcement of the Hertz deal; UAL would pay $587.5 million for the auto leasor.

It made sense for both companies. Hertz fit in well with UAL's airline and its string of fifty-four hotels. At the same time, RCA was selling an operation that in 1984 had reported earnings of $50 million on revenues of $1.4 billion, and which in recent years had turned in a ragged performance. It should be recalled that in 1967 the Sarnoffs had paid slightly more than $200 million in convertible and common shares for the company, which at the time had revenues of $330 million and earnings of $12 million. Hertz had been one of the better acquisitions, and all things considered, the price was not only fair but generous. That it might have remained part of RCA and made further contributions was clear, but equally evident was the fact that Frederick and Bradshaw did not believe it fit into the company they were refashioning.

However, MCA did. That summer rumors abounded that RCA would soon make a tender offer for the entertainment giant. Indeed, Wall Street had known that the two companies had been holding discussions for over a year. As a major producer of theatrical and television films, MCA would have made a nice fit for NBC. Funds generated from the sales of CIT and Hertz could have hardly been put to better use. In early September, however, officials at both companies announced a failure to agree on terms, and the matter was dropped for the time being.

The negotiations for MCA were genuine enough, but Bradshaw had other companies in mind as well. That autumn GE's John Welch asked Felix Rohatyn, who had become a senior partner at RCA's banker, Lazard Freres, if he could arrange for a meeting between himself and Bradshaw. Cash-rich after a campaign of divestitures and cost-cutting, GE viewed RCA as a likely partner. Knowing that Bradshaw was interested in a merger, Welch thought the matter worth exploring. The two men met on November 6, and from the first it was evident each had something the other wanted. With the approval of both boards serious negotiations began. Attempts were made to keep the talks secret, but as usual with anything involving RCA there were leaks, not only to the press but to stock speculators. The second week in December, RCA common showed unusual activity, rising sharply on rumors.

By then everything was in place. According to all accounts Frederick knew of the discussions but played no role in them and in fact made clear his belief that RCA would be better off on its own. Now Bradshaw contacted the CEO to tell him of the deal, and Frederick had no option but to give his assent.

The announcement came on December 12: GE would purchase RCA for $66.50 per share, the total coming to $6.28 billion in cash, an all-time record for a non-oil company, bringing together two firms that had separated more than half a century earlier—and providing Frederick with the prospect of having to work once again with the man and company he had left under not particularly pleasant circumstances. He remained silent then and later on. Only eight months earlier he had assumed leadership at RCA, and now his position there was in doubt. One might have observed that this went with the territory. Perhaps so, but it did seem a rather unmerited twist for the man who as much as anyone was responsible for RCA's turnabout and was providing the company with what was arguably the best management in its history.

Immediately there were cries of foul from Wall Street, where RCA's breakup value was being estimated at around $90 per share. Why was Bradshaw selling for so low a price? And might there be another offer in the wings? Would the FCC challenge the sale of NBC? Would the Justice Department or the Pentagon object to the merger of two major defense contractors? By the end of the year it appeared the merger would take place without a challenge, probably to be completed in the late summer of 1986.

When the smoke cleared the rationale behind the merger, if not the price, became clearer. General Electric was troubled by its exposure overseas and dependence upon manufacturing; RCA would provide Welch with more domestic business (especially in the case of NBC) and greater presence in the service sector. "We've looked at 3,000 companies in the past five years," said GE Executive Vice President Lawrence Bossidy. "But this one is a blockbuster." Bradshaw chimed in, "It gives us the financial capacity to do what we have to do."

What RCA will become in the late 1980s and how it will perform for the rest of the century is a clouded matter at the time of this writing. Perhaps the GE corporate culture will envelop that of RCA; they certainly are different, and watching developments will be fun for the bystanders and press. Will RCA's acknowledged expertise in defense electronics complement GE's in the same area?

Undeniably RCA has ever been a company about which questions have been asked. More than most, the answers were unexpected. This much may not change in the future.

Bibliography

BIBLIOGRAPHIC ESSAY

UNABLE TO GET cooperation from RCA, I was obliged to seek out present and former employees for interviews. Many already were known from earlier work on the histories of ITT and IBM. They put me in touch with others, and this aspect of the research was pretty much on a catch-as-catch-can basis.

As indicated, RCA has always been a veritable rumor factory, with former executives eager to talk on condition they not be quoted directly or mentioned in the book.

The old journalistic practice of getting verification for every contentious statement was attempted but proved not particularly useful. Several times I was told stories about incidents that simply couldn't be true because those involved either weren't at the company at the time or held positions at which participation was improbable. In all instances where the stories have been mentioned I have indicated that such was the case, but the rest were simply omitted.

The basic source for RCA's early years and the David Sarnoff saga is the Elmer Bucher manuscript, described in Chapter 2. A librarian at the David Sarnoff Library in Princeton told me that "four or five" people a year work on the volumes, which are available to all interested scholars, as is the Library itself.

Bucher appears to have relied upon the two volumes by Gleason Archer included below. President of Suffolk University and trained in history, Archer performed his task well. The work is an invaluable source for the early history of both the industry and RCA.

Throughout its history RCA was covered closely and well by magazines and newspapers, the task all the easier because whenever something developed, employees popped up to spill everything to reporters willing to listen and write. If IBM is the quintessential closed-mouth company, RCA was wide-open, and more than six decades of such magazine articles were of immense importance to me. The more important of these publications are listed at the end of the Bibliography.

Among the more important government documents are the *Report on Chain Broadcasting,* the *Color Television Hearings,* and David Sarnoff's testimony in *Edwin H. Armstrong against RCA and NBC,* a copy of which is on deposit at the Sarnoff Library.

While many fine histories of radio and television exist, all of these touch only peripherally upon RCA and even NBC, concentrating for the most part on programming. There is no worthwhile history of the FCC, while Laurence Schmeckebier's history of the FRC is outdated. Dozens of monographs could be undertaken on subjects covered in this book—a history of RKO, for example, and biographies of Allen DuMont and Robert Sarnoff. We had to wait until 1982 for a biography of Owen Young, and then from his daughter and son-in-law, without whose personal interest this fine book would not have been written. The lives and works of Fessenden, De Forest, Armstrong, and others are covered inadequately in those works cited below; each should receive serious attention. The biggest gap is that of a worthwhile biography of David Sarnoff. That none exists is one of the puzzles of American business history.

SELECTED BIBLIOGRAPHY

Books

Aitken, Hugh. *Syntony and Spark: The Origins of Radio.* New York: Wiley, 1976.

Amigo, Eleanor, and Neuffer, Mark. *Beyond the Adirondacks: The Story of St. Regis Paper Company.* Westport: Greenwood, 1980.

Archer, Gleason. *Big Business and Radio.* New York: American Historical Society, 1939.

———. *History of Radio to 1926.* New York: American Historical Society, 1938.

Baker, Ray Stannard. *Woodrow Wilson and World Settlement.* 3 vols. Garden City: Doubleday, Page, 1922.

Baker, W. J. *A History of the Marconi Company.* New York: St. Martins, 1971.

Banning, William. *Commercial Broadcasting Pioneer: The WEAF Experiment, 1922–1926.* Cambridge: Harvard University, 1946.
Baranson, Jack. *The Japanese Challenge to U.S. Industry.* Lexington: Lexington Books, 1981.
______. *Technology and the Multinationals.* Lexington: Lexington Books, 1978.
Barnouw, Erik. *A Tower in Babal: A History of Broadcasting in the United States to 1933.* New York: Oxford, 1966.
______. *The Golden Web: A History of Broadcasting in the United States, 1933–1953.* New York: Oxford, 1968.
______. *The Image Empires: A History of Broadcasting in the United States from 1953.* New York: Oxford, 1970.
______. *Tube of Plenty: The Evolution of American Television.* New York: Oxford, 1975.
Bedell, Sally. *Up the Tube: Prime Time in the Silverman Years.* New York: Viking, 1981.
Bergreen, Laurence. *Look Now, Pay Later: The Rise of Network Broadcasting.* New York: Doubleday, 1980.
Bernays, Edward. *Biography of an Idea: Memoirs of Public Relations Counsel Edward L. Bernays.* New York: Simon & Schuster, 1965.
Bernstein, Marver. *Regulating Business by Independent Commission.* Princeton: Princeton University, 1955.
Bitting, Robert. "Creating an Industry: A Case Study in the Management of Television Innovation." M.S. Thesis. Massachusetts Institute of Technology, 1963.
Bogart, Leo. *The Age of Television.* New York: Ungar, 1972.
Bradshaw, Thornton, ed. *Corporations and Their Critics.* New York: McGraw Hill, 1981.
Briggs, Asa. *The Birth of Broadcasting: The History of Broadcasting in the United Kingdom.* Vol. 1. London: Oxford University, 1961.
Brown, George. *Recollections of a Research Engineer.* Princeton: Angus Brown, 1982.
Brown, Les. *Television: The Business Behind the Box.* New York: Harcourt, Brace, Jovanovich, 1971.
Brooks, John. *Telephone: The First Hundred Years.* New York: Harper & Row, 1976.
Cantril, Hadley, and Allport, Gordon. *The Psychology of Radio.* New York: Harper, 1935.
Carneal, Georgette. *A Conqueror of Space: An Authorized Biography of the Life and Work of Lee de Forest.* New York: Liveright, 1930.
Case, Josephine Young, and Case, Everett. *Owen D. Young and American Enterprise.* Boston: Godine, 1982.

Castleman, Harry, and Podrazik, Walter. *Watching: Four Decades of American Television.* New York: McGraw-Hill, 1982.
Chase, Francis. *Sound and Fury: An Informal History of Broadcasting.* New York: Harper, 1942.
Cole, Barry, and Oettinger, Mal. *Reluctant Regulators: The FCC and the Broadcast Audience.* Menlo Park: Addison-Wesley, 1978.
Cowan, Sidney. *Broadcasting in My Time.* London: Rich & Cowan, 1935.
Davis, John. *The Kennedys: Disaster and Dynasty, 1848–1983.* New York: McGraw-Hill, 1984.
Davis, Kenneth. *FDR: The Beckoning of Destiny.* New York: G. P. Putnam's, 1972.
De Forest, Lee. *Father of Radio: The Autobiography of Lee de Forest.* Chicago: Wilcox & Follett, 1950.
Donner, Stanley, ed. *The Meaning of Commercial Television.* Austin: Texas, 1966.
Dreher, Carl. *Sarnoff: An American Success.* New York: Quadrangle, 1977.
Dunlap, Orrin. *The Story of Radio.* New York: Dial, 1935.
———. *Radio's 100 Men of Science.* New York: Harper, 1944.
———. *The Future of Television.* New York: Harper, 1942.
Eddy, William. *Television: The Eyes of Tomorrow.* New York: Prentice-Hall, 1945.
Emery, Walter. *National and International Systems of Broadcasting.* East Lansing: Michigan State, 1969.
Erickson, Don. *Armstrong's Fight for FM Broadcasting.* Alabama: Alabama University, 1973.
Fessenden, Helen. *Fessenden: Builder of Tomorrows.* New York: Coward-McCann, 1940.
Francisco, Charles. *The Radio City Music Hall.* New York: Dutton, 1979.
Freidel, Frank. *Franklin D. Roosevelt: The Apprenticeship.* Boston: Little, Brown, 1952.
Gammond, Peter, and Horricks, Raymond, eds. *The Music Goes Round and Round: A Cool Look at the Record Industry.* London: Quartet, 1980.
Ginsberg, F. W. *The Music Goes Round and Round.* New York: Macmillan, 1942.
Goldmark, Peter. *Maverick Inventor: My Turbulent Years at CBS.* New York: Dutton, 1973.
Goldsmith, Alfred, and Lescarboura, Austin. *The Thing Called Broadcasting.* New York: Holt, 1930.
Gross, Ben. *I Looked and Listened: Informal Recollections of Radio and TV.* New York: Random House, 1954.
Halberstam, David. *The Powers That Be.* New York: Knopf, 1979.
Hampton, Benjamin. *History of the American Film Industry: From Its Beginnings to 1931.* New York: Dover, 1970.

Harlow, Alvin. *Old Wires and New Waves: The History of the Telegraph, Telephone, and Wireless.* New York: Appleton-Century, 1936.
Harris, Credo. *Microphone Memories.* New York: Bobbs-Merrill,1937.
Heighton, Elizabeth, and Cunningham, Don. *Advertising in the Broadcast Media.* Belmont, Cal: Wadsworth, 1977.
Heittig, Mae. *Economic Control of the Motion Picture Industry.* Philadelphia: University of Pennsylvania, 1944.
Hoover, Herbert. *Memoirs: The Cabinet and the Presidency, 1920–1933.* New York: Macmillan, 1948.
Hutchinson, Thomas. *Here Is Television.* New York: Hastings House, 1946.
Jacobs, Lewis. *The Rise of the American Film: A Critical History.* New York: Teachers College Press, 1939.
Jewell, Richard, and Harbin, Vernon. *The RKO Story.* New Rochelle: Arlington House, 1966.
Jobes, Gertrude. *Motion Picture Empire.* New York: Archon, 1966.
Johnson, Nicholas. *How to Talk Back to Your Television Set.* Boston: Little, Brown, 1970.
Jome, Hiram. *Economics of the Radio Industry.* Chicago: Shaw, 1925.
Kahn, Frank, ed. *Documents of American Broadcasting.* New York: Appleton-Century-Crofts, 1973.
Kennedy, Joseph, ed. *The Story of the Films.* Chicago: Shaw, 1927.
Koskoff, David. *Joseph P. Kennedy: A Life and Times.* Englewood Cliffs, N.J.: Prentice-Hall, 1974.
Landry, Robert. *This Fascinating Radio Business.* Indianapolis: Bobbs-Merrill, 1946.
Layton, Christopher, in collaboration with Harlow, Christopher and De Houghton, Charles. *Ten Innovations.* New York: Crane, Russak, 1972.
Lessing, Lawrence. *Man of High Fidelity: Edwin Howard Armstrong.* Philadelphia: Lippincott, 1956.
Levin, Harvey. *Broadcast Regulation and Joint Ownership of Media.* New York: New York University Press, 1960.
Lichty, Lawrence and Topping, Malachi, eds. *American Broadcasting.* New York: Hastings House, 1975.
Lilienthal, David. *The Journals of David Lilienthal.* 4 vols. Vols. 2 and 3. New York: Harper & Row, 1966, 1969.
Lundberg, Ferdinand. *America's 60 Families.* New York: Vanguard, 1937.
Lyons, Eugene. *David Sarnoff: A Biography.* New York: Harper, 1966.
MacLaurin, W. Rupert. *Invention and Innovation in the Radio Industry.* New York: Macmillan, 1949.
McMahon, Robert. *Federal Regulation of the Radio and Television Broadcast Industry in the United States, 1927–1959.* New York: Arno, 1979.
McNicol, Donald. *Radio's Conquest of Space.* New York: Arno, 1974.
Matusow, Barbara. *The Evening Stars.* New York: Houghton Mifflin, 1983.

Mayer, Martin. *About Television.* New York: Harper & Row, 1972.
Metz, Michael. *CBS: Reflections in a Bloodshot Eye.* Chicago: Playboy, 1975.
Myers, William, ed. *The State Papers and Other Public Writings of Herbert Hoover.* 2 vols. New York: Doubleday, Doran, 1934.
National Opinion Research Center. *The People Look at Radio.* Chapel Hill: University of North Carolina, 1946.
Okimoto, Daniel, ed. *Japan's Economy: Coping With Change in the International Environment.* Boulder: Westview, 1982.
O'Toole, Patricia. *Corporate Messiah: The Hiring and Firing of Million-Dollar Managers.* New York: Morrow, 1984.
Oxenfeldt, Alfred. *Marketing Practices in the TV Set Industry.* New York: Columbia, 1964.
Paley, William. *As It Happened.* Garden City: Doubleday, 1979.
The Radio Industry: The Story of Its Development. Chicago: A. W. Shaw, 1928.
Radio Corporation of America. *The First 25 Years of RCA.* New York: RCA, 1944.
______. *Thirty Years of Pioneering and Progress.* New York: RCA, 1949.
RCA Review. *Television: Volume I, 1933–1936.* Princeton: RCA, 1936.
______. *Television: Volume II, 1936–1938.* Princeton: RCA, 1938.
______. *Television: Volume III. 1938–1941.* Princeton: RCA, 1947.
Read, Oliver, and Welch, Walter. *From Tin Foil to Stereo: Evolution of the Phonograph.* Indianapolis: Howard W. Sams, 1976.
Reel, A. Frank. *The Networks: How They Stole the Show.* New York: Scribner's, 1979.
Reich, Cary. *Financier: The Biography of André Meyer.* New York: Morrow, 1983.
Rochester, Anna. *Rulers of America: A Study of Finance Capital.* New York: International, 1936.
Roosevelt, Elliot. *F.D.R.: His Personal Letters, 1905–1928.* New York: Duell, Sloan & Pearce, 1948.
Rose, Cornelia. *A National Policy for Radio Broadcasting.* New York: Harper, 1940.
Rosen, Philip. *The Modern Stentors: Radio Broadcasting and the Federal Government, 1920–1934.* Westport: Greenwood, 1980.
Sagi-nejad, Tagi; Moxon, Richard; and Perlmutter, Howard. *Controlling International Technology Transfer.* New York: Pergamon, 1981.
Sarnoff, David. *Looking Ahead: The Papers of David Sarnoff.* New York: McGraw-Hill, 1968.
______. "Twenty Years of RCA, 1928–1940." Typescript.
Schiller, Herbert. *Mass Communications and American Empire.* New York: Kelley, 1969.

Schoenberg, Robert. *Geneen.* New York: Norton, 1984.

Schmeckebier, Laurence. *The Federal Radio Commission: Its History, Activities and Organization.* Washington: Brookings Institution, 1932.

Schubert, Paul. *The Electric Word: The Rise of Radio.* New York: Macmillan, 1928.

Seldin, Joseph. *The Golden Fleece: Selling the Good Life to Americans.* New York: Macmillan, 1963.

Shanks, Bob. *The Cool Fire: How to Make It In Television.* New York: Norton, 1976.

Shulman, Arthur, and Youman, Roger. *The Television Years.* New York: Popular Library, 1973.

Shurick, E.P.J. *The First Quarter-Century of American Broadcasting.* Kansas City: Midland, 1946.

Siepman, Charles. *Radio's Second Chance.* Boston: Little, Brown, 1946.

Skinner, Wickham, and Rogers, David. *Manufacturing Policy in the Electronics Industry.* Homewood, Ill.: Irwin, 1968.

Skornia, Harry, and Kitson, Jack, eds. *Problems and Controversies in Television and Radio.* Palo Alto: Pacific, 1968.

Smith, W. Novis, and Larson, Charles. *Innovation and U.S. Research.* Washington: American Chemical Society, 1980.

Sobel, Robert. *IBM: Colossus in Transition.* New York: Timesbooks, 1981.

______. *ITT: The Management of Opportunity.* New York: Timesbooks, 1983.

______. *The Manipulators: America in the Media Age.* New York: Doubleday, 1976.

Southworth, George. *Forty Years of Radio Research.* New York: Gordon & Breach, 1962.

Stanley, Robert. *The Celluloid Empire: A History of the American Movie Industry.* New York: Hastings House, 1978.

Tarbell, Ida. *Owen D. Young: A New Type of Industrial Leader.* New York: Macmillan, 1932.

United States Department of the Army, Office of the Chief of Military History. Dulany Terrett. *The United States Army in World War II. The Technical Services. The Signal Corps: The Emergency.* Washington: USGPO, 1956.

______. George Thompson, Dixie Harris, Pauline Oakes, and Dulany Terrett. *The United States Army in World War II. The Technical Services. The Signal Corps: The Test.* Washington: USGPO, 1957.

______. George Thompson and Dixie Harris. *United States Army in World War II. The Technical Services. The Signal Corps: The Outcome.* Washington: USGPO, 1966.

______. Congress. Senate. 76th Congress. 3rd Session. Temporary National

Economic Committee. *Investigation of Concentration of Economic Power. Part 21, War and Prices*; Part 23: Investment Banking. Washington: USGPO, 1941.

______. Congress. Senate. 76th Congress. 3rd Session. Temporary National Economic Committee. *Investigation of Concentration of Economic Power. Monograph 43: The Motion Picture Industry: A Pattern of Control.* Washington: USGPO, 1941.

Federal Communications Commission. *Federal Trade Commission vs. General Electric, American Telephone and Telegraph, Westinghouse, United Fruit, and Radio Corporation of America.* Washington: USGPO, January 11, 1922.

______. *Color Television Hearings,* May 3, 4, 1950. Washington: USGPO, 1950.

______. Commission Order No. 37, Docket No. 5060. *Report on Chain Broadcasting.* Washington: USGPO, 1941.

______. Congress. House of Representatives. 97th Congress. 1st Session. Committee on Energy and Commerce. *Telecommunications in Transition: The Status of Competition in the Telecommunications Industry.* Washington: USGPO, 1981.

United States District Court for the District of Delaware. Edwin H. Armstrong against RCA and NBC. Deposition of David Sarnoff. February 20, 1953.

Waldrop, Frank, and Borkin, Joseph. *Television: A Struggle for Power.* New York: Morrow, 1938.

Walton, Francis. *Miracle of World War II.* New York: Macmillan, 1956.

Wasco, Janet. *Movies and Money: Financing the American Film Industry.* Norwood, N.J.: Ablex, 1982.

White, Llewellyn. *The American Radio.* Chicago: University of Chicago, 1947.

Wicklein, John. *Electronic Nightmare: The New Communications and Freedom.* New York: Viking, 1981.

Wilk, Max. *The Golden Age of Television.* New York: Delacorte, 1976.

Wolf, Marvin. *The Japanese Conspiracy.* New York: Empire, 1983.

Wright, John, ed. *The Commercial: Advertising and the American Mass Media.* New York: Delta, 1979.

Zworykin, Vladimir, and Morton, G. A. *Television.* New York: Wiley, 1940.

Periodicals and Newspapers

Annual Report of the Federal Radio Commission 1927–1933.
Billboard
Barron's
Business Week

Forbes
Fortune
Newsweek
The New York Times
Time
TV Guide
Variety
The Wall Street Journal
The Washington Post

Index